Hear Me, O God

Meditations
on the
Psalms

W A Y N E   B R O U W E R

Preface

The book of Psalms is a collection of 150 worship songs and poems. Written by a variety of authors, they reflect almost every human thought and emotion: anger and fear, longing and wonder, sorrow and comfort, complaint and trust, praise and thanks. The psalms serve as a model, lesson, and guide to believers on how we may and should speak to our God.

In his meditations on these 150 psalms, Wayne Brouwer captures both the thought and emotion of each one. He makes each psalm come alive in our present-day cultural context and in our own lives. For instance, he writes of Psalm 64, the one providing a title for this collection:

> When [British poet Matthew Arnold] died, one of his neighbors said of him, "Poor Matthew; he won't like God!" Perhaps you're tempted to say that about David when reading Psalm 64. . . . After all, he opens his prayer by telling God he's got a complaint. . . . Isn't that a bit sacrilegious?

> Probably much of our mean-spirited whining is. But consider this: our excessive complaining is actually a reflection of the excessive evil that surrounds us and even spills out from our own hearts. Perhaps if we ever stop complaining about that, we won't have a prayer left.

Wayne Brouwer, author of *Hear Me, O God*, is pastor of the Harderwyk Christian Reformed Church in Holland, Michigan. He has also written the book of devotions *Walking on Water: Faith and Doubt in the Christian Life*. We offer you this collection with the prayer that it will enrich your own ability to talk to God, knowing that you will certainly be heard.

Harvey A. Smit
Editor in Chief
Education, Worship, and Evangelism Department

Blessed

Blessed is the man . . .
—Psalm 1:1

There's an ancient Chinese teaching riddle that tells the story of a man who's running from a hungry bear. Suddenly he's at the edge of a cliff. It's either jump or be eaten, so he throws himself over. Fortunately, there's a tiny sapling to grab as a lifesaver. Jerked to a halt, he sees a tiger beneath his feet, just waiting to devour him. And two gophers have chosen that moment to gnaw at the wood that suspends him between death above and death below!

What to do? What would you do? The story continues: all at once he spies a wild strawberry bush, an arm's reach away. It's loaded with ripe red berries. He plucks one, pops it in his mouth, and with a look of sheer contentment sighs, "Mmmmm! Delicious!"

Quality Life
That man is blessed, says the parable. He knows how to find joy and contentment in life, no matter what his circumstances. No one will take from him the quality of life that flows from his heart!

Psalm 1 is about quality life. But there is a very clear focus as to what makes it that way. For some people, contentment might come from a stable family life. It may result from financial success or achieving a degree. It may even begin with a good job. "Blessed is he who has found his work" says Thomas Carlyle, "let him ask no other blessedness."

But Psalm 1 doesn't suggest any of these. And you know why. Circumstances change. Happenings happen for a while, and then stop happening. We need to pin our goals and values on something deeper than shifting sands.

And that's precisely the point. "His delight is in the law of the Lord!" shouts the psalmist. When you're in tune with the Creator and the creation, temporary dissonance and discord are momentary ripples that soon will be smoothed into the larger patterns of life's fabric.

Knowing that, you can savor the taste of a strawberry, even on a hospital bed.

Abide with Me

Henry Francis Lyte was only fifty-four, but several years of illness had kept him from functioning to full potential in his congregation in a small fishing village. His limitations seemed to have fostered problems in the church. At one time worship services were crowded, and over eight hundred children were taught by seventy teachers in the Sunday school program. At one time he knew the names of every boat in the harbor and every man who walked the docks. At one time his tireless care and enthusiasm drew even skeptics to Christ.

But now he was failing rapidly. His doctor told him to quit the ministry. His congregation was falling apart. And here he sat, on a bluff above the sea, wondering what message to bring for his last Sunday evening sermon.

The points and outline wouldn't come. They were crowded out by the cares and troubles that surrounded him. But then a prayer began to form in his mind that softly caressed his vision back into focus. The prayer began to sing itself. And by the time his people gathered for worship, a new hymn called them into the presence of God.

Henry Lyte died a few months later. But he died a blessed man. And people in churches around the world know that, each time they open their hymnbooks to sing his prayer: "Abide with Me!"

> I need your presence every passing hour;
> What but your grace can foil the tempter's power?
> Who like yourself my guide and strength can be?
> Through cloud and sunshine, O abide with me!

Political Religion

*The kings of the earth take their stand and the rulers gather
together against the LORD and against his Anointed One.*
—Psalm 2:2

"Politics are almost as exciting as war, and quite as dangerous!" said
Winston Churchill. "In war you can only be killed once, but in politics
many times."

Politics and Power

Politics is about power. Dale Carnegie knew that, and created his popular
seminars on "How to Win Friends and Influence People." In his famous
treatise on politics, *The Prince,* Machiavelli said, "All the armed prophets
conquered, all the unarmed ones perished!" In the end, it seems, what
matters is your ability to create your dream, not the rightness of the
dream itself. Napoleon even confided in his journals that "justice means
force as well as virtue." Your ideal can be noble, but you must be able to
force it upon others you consider less noble than yourself.

Politics and Passion

In one of his essays, Albert Camus describes a powerful scene. John Huss,
the great Czech Reformer of the church, is on trial. His accusers twist all
his ideas out of shape. They refuse to give him a hearing. They maneuver
the political machine against him and incite popular passion to a lynch-
mob frenzy. Finally Huss is condemned to be burned at the stake. As the
flames surround him, people who couldn't possibly have read his writings
and who have no interest in either his perspectives or those of the governing authorities, line up to assist in the murder. "When they were burning
John Huss," writes Camus, "a gentle little old lady came carrying her fag-
got to add it to the pile."

The tragedy of politics often lies in passions, not platforms. "Private
passions grow tired and wear themselves out; political passions, never!"
says Lamartine. That's why there's an unwritten rule in many communities that when all the in-laws and out-laws get together for the annual
"family rebellion" you can't talk about politics or religion. Both grab a person so deeply!

Politics and Religion

But maybe, when it comes right down to it, politics and religion are much the same thing. The kingdom of God is *very* political. It's a perspective on all of life. It's a way of holding things together and giving them meaning. It's a movement that's out to change the world, to reclaim lost territory in the civil war of the universe.

That's why Jesus' followers got into trouble with the political leaders of their day. Two visions of reality collided. Two perspectives on life challenged each other. Six times over in the book of Acts, the Christian community is called "The Way." Not "The Society," nor "The Institution," but "The Way"!

The church of Jesus Christ is a political movement. It's *on the way* to somewhere. Every worship service is a political rally; a time when we refocus our energies, study our political platform and policies, and pay homage to the Party Leader.

In Acts 4 the church leaders are arrested by the political leaders of their day. Peter and John have just healed a man with bad legs and have counseled a large crowd of troubled people. And then the high council challenges them: "What right do you have to practice medicine without a license?"

Peter and John have the answer. "We're under marching orders!" they say. "We must obey God rather than men!"

When they're released, Peter and John hold a prayer service that's really a political rally. They raise the song of Psalm 2 to heaven. And the King of heaven and earth shakes the world as a promise of things to come (Heb. 12:25-29).

"Onward Christian Soldiers" may sound too combative in an age of growing world accommodation and pluralism. But the community of God's people that speaks "Peace!" while the final armistice has not yet been signed before the judgment seat of heaven has capitulated to the Enemy.

Security

But you are a shield around me, O LORD. . . .
—Psalm 3:3

Mike Maryn has a rough life. And he's become famous enough to have reporters from all over North America interviewing him. Why? In five years he's been mugged and robbed *eighty-three* times!

Is somebody out to get him? No, say the police; each incident happened at the hands of a different person or group. The list of his attackers includes young boys, teenagers, able-bodied men, and even several women!

Does Mike give a show of wealth that attracts thieves? No, say his neighbors; he's a rather plain man who never wears any jewelry except for his wedding ring and a cheap watch. He's an ordinary fellow, with no excess of money or possessions.

Well, then, does Mr. Maryn tend to frequent the rough parts of Chicago, and get himself into trouble? Not according to the crime reports. Each of the eighty-three attacks happened in a different location at various times of the day or night. Sometimes he was on a bright and busy sidewalk; sometimes he was just walking along in a shopping plaza; once he was even sitting in a taxi at a traffic light, and two fellows opened the door, dragged him out, and grabbed his wallet!

Police don't know what to make of it. They're as puzzled as poor Mike is. All they can say is "he just happens to be in the wrong place at the wrong time!"

Vulnerable

Did you ever feel like you were in the wrong place at the wrong time? Have you bumbled into a crowded room wearing the wrong clothes? When that happens, we protect ourselves with a blush and a hasty exit. One fellow I know invited a neighbor to church. Finally the fellow gave in. But when he showed up, he was the only man there without a tie. And he never came back!

Sometimes, though, being in the wrong place at the wrong time is much more traumatic. A brutal rape. A rare disease. An untimely explosion. A ticket on the wrong airplane. And in a startled heartbeat, we look at a foreboding world through victim's eyes.

SOS

That's the way David felt when he first sang Psalm 3. His cherished son Absolom had run off with his counselors, his people, his kingdom, and even some of his wives! The world was against him! The deck was stacked; the dice were weighted. Every whisper brought a new word of gloom. He tossed the nights away, running scared in his dreams. And the morning mirror called him a loser.

But somehow David's distress signal SOS balances a plea for help with a profession of hope. Somehow he manages a sense of serenity on the battlefield of strife. Somehow the victim carries himself with the wearied bearing of a victor.

Sustaining Secret

What is the secret that sustains David? Part of it has to be a good memory. He's been in tough scrapes before, and he knows how God got him through. But another part of it is the secret knowledge all God's children have that God takes sides in the conflicts of life. Justice is not blind. In fact, in the larger scope of cosmic realities, it is weighted heavily in favor of those who believe in God's promises.

You see, God is a victim too. His angel Satan (Job 1:6) tried to take over God's kingdom. And in a startling turn of events, God joined hands with the weak and helpless children on the battlefield. He allowed the Dragon to roar for a time so that his voice would be stilled for eternity. And while Adam's descendants cowered in fear, always in the wrong place at the wrong time, God absorbed the mugger's death blow in his own body.

For thousands of years, reporters have been trying to make sense out of that story. Isaiah the prophet once asked: "Who has believed our message?" (53:1). David would probably answer, "Only the lost and the last and the least. Only the vulnerable and the victims. Only people like you and me."

Peace

I will lie down and sleep in peace, for you alone, O LORD,
make me dwell in safety.
—Psalm 4:8

In the spring of 1963, Martin Luther King, Jr., sparked a Birmingham, Alabama, campaign to end discriminatory hiring practices and racial segregation in restaurants. The drama gained worldwide attention when police attacked the participants with dogs and fire hoses. Many were arrested, including hundreds of schoolchildren.

A coalition of white clergy issued a public denunciation of such activities and called on blacks to boycott the demonstrations. Twenty men sent a letter to King, who was being held in the Birmingham jail, begging him to be more cautious, less troublesome. His reply carried the famous line: "Peace is not the absence of tension but the presence of justice."

Untroubled Sleep

Generations ago, the philosopher Spinoza said it too: "Peace is not an absence of war; it is a virtue, a state of mind, a disposition for benevolence, confidence, justice." And in Psalm 4, the harried fugitive David powerfully declares the same truth. On the run from Saul, a homeless vagabond surrounded by enemies, David lies down to sleep in peace. Parents who have stolen quietly into the bedrooms of their sleeping children have a perfect image of that repose.

Some hospitals have ingeniously stimulated a peaceful environment on maternity wards. Where the cry of a single baby once stirred others into a chorus of wailing, a tape recording is piped in over the speakers above. Is it a quiet lullaby? A meditative classical work? The soothing sounds of winds and waves?

No. These babies are surrounded with the gentle thumping of a human heartbeat. It is the echo of a mother's breast, a parent's pervasive caring. It is the heartbeat of love. And the young children, challenged by a bright and noisy world, sleep in peace.

Waking Confidence

David is not sleeping while he sings this psalm. He is awake, alert, sword in hand. No comfortable silky sheets or puffy pillows. And that's the power of his song. David has confidence, inner security, in a noisy and troublesome world.

C. S. Lewis, in *The Screwtape Letters*, pictures a devil banishing both music and silence from the world, filling it instead with noise. It is "noise which alone defends us from silly qualms," he declares. "We will make the whole universe a noise in the end."

But the Prince of Peace will never allow it. As a poet once put it:

> Thou shalt know Him when He comes,
> Not by any din of drums . . .
> But His presence known shall be,
> By the holy harmony
> Which His coming makes in thee.

A Song

There's a marvelous tale about a painting contest. Artists were encouraged to submit their most descriptive canvases portraying "peace." The offerings were as varied as the colors of the spectrum. One bright scene showed a pastoral countryside. Another found peace on the wide expanse of sea coast, drummed by the steadying rhythm of the waves. A third found its glow in the setting sun at day's end.

The winning painting, though, portrayed a chaotic and troubled scene. Torrents of water cascaded over jagged rocks. Black storm clouds reached down to earth with destructive claws of lightning. Fierce winds tore at the leafy clothing of trees. Hailstones mixed with rain punished the world with a sound beating.

But these were not the things that grabbed the viewer's attention. There, just to the right of center, in a nest supported by a gnarled old tree limb and sheltered by overhanging rocks, was a small bird. Singing. Peaceful.

That's David in Psalm 4. That's the child of God, resting confident in the heartbeat of heaven. As Isaiah put it: "You will keep in perfect peace him whose mind is steadfast, because he trusts in you" (26:3).

Lies

You destroy those who tell lies; bloodthirsty and deceitful men
the LORD abhors.
—Psalm 5:6

A mother was shocked to learn that her young son had told a bold-faced lie. She took him aside and tried to scare such behavior right out of him. "A tall dark man with fiery red eyes and two sharp horns grabs little boys who tell lies," she said, "and carries them off at night! He takes them to Mars were they have to work in a black cavern for fifty years! Now, you don't want that to happen to you, do you? You won't ever tell a lie again, will you, dear?"

"No, Mom," he replied gravely. "You tell better ones than I ever could!"

A Society without Conscience

Brux Austin, the editor of *Texas Business,* describes our society as staring at the dollar sign with one eye and winking in dishonesty with the other. "We have no built-in beliefs," he says, "no ethical boundaries. Cheat on your taxes, just don't get caught. Cheat on your wife, just don't get AIDS." Our high-tech society has given us everything, he writes, "everything but a conscience."

A year ago the *Calgary Herald* carried an article about a new dictionary created by Professor Robert Thornton of Lehigh University. The *Lexicon of Inconspicuously Ambiguous Recommendations* (appropriately tagged LIAR) is a tongue-in-cheek sourcebook of statements that mean exactly the opposite of what they seem to say. A teacher who's asked to write a letter of endorsement for a questionable student might say, for instance: "I most enthusiastically recommend this candidate with no qualifications whatsoever!" Or he might choose this twist: "I can assure you that no person would be better for the job!"

We feel the clutch of Ralph Waldo Emerson's line, "The more he talked about his honor, the faster we counted our spoons."

Roots of Lying

Recently *Chatelaine* magazine described five personality types that are most prone to lying. The *narcissist* lies to make others think he's better than he really is. The *compulsive* person is usually honest, but hates to admit any imperfections. She might stretch the truth just to cover herself in a crisis. Someone who is *hysteric* exaggerates nearly everything in order to get a reaction from people around him. A *borderline* personality can't tolerate frustration, and throws blame to others. And the person who is *antisocial* will do anything to get his way.

This last personality type has victimized David as he cries out his frustrations in Psalm 5. A person who cares nothing for people, cares neither for truth or for God. David is hurt. But so is God.

Intolerance

Sometimes we chuckle at little deceits and the exaggerations of humorous conversation with friends. But only the antisocial person laughs when he cheats on his wife. Only the sadistic woman smiles when she destroys a relative's reputation. Only the mean-spirited child giggles as he tears the dignity from a younger playmate.

Certainly God doesn't laugh. God takes great delight in much that is good and right and fun, and even in things that are marvelously hilarious. But the lie of hurt, the doublespeak of evil, the sneer of malice, move him to anger. God has no tolerance for such "comedy."

Neither should we.

Mercy

The LORD has heard my cry for mercy;
the LORD accepts my prayer.
—Psalm 6:9

A rather distinguished matron of high society felt the need to commission a lavish portrait of herself. But her demands and desires drove her from one artist to the next. None could do it right! Finally she stormed into the studio of still another candidate. As they settled on a fee, she told of her disappointment with others of his profession.

"Young man!" she said, "I want you to do me justice!"

By now the artist was having second thoughts. He looked her up and down and finally let it slip: "Madam," he said, "it's not *justice* you need. It's *mercy!*"

Beggar's Refuge

"Mercy is a beggar's refuge," said George Bernard Shaw, "a man must pay his debts!" That's how we feel when someone hurts us. Can you imagine a rape victim suffering a lifetime of psychological scars while her attacker gets a mild reprimand? Or a family carrying on with the knowledge that the drunk driver who senselessly slaughtered their son didn't even have his license suspended? "It isn't fair!" we shout. A cry for mercy from such trash is a beggar's refuge. We spit on it.

When Austrian Prince Schwarzenberg put down the Hungarian rebellion of 1849, some counselors advised mercy for the captives. "Yes, indeed," he replied, "a good idea; but first we will have a little hanging!" Our hearts nod in assent.

Spite

Even our mercy can be laced with spite. When the first Elizabeth finally came to England's throne after the political and religious wrangling of the sixteenth century, a knight who had formerly despised her came seeking pardon. He threw himself at her feet begging mercy. With a flick of her hand she dismissed him, saying, "Do you not know that we are descended of the lion, whose nature is not to prey upon the mouse or any other such small vermin?"

A royal put-down indeed! But husbands do it to wives, and vice versa; neighbors condescendingly do it to each other; church members justify their cases and offer mean-spirited "forgiveness." "Community" becomes a shining ideal that we can't buy with our smoldering bitterness.

Love's Second Name

In Shakespeare's *The Merchant of Venice,* the main character borrows a great sum of money from Shylock. Due to adverse circumstances, he is unable to pay it back. Shylock demands justice, but seethes with vengeance. And, in a marvelous speech, Portia slices to the heart of human need:

> The quality of mercy is not strain'd,
> It droppeth as the gentle rain from heaven. . . .
> Though justice be thy plea, consider this,
> That in the course of justice none of us
> Should see salvation. We do pray for mercy,
> And that same prayer doth teach us all to render
> The deeds of mercy.
>
> —*Act IV, Scene 1*

That's the kind of mercy David sings of in Psalm 6. Enemies surround him. Terrors press on him. Behind it all he feels the blazing wrath of God.

David knows he deserves God's wrath. He knows he's done great wrong, that even the little right he claims to do is a paltry pittance. He knows he's not caught in an unfair tragedy of blind circumstances; he is caught in the grip of justice. Divine "discipline" (v. 1) demands its pound of flesh.

Will he "stand like a man" and pay his debts? No, for in this courtroom there is no limit to the punishment and no door marked "Exit." All that's left is Love's second name: Mercy!

And in the scent of that whisper, life begins again.

Righteous Judge

---

*God is a righteous judge, a God who expresses his
wrath every day.*
—*Psalm 7:11*

Oscar Wilde penned a powerful story about justice called *The Picture of
Dorian Gray*. Dorian was a handsome young man, a model of physical
beauty and moral virtue. People complimented him on his good graces.
Parents pointed to him as an example to their youth. One artist even
painted an exquisite portrait of him.

Dorian idolized the painting. He woke each morning to admire it. He
ended every day with a gaze at his mirrored perfection. Someone so lovely
could do no wrong, he began to think, or at least would not be punished
for it. In his vanity, he became selfish and indulgent. He sampled the sins
of the streets. He debauched himself in the opium dens of London's darker dives.

Of course, Dorian's crimes and carelessness took their toll. Soon the
perfect portrait on the wall began to haunt him. The picture of a radiant
and wholesome young man gleamed down on his puffy face and diseased
body and glazed eyes. If only he could look that way again! If only the
portrait could absorb the marks of his sin!

And miraculously, that's what happened. Before long, his youthful
glow returned. The more he caroused at night, the healthier and hand-
somer he became. And on the wall, the painting slowly became etched
and lined with the wickedness of Dorian Gray.

What a life! Each day, people marveled at his virtue and eternal youth.
And by night he wallowed in every vice, with no recrimination. The now-
ugly painting on the wall absorbed every evil, and tallied each painful
degradation.

Dorian could no longer endure even a casual glance at the horrible picture. He hid it in the attic and only occasionally sneaked up to survey the
damage. Over the years, what little resemblance there may have been between young Dorian Gray and the grotesque monster in the painting was
all but lost.

But the painting remained a sacramental testimony of his wickedness. It was a haunting conscience, an inviolate judge on the life and times of Dorian Gray. It stood as accuser. It never lied. It drove him mad.

One night he could stand it no longer. Knife in hand, he ascended the stairs to the attic courtroom and attacked the awful witness that spoke silently for the prosecution.

When his servants searched the house the next day, looking for Master Gray, they found only the wretched body of a ghastly old man in the attic, knife through his heart. And on the wall beamed the handsome and virtuous face of the painting of Dorian Gray.

Blind Justice

Wilde's story summarizes two themes that linger within each of us. The first is a sense of morality. Dorian knew right from wrong. He realized there was a proper way to live and a style of life that was evil and degrading. God made us with a conscience, says the apostle Paul, and no one is without excuse in matters of morality.

Second, Wilde pointed a finger to justice. Blind justice. Standing there weighing our deeds with her scales, meting out punishments. We'd like to be excused. We'd like a way out, a miraculous painting that absorbs our punishments and lets us off with only an ugly glance. But we know it'll never happen. We get what we deserve, if not now, then when we die. Dorian Gray got his; we'll get ours.

The Eye of God

Such might also seem the theme of Psalm 7. Certainly the challenge of morality is there. But justice, for David, is not sightless. Rather, it is God's second name. God wields his "deadly weapons" (vv. 12-13) with keen perception. God's justice is aimed by mercy. The threat to wickedness is at the same time a comforting shield for those who call God by name.

The warning of Psalm 7 is clear: sin, evil, and immorality get their due in the cosmic courtroom presided over by God, the righteous Judge. But thanks to mercy, David can claim "righteousness" and "integrity" at the same bar (v. 8).

And only in that courtroom is it possible to sing for joy (v. 17).

Majesty

O LORD, our Lord, how majestic is your name
in all the earth!
—Psalm 8:1

Once King George and Queen Elizabeth went to a London theater to see a Noel Coward/Gertrude Lawrence production. As they entered the royal box, the whole audience rose to its feet to honor them. Standing in the wings, Gertrude Lawrence said, "What an entrance!"

And Noel Coward added, "What a part!"

Expanding Circles

What a part God has to play in the drama of time and space! Says Joan of Arc in the first installment of Shakespeare's *King Henry VI:* "Glory is like a circle in the water, which never ceaseth to enlarge itself" (I.ii). For human rulers, she pointed out, that was disastrous. Eventually the reach would exceed the substance.

But what a part for God! David draws the ever-expanding circles of God's glory in Psalm 8, and marvels at the way in which each successive wave grows more majestic. Every element of creation, from the star-spangled skies to the thumb-sucking baby, stands and shouts at God's entrance.

Eyes to See

One ring, though, among the circles of expanding glory, heaves a mixed applause toward heaven. It's the circle of humanity. Elizabeth Barrett Browning put it this way:

> Earth's crammed with heaven,
> And every common bush afire with God;
> But only he who sees takes off his shoes;
> The rest sit round and pluck blackberries.

Some would say that "he who sees," sees God. And because so few people see God today, Psalm 8 has died on our lips.

But David wouldn't quite put it that way. The marvel of God's majesty is not merely some quality we see in *God*, but the wonder of the way in which God sees *us*. "What is man that you are mindful of him?" asks David. "You've crowned him with glory and honor" (v. 4).

In other words, our ability to see God is quite directly related to our understanding of ourselves. Those who carelessly toss aside human life will never worship God as they stuff blackberries into their mouths. John Calvin started his magnificent survey of the Christian faith, *The Institutes of the Christian Religion,* by reflecting that our knowledge of ourselves and our knowledge of God are so intertwined that the one has little power to grow without the other.

The Weight of Glory

C. S. Lewis thought of that. He wondered why we humans, who have so much to live for here, might ever be enticed to long for "heaven" or "eternal life." Often religion turns worship of God into a duty that exacts a tax of begrudging acknowledgment from us. We *have* to go to church. We *must* be good. We are *obligated* to pray.

But such feelings arise from the pagan notion that we can somehow increase the majesty of our tribal god in the clash of worldly power plays. Rather, says Lewis, echoing David, it is God's amazing thoughts about us that make biblical religion special. It is God who creates us in his image. It is God who loves us when we are unlovely. It is God who declares us to be kings and queens. It is God who thinks wonderful thoughts about us, even when we can't be bothered to think much of ourselves.

Holy Hilarity

When the German prince, George II, became king of Great Britain, he had a special fondness for the music of his fellow countryman, George Frideric Handel. At the premiere concert of Handel's *Messiah* in 1743, the king and the crowds were deeply moved by the glory and grace of the masterpiece. When the musicians swelled the "Hallelujah" chorus, and thundered those mighty words, "And He shall reign for ever and ever!" King George (whose English wasn't all that great) jumped to his feet, thinking they sang of him! The whole crowd followed suit—for a different reason, of course, and a different King!

The comedy of that moment reflects Psalm 8. God in heaven claps his hands and shouts of our greatness. And in the expanding circles of God's glory, we rise, singing the "Hallelujah" chorus.

Vindication

O Lord, see how my enemies persecute me!
—Psalm 9:13

A truck driver pulled his rig into a truck stop and went to the restaurant for a meal. While he was eating, a rough crowd drove up on motorcycles. They invaded the restaurant, wandering around annoying the guests and pestering the staff. They came to the trucker's table and demanded: "We want this table. Get out of here!"

"But I'm not done yet!" he protested.

The leader of the gang took his coffee and poured it all over his food. "Now you're done! Get goin'!"

Without a word, the truck driver picked up his cap, got up from the table, and walked out. The motorcycle gang had a good laugh. "Not much of a man, are ya?" roared the leader after him.

A waitress clearing tables over by the window said, "He's not much of a truck driver either! He just ran over six motorcycles!"

Violence

It's easy to laugh at the problems of others. In fact, virtually the entire entertainment industry in North America earns its billions from our delight in the conflict situations of those around us. News reports sensationalize scandal. Soap operas sneak through steamy bedrooms. Sitcoms revel in family tensions. Crime dramas smear blood. And the ratings soar.

But whenever problems come closer to home, laughter gives way to anger and fear and bitterness. A few years ago this letter appeared in the *Philadelphia Evening Bulletin*:

> I write to you this morning, at the rise of the dawn, still in the midst of a tormented wake, the most terrible grief which has ever seared my soul. Yesterday afternoon, on June 4, I lost the most precious thing that life ever gave to me—a three-and-a-half-year-old girl child of surpassing purity and joy; a being profoundly close to the sacred wellsprings of life itself—a closeness from which she derived great unconscious strength which made her irresistibly attractive to human beings with whom she came in contact. She was murdered at three in the afternoon, in a basement of a house only a few doors

away from ours, by a fifteen-year-old boy. . . . I am hurt to the depths of my being. Had I caught the boy in the act, I would have wished to kill him. . . . A Sick Father

Vengeance

Such evil demands retribution. But often it seems that crime *does* pay, and the innocent bear the scorn of a laughing world. The *New York Times* reports that ninety-nine out of a hundred persons arrested for felonies never go to prison. Embezzlement in North America is growing by 15 percent annually. Nearly half a million students in the U.S. have defaulted on government loans. Hotel and motel rates climb because over 1.5 billion dollars of supplies and equipment is stolen from them *each year.* Hospitals estimate that every bed must be charged an extra thousand dollars per year to pay for thefts from their systems.

"Unfair!" we say. Crimes against property lead us to cry for justice. But when the crimes are against persons, against people we know, against ourselves, we want more than justice—we want revenge.

Vindication

David gets as close to a rage of vengeance in Psalm 9 as we ever hope to find in the Bible, from a human perspective. He stops short of spite, though, and hands the matter over to God. His focus is not ultimately on how badly he's been hurt, but on the glories of God, which transcend these matters, and which ultimately set all things in their proper places.

David echoes what the Heidelberg Catechism states so powerfully in Lord's Day 19: "In all my distress and persecution I turn my eyes to the heavens and confidently await as judge the very One who has already stood trial in my place before God and so has removed the whole curse from me. All his enemies and mine he will condemn to everlasting punishment; but me and all his chosen ones he will take along with him into the joy and the glory of heaven."

Is that a cop-out? Is that pious prejudice or religious retaliation? Only the person who, like David, has been hurt to the core of his being, will be able to answer that question honestly. All others keep silent.

A Small Mind

In all his thoughts there is no room for God.
—Psalm 10:4

Frank Fowler tells this amazing story: during World War II, fifteen hundred international noncombatant prisoners of war were held by the Japanese in a prison camp. Three hundred were Americans, twelve hundred were of other Allied nationalities. The American Red Cross sent twenty-one hundred "care packages" to the camp, each with some necessities and some conveniences.

The Japanese decided that since these came from America, each American should get three packages, and all of the non-Americans would get one package apiece. But the Americans protested; as a group they demanded that they each get seven Red Cross packages, and their non-American allies get none!

Self-centeredness dies slowly in the human heart. We are born frail and helpless, but spend our years asserting our importance. When the French philosopher Auguste Comte was about to die, he murmured to those at his bedside, "What an irreparable loss!" As Nero, the mad emperor of Rome, prepared to commit suicide, he wept for himself, crying, "How great an artist dies here!" And the German philosopher Hegel took this parting shot: "Only one man ever understood me. . . . And he didn't understand me!"

Bitterness

Humility is part of the Christian gospel. We aren't the best. We can't make it on our own. We have no boast in ourselves. Sometimes that can engender a bit of bitterness toward those around us who seem rather self-accomplished and self-fulfilled. Asaph spoke that way in Psalm 73. "I decided at one point to stop training my children in the ways of the Lord," might be a paraphrase of what he says in verse 15, "since godliness kept them from enjoying life!" And David seems to feel the same way here in Psalm 10: "Why do you let others get away with so much, God?"

Simon Darcourt expresses similar sentiments in Robertson Davies's novel *The Lyre of Orpheus*. He's a priest by training and vocation, working now as a university professor. He knows he should be more devout and humble and loving, but there's too much to enjoy in the world around him. He even pulls off an art theft at one point and muses about what it might do to the eternal destiny of his soul. Finally he decides that his sins and deceit won't matter: "A deathbed repentance would probably square things with God. Meanwhile, this was Life."

Resolution

So where does David end up? Is he left a cranky old man, spitefully religious, spouting off doomsday sarcasm ("God's going to get you someday") to the godless millionaires around him?

Not quite. Psalm 10 ends with David's attention turned toward those who are used and abused in society. The helpless. The homeless. The manipulated. Sure, he's gotten ripped off a time or two. Sure, there are moments when he would sell his soul to the devil, if it would gain him some of the cravings that whet his appetite here. But when he sees others who are cast off by the system, he realizes how small the system is. It's big enough for lust, but not for love. It's grand enough for consuming, but not for communion. It's large enough for taking, but never tending.

In the end, David sees beyond the facade of a materialistic society. He longs for a bigger mind that sees God and a larger heart that cares about people. Some might think David is opting out of a dog-eat-dog world because he hasn't got what it takes to make it.

Maybe he hasn't. But should he? Is the mark of human accomplishment the ability to live without God?

Exam Time

He observes the sons of men; his eyes examine them.
—Psalm 11:4

J. Robert Oppenheimer was the brilliant physicist who supervised the development of the atomic bomb. When he was examined for his doctorate at Gottingen University, Professor James Franck discovered that his principle questioner, the young Oppenheimer, was unusually well prepared for the ordeal. When Franck emerged from the interview, he remarked to a colleague, with obvious relief, "I got out of there just in time. *He* was beginning to ask *me* questions!"

Tough Questions

Examinations are rarely fun. They are meant to find out where we are, what we know, and who we are. Sometimes we can bluff our way through. Writer Gertrude Stein happened to be a special favorite of her professor, William James, at Radcliffe College. Unprepared for a test after a night of partying, she boldly wrote, "Dear Professor James, I am so sorry but I do not feel a bit like writing an examination paper on philosophy today." Her brash honesty and his feelings toward her resulted in a full pardon: she passed anyway!

But most times examiners have little mercy. When William Lyon Phelps was a professor of English literature at Yale University, he received a student's test paper shortly before Christmas with this note: "God only knows the answer to this question. Merry Christmas!"

Phelps added a line of his own: "God gets an **A**. You get an **F**. Happy New Year!"

Quality Control

"God gets an **A**." That's really David's affirmation in Psalm 11. God is the great Examiner of hearts who always knows the right questions and never fails at the answers. Nobody pulls a fast one. Nobody bluffs her way through.

Our standards rarely match God's assessment of our lives. We're more like the major Canadian corporation that has this official policy: if less than five lawsuits or grievances are filed against it over any single product or service, quality is deemed satisfactory. It's no longer a matter of doing things right, but what margin of deficiency will allow for maximum profits.

Absolutes

With God there is no margin of deficiency. God's assessment is always accurate; God's grading is never done on the curve. And that is David's great comfort. Where there is wickedness and violence, God will not turn a polite smile of social kindness. He examines. He sees. He tests according to absolute standards. And he will mark with profound judgment the final grade.

But isn't David also afraid? He knows the failings in his own life. "What's good for the goose is good for the gander!" we say. Shouldn't he, too, fear the last report card?

He might, except for one thing. Verse 4 opens by reminding us that "the LORD is in his holy temple," and that makes all the difference in the world. You see, the temple was the one place where Fs could be traded for As, and failures could become successes. The secret was not in bluffing the Examiner or sliding the grading scale; the secret was in the mercy seat at the heart of the temple on which the official Examiner of human hearts sat.

During the nineteenth century, all Oxford graduates were required to translate a portion of the Greek New Testament aloud. Oscar Wilde was assigned a passage from the passion story of Jesus. His translation was fluent and accurate. Satisfied with his skill, the examiners told him he could stop. But he ignored them and continued to translate. Several times more they tried to call a halt to his reading. Finally he looked up and said, "Oh, do let me go on! I want to see how it ends!"

That's the end that matters: the grades are accurate and the results are posted for all to see. No one emerges innocent. But those who are tired of wickedness can become righteous. And only they will see the great Examiner with no fear (v. 7).

Endangered Species

*Help, LORD, for the godly are no more; the faithful have
vanished from among men.*
—Psalm 12:1

The latest word arrived from *Greenpeace* in this morning's mail: "The world's dolphins are being decimated through a deadly combination of commercial greed and plain human carelessness." Without public outcry, "more than 375,000 of these sensitive, intelligent animals" will be slaughtered in the next year.

It's a tragedy, and no human being, authorized by the Creator to mind the world, can ignore the scandal.

Causes

"Commercial greed," says Lesley Scheele of *Greenpeace*, "and plain human carelessness." That's what does it. When those two forces rule, life loses its importance. Commercial greed defines values in terms of profit. Carelessness takes the heart out of our relationships with things or people.

Albert Camus has a little scene reflecting that in his powerful novel *The Fall.* A well-known gentleman is walking the streets of Amsterdam one night, and he hears a sharp cry. A woman has fallen into the canal. She's splashing about, yelling for help. Thoughts come rushing to his mind: of course he must help; but . . . he's a respected lawyer; should *he* be the one to get involved in this? After all, who knows what's been going on? Maybe she's a woman of the streets, and people would assume he'd been with her! Maybe she's been attacked, and her assailant is still lurking in the shadows! Maybe . . .

But by this time, he doesn't have to worry anymore. The splashing has stopped. The woman has drowned. The lawyer is safe, all his marketable values still intact. Camus closes the scene with these words: "He did not answer the cry for help. That is the man he was."

Tragedy

The same tragedy is reflected in Psalm 12. David laments for an endangered species, a vanishing breed. It's not the dolphins and it's not the dinosaurs. It's the community of faithful and godly people who once testified of their religious commitments. It's the race of humans who had a measure of integrity and carried themselves with divine dignity.

"The godly are no more!" cries David. In the words of that mournful folk song: "Where have all the flowers gone, long time passing?"

Commercial greed got them, he says. "Who is our master?" they say (v. 4), and the weak are sold for a mess of pottage (v. 5). Carelessness is their way of life. "The wicked freely strut about when what is vile is honored among men" (v. 8).

And when the godly vanish, the conscience of the people disappears. Babies are aborted, ethnic groups are brushed aside in bigoted disdain, the earth is raped, and the skies are polluted. Jesus once asked, "When the Son of Man comes, will he find faith on the earth?" (Luke 18:8). "I don't know," David would reply. "I'm not sure anymore."

Hope

But David doesn't allow our righteousness to take on Elijah's martyr complex: "I, only I, am left, and they seek to take away my life as well." Nor does he abandon us in remnant suffering: "Well, that's just the way it is these days."

He expects God to do something about it, to enact a new law of protection or to revitalize the species with fresh energy and life. And that's what God does, when Psalm 12 becomes a regular prayer. "O Lord, you will keep us safe" (v. 7).

There's no magic formula, though. There's only the church. A school of dolphins swimming together can break the nets hung for them in the sea. A company of those faithful to God can shatter the grip of commercial greed and carelessness.

The race is endangered. The species is vanishing. The conscience of society is dying. But there's the church. . . .

When God Plays Hide and Seek

How long, O LORD? Will you forget me forever?
How long will you hide your face from me?
—Psalm 13:1

Baptist minister Stephen Winward says that when he was growing up, his mother used to quote a little proverb to him: Patience is a virtue: possess it if you can! Seldom in a woman, and *never* in a man!

Is that true? How patient are you?

Probably each of us has prayed that prayer of patience at one time or another: "Lord, give me patience, and give it to me *right now!*" In the sixteenth century, when life moved at a much slower pace, one man wrote these words: "I have not so great a struggle with my vices, . . . numerous as they are, as I have with my *impatience.* . . . I have never been able to conquer this ferocious wild beast!"

Sound familiar? John Calvin wrote that. And his words will probably always be true for each of us. Even if technology allows us to experience things faster and faster, we will never have enough patience for some things that happen around us in the world, or for specific people that keep getting in our way, or for God, who sometimes seems so distant.

The Silence of God

That last is the tough one, isn't it? We can get over our other frustrations in life, but what do we do when God is silent?

A short while ago I sat with a mother in one of London's hospitals. We prayed for the life of her daughter. She had no peace that God was there. And then, after we prayed for God's healing, her daughter died anyway. Why?

Elie Wiesel endured the horror of the Nazi death camps. He watched women and children herded into gas chambers. He cried with the men who were beaten to death by cruel soldiers. He saw a young boy hanging on a gallows. "Where is God?" he cried.

It's the cry of David in Psalm 13. It's the cry of Job. It's the haunting whisper of every generation that feels the stress of a groaning world and hungers in cosmic silence for a reasonable answer or some tangible touch from heaven. "Where are you, God?"

Where is God when a child dies? Where is God when a mother is snatched from her family? Where is God when nuclear reactors blow up, and airplanes crash, and mines collapse? Where is God? "How long?" cries David.

And Satan laughs. He knows he's got us now. He knows the cards in his hand are the winning draw. Can faith remain when God is silent? Can trust carry on when there seems to be no one at the other end of the line? "No!" shouts Satan.

The Endurance of Faith

But Satan doesn't have the last word.

"Yes!" whisper Job and David and a thousand million other little people crushed by the circumstances of life. "I trust in your unfailing love! I *know* my Redeemer lives!"

That's the deepest level of patience, you know. In the New Testament James calls it "perseverance" (5:11). We love God, not because of the miracles that turn everything our way, but because there is no other way that life makes sense. We trust in God, not because we always feel the wonder of his presence, but because, even in his absence, *there is nowhere else to turn.*

That's the cry of David. That's the patience of Job. That's the heart of Christian faith. You can't explain it. Those of you who have been there can never really share the experience. But you can talk about it later, when God seems close again. It's the awful agony of faith, when we stand undressed and alone.

Not a Pretty Picture

The LORD looks down from heaven on the sons of men to see if there are any who understand, any who seek God. All have turned aside, they have together become corrupt; there is no one who does good, not even one.
—Psalm 14:2-3

Kendrick Strony tells of a seminary classmate who was being examined for ordination as a pastor. All went well till this question came: "Do you believe in the doctrine of the total depravity of the human soul?"

"Yes," he said with a smile, "but I find it very difficult to live up to!"

Easy Enough
For most people, total depravity doesn't seem that hard to live up to. Oscar Wilde put it this way: "I can resist every thing except temptation." In fact, he said, "the only way to get rid of temptation is to yield to it!" Even the saintly Corrie ten Boom admitted late in her life, "I am constantly doing things to others that cause me to have to go back and ask their forgiveness" *(Tramp for the Lord)*.

What one wit has said is probably true: "Most people who fly from temptation usually leave a forwarding address." That's the way it looks from God's perspective, according to David in Psalm 14. Can you imagine all of the rottenness in the world collecting itself into one ugly portrait, and then assaulting the good senses of heaven? Even worse, says David, all the while fools shout, "There is no God" (v. 1).

Silly Sadness
It must seem a little like the silly sadness that surrounded one of Frederick the Great's inspection tours of a Berlin prison in the late 1700s. All of the prisoners crowded the Prussian king, begging for clemency with ringing declarations of innocence. Only one fellow remained silent and aloof. Frederick called to him, "You there! Why are you here?"

"Armed robbery, Your Majesty!" came the reply.

"And are you guilty?" asked Frederick.

"Yes, indeed, Your Majesty. I entirely deserve my punishment."

Frederick summoned the prison warden. "Release this guilty wretch at once!" he ordered. "I will not have him kept in this prison where he will corrupt all the fine innocent people who occupy it!"

In a sense, that's the picture of Psalm 14. Crowded by the blatant godlessness of a self-righteous world, the few who know their guilt are almost afraid to cower in the folds of God's just, though merciful, robes. And while the world carries on with a drunken orgy of war, crime, and immorality, the lonely who buck the evil system seem swallowed up in its aftershocks. Even God appears powerless for the moment to change things. Says the German poet, "If I were God, this world of sin and suffering would break my heart."

Comfort

But David, as always, sees the end of the matter. It may seem that no major counterattack has been launched from heaven's gates since Jesus last appeared on earth. But there are still those who know that "the LORD is their refuge" (v. 6). The essence of biblical religion is comfort—comfort that takes the sting out of pain and death, comfort that encourages in the darkness, comfort that reinvigorates for a new lifestyle (see 2 Cor. 1:3-7).

That comfort is forward-looking. History is not an endless cycle of downs and ups and more downs. Rather, it's a movement toward a climax. It's a promise and a hope of God's next earth-shaking appearance (v. 7).

And when that day comes, the Name that is snubbed now in practical atheism by a self-serving world will be shouted in worship of the King of kings, and the Lord of lords!

Holiness

LORD, who may dwell in your sanctuary?
Who may live on your holy hill?
—Psalm 15:1

In 1928, the annual synod of the Christian Reformed Church debated a weighty matter. Should Dr. B. K. Kuiper be reappointed to a teaching position at Calvin Theological Seminary? After significant discussion and sometimes heated argument, the decision became clear. By a vote of seventy against and only ten in favor, Dr. Kuiper's tenure was denied. He was no longer qualified to shape the minds and lives of future denominational leaders.

Why? What gross heresy was he propounding? How had his theology changed?

No one could deny that Dr. Kuiper was a keen scholar. And no one wished to declare him un-Reformed. In fact, his demise as a professor had little to do with his teaching skills or his theological perspectives.

Instead, it had everything to do with some reported sightings of the venerable gentleman entering a movie theater! "Is it true?" they asked him. And he would not deny it.

Mixed Signals

Holiness is a hard quality to define. Sometimes the signals are all mixed up. Tony Campolo tells of arriving in Philadelphia by bus late one evening. As he turned down the dark street toward home, something hard was pressed against his back. "Give me your money!" came the ominous command.

So Tony handed his wallet to the unseen mugger. After a moment of rustling, there was a cry: "Three dollars? Only three dollars in your wallet? What do you do for a living anyway?"

Tony said that he was a Baptist minister.

"Hey! That's great!" came the reply. "I'm a Baptist too!"

Visible Godliness

Holiness is visible expression of godliness. But what would God look like if he were living among us as a human, not just in Palestine twenty centuries ago, but right here, right now, just down the street? The way Christians answer that question shapes their perspective on what a Christian lifestyle looks like.

Members of one congregation demanded a policy from the elders regarding the Sunday afternoon pastimes of the young people. "How can you let them play ball on the Lord's day?" questioned some. But for others, playing ball was preferred over swimming. "Let them play ball! Just keep them out of the water!"

During the winter it was hockey. Some thought Sunday afternoons were made for skating on the local pond. Others felt their commitments to organized clubs required tourney play at the nearby arena. Still another group was certain that any sporting activity, including all forms of hockey, had no place in a Christian's life on Sunday.

Matters of the Heart

Until Jesus returns, we will debate issues of holiness. Few of us will be completely satisfied with others' perspectives. Part of the problem is that there is no concrete "code of ethics" in Scripture that defines behavior in all situations of life. The Ten Commandments brush colors in broad strokes, which, as Jesus says in the Sermon on the Mount, have a variety of more specific applications. Even David's list in Psalm 15 is too general to be a final code of conduct. He speaks of the heart and expects some change in lifestyle. But the emphasis is on the heart. The person who lives with God carries himself or herself with a certain air in society. It's hard to define in exact terms, but others can sense it. And they can sense its absence too.

One morning in 1872, David Livingstone wrote this in his diary:

> March 19, my birthday. My Jesus, my King, my Life, my All, I again dedicate my whole self to Thee. Accept me, and grant, O gracious Father, that ere the year is gone I may finish my work. In Jesus' name I ask it. Amen.

Just one year later, servants came to check on their master's delay. They found him on his knees in prayer. He was dead.

Friends in England provided a final resting place for his body. And they posted a note that testifies yet today:

> He needs no epitaph to guard a name
> Which men will prize while worthy work is known;
> He lived and died for good—that is his fame;
> Let marble crumble: this is Living-stone!

Hi! How Are You?

LORD, you have assigned me my portion and my cup; you have made my lot secure. The boundary lines have fallen for me in pleasant places; surely I have a delightful inheritance.
—*Psalm 16:5-6*

"Hi! How are you?" We probably say that to people around us a hundred times a day. Usually we're not really looking for an answer. It's just a polite way to acknowledge somebody else's presence.

In fact, if we know of people who take us seriously and start dumping all their problems on us, we'll probably not ask them how they are tomorrow.

There's a story about a little girl who came home from school one day, and her mother met her at the door: "Hi! How was school today? How are you doing?"

With the honesty of little people, the girl replied, "Oh, not so well, Mommy. My tummy hurts!"

Mothers know everything, and this Mommy had the cure: "Well, that's probably because you don't have anything in it. Let's find you something to eat." Sure enough, after a snack the little girl's tummy didn't ache anymore.

Mother had to go to the store for a few items, and the little girl was left home alone. When the phone rang, she answered it politely, just as she had been taught. It was the minister. "Hello!" she said. "How are you today?"

"Well," he replied, "to tell you the truth, I've got a bit of a headache!" And before he could go any further, the young girl had him diagnosed: "My Mommy says that's probably because you don't have anything in it!"

How Are You?

"Hi! How are you?" How would you answer that today? Could you answer the way David did in Psalm 16?

David says that his joy and confidence have very conscious roots: "I said to the LORD, 'You are my Lord; apart from you I have no good thing'" (v. 2).

David doesn't rationalize his happiness and contentment in Psalm 16. In fact, he acknowledges a number of nasty things that are happening to him and around him: he's being threatened by enemies (v. 1), he lives in a wicked society (v. 4), he's had some sleepless nights (v. 7), troubling circumstances have surprised him (v. 8), and an illness has brought him face to face with death (vv. 9-10). Not a pretty picture! What would you say if you were in his shoes, and somebody asked you, "How are you today?"

Samuel Beckett wrote a little drama called *Happy Days.* The main character is a woman named Winnie. In the first half of the play she stands in a pile of sand that comes up to her waist. In the second half, she's there at center stage again, but now the sand is up to her neck. And the whole time she keeps cheering herself on with an endless monologue—little witty sayings, bits and pieces of songs and hymns, things like that.

But you end up feeling sorry for her. She's not really happy. She's just putting on a show. If she would ever stop singing to herself, stop giving herself a pep talk, the sands would swallow her up.

Fooling Ourselves?

You and I could be in the same spot. And some around us will say that our religion is to us what it seems to be for Winnie: a disgusting, mindless, self-deluding pep talk.

But don't accuse David of that. He's a realist. He'll tell you his troubles if you ask him. But he'll also tell you about the One who shares his troubles and gives him a delightful sense of security. Happiness isn't what you have; it's Who you know!

Years ago, when I was an announcer at a U.S. radio station, I hosted a request program. One song that people asked for dozens of times one year spoke about people in trouble, like David. It told a story about Abe Lincoln, the famous U.S. president. And the story is supposed to be true. During the bloody days of the Civil War, when Christians on both sides were praying for God to help them . . . Well, listen to these lines from the song:

> Abe Lincoln was a president, fought hard for liberty.
> Was asked if he considered God upon his side to be. . . .
> "The thing," he said, "that bothers me, as I consider this
> is not if God is on *my* side, but whether I'm on *His!*"

David would say, "Now you've got it straight! How are you doing?"

Night Thoughts

You probe my heart and examine me at night. . . . When I
awake, I will be satisfied. . . .
—Psalm 17:3, 15

A young playwright was anxious about the new drama he had written. He decided to ask the great poet Carl Sandburg to attend the dress rehearsal and critique the play. Sandburg came alright, but he slept through the entire performance. When the young writer complained, reminding Sandburg how much he had wanted the master's opinion, Sandburg replied, "Sleep *is* an opinion!"

Yawn!

Sleep comes rather easily for some people. Alfred Hitchcock had a nasty habit of falling asleep at parties. On one occasion, he had been asleep for nearly four hours when his wife woke him and suggested that they go home. "But it's only one o'clock!" he protested. "They'll think we aren't enjoying ourselves."

Or take Prince Albert, husband of the great Queen Victoria. A typical line in a review of a concert given at Buckingham Palace was this: "The queen was charmed, and cousin Albert looked beautiful, and slept as usual."

Insomnia

Some people can sleep anywhere, anytime. But most of us have moments of anxiety when even the darkest night is crowded with thoughts and fears. Sleep takes a holiday, and we toss under the restless persecution of unwanted memories. David's waking nightmare in Psalm 17 is a picture of enemies ready to pounce (vv. 10-12). But it could just as well be a financial crisis, the agony of a lonely bed after death or divorce, or the problems developing in family relationships.

What do you do when you can't sleep at night? British Roman Catholic priest and author Ronald Knox suffered from insomnia all his life. His parents remember the time when he was only four years old and a friend asked him what he did during his sleepless nights. "I lie awake," he said, "and think about the past."

But sometimes the past has problems of its own. David, who wrote this psalm one sleepless night, also wrote Psalm 25, where the sins of his younger days continue to worry him as well (25:7). And here in Psalm 17, the probing, unsleeping eye of God is threatening challenge (v. 3). On those sleepless nights when peace skirts the edges of my sanity, the harder I try to sleep, the more I'm taunted with new problems and bigger worries.

Lullaby of Love

Where do you go on a sleepless night? Where do you turn? What do you think about? Amazingly, Psalm 17 is cut short after a few reflective phrases about the love of God. It's almost as if the worries tumble over each other in jumbled vexation until David remembers that God really cares about him. God's eye may never close. God's eye may search out the evil of his heart. God's eye may probe the nightmares of his daytime existence. But God's eye is always the eye of a Father for his children. When David looks God in the eye, he sees a heart of love.

Before he can even think another anxious thought, a smile has softened his face. And the gentle peace of sleep tugs his eyelids shut.

"Precious Lord, Take My Hand"

I love you, O LORD, my strength.
—Psalm 18:1

There's a place in one of our London, Ontario, parks called "Storybook Gardens." It's a children's village filled with scenes from nursery rhymes and fairy tales. There are animals to touch and feed and watch, and play areas for jumping and running and climbing.

There's also a maze made of four-foot fencing. It's a human puzzle full of blind alleys and dead-ends. Our girls have mixed feelings about the maze. They ran right on into it the first time. Kimberly dashed ahead, finally blundering her way through by trial and error. But Kristyn and Kaitlyn got stuck. The walls closed in on them. There was no way out. All of a sudden a desperate crying and fearful wailing rose above the maze! And Daddy, who can see all things, had to rescue them from the melancholy of the maze!

The Maze of Melancholy

There are times in all our lives when we enter the "maze of melancholy." We feel weak and helpless and lost. The walls start closing in around us. There's no future and no past—just the hopeless grim skies of now.

You can see David walking in his own "maze of melancholy" in Psalm 18: "The cords of death entangled me; the torrents of destruction overwhelmed me" (v. 4). The whole psalm resonates with struggles and bleak moments. It reminds me of the songs of William Cowper, a member of John Newton's congregation in Olney, England, in the 1700s. Some of his poetry has found its way into the hymnals of the church. "God moves in a mysterious way, his wonders to perform," says one song. And in a wonderful confession of confidence:

> What God ordains is always right;
> he guides our joy and sadness.
> He is our life and blessed light;
> in him alone is gladness.
> We see his face, the way of grace;
> he holds us in his mighty arm
> and keeps us safe from every harm.

But William Cowper was a troubled soul. He began to slip in and out of depression. He spent a year and a half in what was then called an "insane asylum." His hymns began to take on a darker color. This song is a cry of spiritual loneliness:

> Where is the blessedness I knew,
> when first I sought the Lord?
> Where is the soul-refreshing view
> of Jesus and His word?

Cowper died of a broken heart and a crushed spirit.

Sometimes we want to die, too, stranded in our own "maze of melancholy." David says "the snares of death confronted me" (v. 5). The weakness of the human spirit is no match for the combined terrors of friendlessness, fear, and fatigue: "The cords of the grave coiled around me."

Scaling the Walls

But another theme plays out Psalm 18. "The LORD is my rock, my fortress and my deliverer" (v. 2). "He reached down from on high and took hold of me; he drew me out of deep waters" (v. 16). "The LORD was my support" (v. 18). "With my God," says David, "I can scale a wall" (v. 29), even a wall in the "maze of melancholy."

And somewhere in between comes the prayer of verse 6: "In my distress I called to the LORD." Somehow, says David, "my cry came . . . into his ears." God opened a door in David's "maze of melancholy."

Early this century, Tommy Dorsey, the "blues" songwriter and musician, had a moment when the world had collapsed around him, and he wandered in his private "maze of melancholy." He sat at his piano and wrote this little prayer:

> Precious Lord, take my hand, lead me on, help me stand;
> I am tired, I am weak, I am worn;
> through the storm, through the night, lead me on to the light;
> take my hand, precious Lord, lead me home.
> When my way grows drear, precious Lord, linger near;
> when my life is almost gone,
> hear my cry, hear my call, hold my hand lest I fall;
> take my hand, precious Lord; lead me home.

A Perfect Pair

The heavens declare the glory of God. . . .
The law of the Lord is perfect, reviving the soul.
—Psalm 19:1, 7

"You can't stand on one leg!" A hostess says that to her mealtime guests, urging second helpings on them. It seems that only the pink flamingos at the zoo know it's not true.

Some things come naturally in pairs: salt and pepper, hammer and nails, sackcloth and ashes. We never use a scissor; only a pair of scissors will do the job. Children in school learn quickly about "show and tell"; you can't do one without the other. And the way we're made demands a pair of pants, a pair of glasses, and a pair of gloves.

An old song says that one is the loneliest number that you've ever heard. It's true in marriage. It's true in friendship. It's true in conversation. Some things have to come in twos in order to exist.

Hand in Hand

Psalm 19 praises the perfect pair: the shout of God's glory in creation and the testimony of his goodness in the Bible. They walk hand in hand. They stand side by side. They know each other face to face.

You can't have the one without the other. Creation is the splash of splendor, and the Bible is its interpretive handbook. Nature speaks of God's power, and the Scriptures define that power in the shape of love. The star-spangled heavens exalt a transcendent deity, while the pages of the Book bring God as close as a good friend.

Bible scholars have tried for centuries to plunge in a knife at verse 7 and divorce the two parts that "obviously" stood separate long ago. But with grudging admiration, all of them finally agree that the balance is perfect, the partnership fits, and the whole is greater than its halves. As C. S. Lewis says, "I take this to be the greatest poem in the Psalter and one of the greatest lyrics in the world!"

Double-Talk

Sometimes double-talk can be deceitful. The ancient Roman god Janus was always depicted with two faces, one facing forward, the other facing to the rear. Originally he was worshiped as the all-seeing one, knowing both the future and the past. But later he became the epitome of contempt, speaking from two mouths at the same time. Today his name describes the liar, the hypocrite, the charlatan. A "Janus" is a deceitful, double-dealing person.

George Orwell's powerful novel, *1984*, portrayed a society in which the official language was Newspeak. But Newspeak was really double-talk; nothing actually meant what it was supposed to. And in a world of double-talk, nobody trusted anybody else.

Two Witnesses
But the delightful thing about God's "double-talk" is that each testimony confirms the other. What creation proclaims in bold patterns is matched by Scripture's poetic narrative. What thunders from the heavens above is validated by the whisper from the page. God is good. God is glorious. God is gracious.

When the famous soprano Jenny Lind was on her way to her first concert tour of North America, she told Captain West of her desire to see sunrise across the expanse of the ocean. One cloudless morning he had her called at early dawn.

Silent and motionless she stood by his side on the rear deck, watching every change of shade and tint in the sky and the reflections on the water below. As the rays of the sun leaped from the horizon, she spontaneously broke out in song. Her message was Job's testimony, set to the magnificent melody of Handel: "I know that my Redeemer liveth!"

In that moment of exaltation, Captain West later wrote, the Word of God was complete. The pair of God's speeches had become one. And the only response possible was the awe-struck prayer of David: "May the words of my mouth and the meditation of my heart be pleasing in your sight, O LORD, my Rock and my Redeemer" (v. 14).

Friends

We will shout for joy when you are victorious and will lift up
our banners in the name of our God.
May the Lord grant all your requests.
—Psalm 20:5

A sign in a nearby restaurant proclaims: *There are no strangers here; only friends we haven't met yet.* Isn't that a nice thought?

Wanted: Friends

In 1985, researcher Donald Posterski surveyed more than 3,600 young people across Canada. "What are the most important values in your life?" he asked. Surprisingly, only 20 percent said "I want to be popular."

Half gave "success," or "freedom," or "a comfortable life" as things they felt strongly about. "Good family relations" were extremely important to 65 percent, and 87 percent hoped they would always be loved.

But more than 90 percent chose *friendship* as the highest value in their lives. And, deep down, we know that's true. When a high school friend of mine committed suicide, he left a note behind saying two things: he felt he had failed his parents, and he believed he didn't have a friend in the world to talk with. If only he had a friend . . .

A few years ago, a senior high school student in Alberta wrote a poem called "Caged Emotions." She said:

> . . . no one knows me.
> I mean the real me.
> The one part of me that
> Counts the most.
> My doubts and fears and emotions.
> > You're so entwined
> > In your own world
> > You have no time for mine.

If only she had a friend, a *good* friend . . .

The American philosopher George Santayana once tragically summarized a marriage he knew like this:

He liked to walk alone;
she liked to walk alone;
so they got married,
    and walked alone together.

If only they had learned to be friends . . .

Companions

Maybe the word "companion" says it best: it literally means "someone who shares bread" with me. A true friend is a companion, someone we eat bread with, someone we sit at table with, someone who shares our provisions and carries our loads down the path of life.

That's the delight of David in Psalm 20. He knew the strength of friends. They listened to him. They laughed with him. They shared his tears. They encouraged and supported him. His bread was their bread, and in the struggles of his life they prayed for him. Companions . . .

Friendship Blossoms

Last year, at one marriage ceremony in our church, the program included this poem written by the bride, summarizing the warm glow confirmed that day:

My heart quickens at the thought of spending time with you!
You put joy in my heart,
    a smile on my lips,
   and a sparkle in my eyes!
When two people care enough to give of themselves,
    friendship blossoms!

It must have felt the same way in another place, long ago, when another Wedding Partner said to us, "You are my friends" (John 15:14).

Strength

O LORD, the king rejoices in your strength. . . .
Be exalted, O LORD, in your strength;
we will sing and praise your might.
—Psalm 21:1, 13

In David Heller's delightful book *Dear God: Children's Letters to God,* one youngster writes about his summer vacation: Dear God, I saw the Grand Canyon last summer. Nice piece of work!

Awe

Big things have a way of overwhelming us, especially big displays of power. Recently an advertisement came in the mail. Associates of a Dr. Frank R. Wallace were promoting his revolutionary "new field of knowledge" called "Neo-Tech." He says he discovered this "scientific" use of intellectual power while playing poker. After some reflection, he figured out how to use this power on a regular basis, to make money, influence people, and take command of any love relationship he wanted with any woman he chose.

"Who exactly is the Neo-Tech person?" asked an interviewer.

Said Wallace: "He's a person of quiet power—a person who cannot lose. He can control anyone . . . man or woman. Within days after gaining this knowledge, people can safely bankrupt opponents . . . immediately extract money and prestige not only from any card game, but from any competitive, personal, business or money situation."

Wow! That's some kind of power. Wallace even makes the claim that "those without Neo-Tech will die unfulfilled . . . without ever knowing wealth, power, and romantic love."

How much for the package? Just $70 for all that power! My only problem was this line: "Dr. Wallace prohibits us from selling Neo-Tech to certain people, such as clergy, politicians, and other professional neocheaters. . . ." So much for me!

Gentleness

Raw power is stunning. But rarely is it warm and personal in the way we think of strength. Power explodes, while strength is channeled energy. Power unleashes force, but strength controls ability in very specific ways.

Someone has even defined the gentle concept of meekness as "strength under control."

An atomic bomb is horrifyingly overwhelming, but the steady nuclear output of the sun is simply amazing. A wild horse can be a terrifying beast; the grace and gentleness of a trained stallion channels all that energy into a magnificent steeplechase run. A powerful person intimidates, but a strong person may tumble in play with children.

Adequate

And that's the delight of David's awe in Psalm 21. He's captivated by the strength God commands and the power God displays for the asking. It's not brute force or raw energy. Rather, it is a sense of justice (vv. 11-12), a victory of "splendor and majesty" (v. 5), and the security of a personal friendship (v. 7).

Alan Redpath tells of a prominent businessman in South Africa who was duly impressed with the luxury of Rolls Royce automobiles. He ordered one for himself and marveled at its speed and handling. He looked through the manual but found no test results listed indicating the horsepower of the engine. So he went to the dealer.

"I'm sorry," the dealer told him. "The company never states the horsepower of their engines."

But the man was not to be put off. And he was too powerful a person to be ignored. So the dealer sent a cable to Derby, England, asking the head office for an answer in the matter.

Within a short time, there was a reply. It was brief and to the point, a response of only a single word. How much horsepower does the Rolls Royce engine develop? "ADEQUATE." That's all. That's enough.

And that's David's celebration in Psalm 21. How much strength does God have? Adequate. Adequate to meet my needs and see me through. Adequate to take care of whatever evil power might throw itself up against God or God's people. Adequate to establish a king on a throne or suckle a child at its mother's breast.

"We will sing and praise your might" (v. 13), say the people, for it is adequate.

Only the Grateful Believe

From you comes the theme of my praise in the great assembly;
before those who fear you will I fulfill my vows.
—Psalm 22:25

A schoolteacher asked her students to make a list of the things for which they were thankful. Right at the top of Chad's list was the word "glasses." Some children resent having to wear glasses, but evidently not Chad! She asked him about it. Why was he thankful that he wore glasses?

"Well," he said, "my glasses keep the boys from hitting me and the girls from kissing me."

Hard Arithmetic

The philosopher Eric Hoffer says, "The hardest arithmetic to master is that which enables us to count our blessings!" That's true, isn't it?

There's an old legend about the angels of heaven coming to earth to gather prayers into large baskets. Thousands return with their baskets overflowing with every request, from a child's prayer: "Bless Mommy and Daddy and Sister and Brother and my pet hamster" to the atheist's cry: "O God! What do we do now?"

But a single lonely angel returns to heaven with a half-empty basket of thanksgiving notes. That's all there are. Like the ten lepers Jesus healed, we run off with the nine and only once in a while stop to think and thank.

Uneasy Union

David overflows with thanksgiving in Psalm 22. We would never think so at first. The early verses of the Psalm are horrible. "My God, my God, why have you forsaken me?" he yells in verse 1. He's surrounded by taunting enemies (v. 12), burning with fever (v. 15), exhausted and starving (v. 17), and facing the prospect of a violent death (v. 16). His experiences find a prophetic parallel in the screaming horror of Jesus' death on the cross—so much so that Jesus himself makes David's opening cry his own (Mark 15:34).

How is it possible to end that song in praise and thanksgiving? We'd like to separate the two, wouldn't we? We'd like to cut Psalm 22 into sections. We want to sing the song of thanksgiving when we're in the mood for it, seldom as that may be. But we don't want to sing the first twenty-one verses. We don't want to know the tragedies of life. We don't want to feel the lostness and the forsakenness that David knew. We don't want his pain. We don't want his problems. It's either/or for us. It's one or the other, the good or the bad, thanksgiving or curses.

Where Faith Begins

But faith begins when we *do* keep the tragedy and thanks of Psalm 22 together, doesn't it? Before another year is over, some of us will die, perhaps painfully. Some of us will find out we have cancer. Some of us will lose our businesses. Some of us will lose our spouses. Some of us will be betrayed by our friends. And some of us will pray, but after a little while, all we'll be able to do is cry out: "My God, my God, why have you forsaken me?"

That's when we'll need to remember Psalm 22. Thanksgiving and faith go hand in hand. My faith in God is not just some polite thanks for the goodies and trinkets that I think he's given me. No, it's the other way around. My thankfulness to him is the cornerstone of my faith. I'm not thankful just because I believe he's given me things. Rather, I believe because it's right to give him thanks, even when I can't point to anything specific. Even when the chips are down. Even when I'm surrounded by trouble.

In 1637, Eilenburg, Saxony, was surrounded by the dark night of the soul. Europe was at war. Eilenburg was tossed back and forth by the armies. Three times during that year it was attacked and severely damaged. When the armies left, refugees poured in by the thousands. Diseases ran rampant. Food was scarce.

There was only one pastor in the city, a fellow named Martin Rinkart. His journal for 1637 indicates that he conducted over 4,500 funerals that year, sometimes as many as forty or fifty a day. Life was a constant death, and each morning stank of disaster.

Still, somehow, even today, 1637 is important for nearly every Thanksgiving celebration around the world. For Christians still sing the song Pastor Rinkart wrote that year. They sing it with gusto. They sing it with faith. They sing it, not because it catalogues a list of reasons for thanksgiving, but because thankfulness is all that is left when the bottom drops out of the world.

> Now thank we all our God with heart and hands and voices,
> who wondrous things has done, in whom his world rejoices;
> who from our mothers' arms has blessed us on our way
> with countless gifts of love, and still is ours today.

Only the grateful believe!

Driven or Led?

The LORD is my shepherd . . .
—Psalm 23:1

Several years ago, Jack Glenn, pastor of a Presbyterian congregation in Mendota, Illinois, decided that the church's nativity scene needed a little repair work. The shepherd figures held staffs made of electrical conduit, bent and rebent and kinked over the years.

Let's get real ones, he thought. But no farm supply store had such a thing. Intrigued, Pastor Glenn asked around until he gained the name of a man who not only owned a large herd of sheep, but was also an expert on their care.

"Where can I get a genuine shepherd's staff?" he asked.

"Nowhere," came the reply. "You have to remember that here in the West, sheep are driven by dogs. It's only in the East that they are led by a shepherd."

Mob Mania

Ours often seems to be a *driven* society. The ideals of the French Revolution have permeated our culture: Life! Liberty! Land! We North Americans have turned the last into a steady pleasure trip by translating it this way: the pursuit of happiness. All too often we're scrambling after more and better and bigger thrills.

One picture from the French Revolution, with its mob mania, perhaps best typifies the whole enterprise of Western life. A wild-eyed man comes charging up to a citizen pausing on a Paris street corner.

"Where's the crowd?" he cries. "Tell me, quick! Which way have they gone? I must follow them. I'm their leader."

Driven by madness! Driven by the dogs! The dogs of desire, the dogs of fame and fortune, the dogs of war . . . it's a dog-eat-dog world.

He Leadeth Me

Maybe it's time to return to the East. Not the East of mysticism and transcendental meditation, helpful as they might be, but rather the One who grew up in the East, the One called "the good shepherd" (John 10:1-18), "the great Shepherd" (Heb. 13:20-21), and "the Chief Shepherd" (1 Pet. 5:4). Maybe it's time to stop being driven and be led again in the simplicity of devotion. Maybe it's time to stop with David on the hillsides of Judea and sing the song of the Shepherd.

What a wonder of peace and tranquility Psalm 23 is! Sometimes, in our mad dashing about, we see only the last verses, the verses about comfort at death and the promise of life beyond the grave. But which of us will hope in such things if the calm serenity of the early verses isn't also a mark of our lives? The closest some people seem to get to Psalm 23 is having its poetic lines etched on the little memorial cards that are handed out at their funerals.

The Japanese Christian Toki Miyashina once surveyed the damage done by Western culture on his hustle-bustle society. He paraphrased Psalm 23 in a way that speaks volumes:

> The Lord is my pacesetter, I shall not rush:
> He makes me stop and rest for quiet intervals;
> He provides me with images of stillness which restore my serenity;
> He leads me in the way of efficiency, through calmness of mind;
> and His guidance is peace.
> Even though I have a great many things to accomplish each day,
> I will not fret, for His presence is here.
> His timelessness, His all-importance keeps me in balance.
> He prepares refreshment and renewal in the midst of activity
> by anointing my mind with His oils of tranquility;
> my cup of joyous energy overflows.
> Surely harmony and effectiveness shall be the fruits of my hours,
> and I shall walk in the pace of my Lord,
> and dwell in His house forever.

If David were with us today, I think he'd like that.

MEDITATION 24

The Earth Is the Lord's

The earth is the LORD's, and everything in it,
the world, and all who live in it.
—Psalm 24:1

J. B. S. Haldane was a British biochemist who died in 1964. He was widely read, and had a keen sense of perception. People used to come to him for simple explanations of profound mysteries. Once, a well-known theologian asked him, "What are you able to say about the character of God, now that you've studied his creation?"

"Well," said Haldane, "He seems to have an inordinate fondness for beetles!"

Do You See What I See?

What do you see when you look at the world around?

Stephen W. Hawking's book *A Brief History of Time* had a place on the best-seller lists for over a year. Dr. Hawking is a tiny man, scrunched up in a wheelchair by a strange and debilitating disease. His body is twisted out of shape; often useless for the simplest tasks in life. But his mind is free and powerful, and from his wheelchair he travels the universe, unraveling the mysteries of time and space.

"Why was the universe formed?" asked Ric Dolphin of *Maclean's* magazine.

"If I knew that," replied Hawking, "there would be nothing else to find out. I would know the mind of God. . . . "

The Mind of God

What do you know of the mind of God?

"God is really only another artist," said Picasso. "He invented the giraffe, the elephant, and the cat. He has no real style; he just goes on trying other things."

"God is a sort of burglar," said Sir Herbert Beerbohn Tree. "As a young man you knock him down; as an old man you try to conciliate him because he may knock you down."

"God seems to have left the receiver off the hook," wrote Arthur Koestler, "and time is running out."

The King of Glory

David's experience of God is something different. It's the amazed shout of joy that happens on a beautiful morning as the colors shimmer in early dawn. "The earth is the LORD's, and everything in it," he sings with gusto.

But it's more than just an emotional outburst, a passing exuberance, a peak psychological experience. David stands above Jerusalem wondering aloud whether the God of great glory notices him (v. 3). Why, indeed, should a God of glory pay attention to any of us?

For one reason. For one reason alone. Because God *chooses* to! Psalm 24 is the song sung as the ark of the covenant enters Jerusalem. The ancient doors, long closed in foreboding, long darkened with dread and deceit, swing wide (vv. 7-10), and the royal throne of the King of glory enters in triumph. The God who holds the world in the palm of his hand sets up housekeeping with his people in Jerusalem. God chooses to care.

And that's why life matters. Not just on Sunday at church. Not just devotions and Bible reading. But all of life. Even beetles!

Anguish

The troubles of my heart have multiplied;
free me from my anguish.
—Psalm 25:17

The world received it as a smash hit. The song topped the charts and was crooned from the stages of a thousand North American dance halls. Everyone wanted to hear Ruth Lowe's new melody.

But in her Toronto home, the young widow could care less. A vibrant marriage to a handsome young pianist had been cut short by his death. Life was cruel, and anguish etched the dark rooms of their home. Even the old piano they had played together seemed a taunting monster, and Ruth couldn't bring herself to touch it.

Family and friends tried to help, but Ruth was beyond comfort. In a moment of exasperated helplessness, her father threw up his hands and challenged her to *do something,* anything. "Take it out on the piano!" he shouted. "Write a song! Pound the keys!"

When he left, Ruth Lowe hammered out the mournful dirge that all the world begged to sing with her: "I'll Never Smile Again."

All Sizes

"Afflictions sorted," wrote George Herbert, "anguish of all sizes, fine nets and stratagems to catch us in . . . " George Eliot read the tragic story of a burdened man, and called it "the chronicle of a solitary hidden anguish. . . . " It could have been the story of David in Psalm 25. One feels a heartbreak like that in Hemingway's tale *Islands in the Stream.* An anguished father mourns the loss of his oldest son, killed in the war. There is no consolation. He won't eat. He can't sleep.

At one point he walks the beach for hours and hours till a friend tries to steer him out of his depression. "No," he says, "I have been out here all day thinking about him and wanting to have him with me always. I know I have to let him go. I have *got* to . . . but I cannot do it today!"

Tomorrow may be brighter, but not today, never today.

Faith in Focus

In my childhood home there was a wall plaque, unadorned except for three words: "Keep looking up." For us children, it was a comic command, and we would stumble about with our eyes glued to the ceiling. But for those of us who have known the adult anguish of David, there is no other hope or help. "To you, O LORD, I lift up my soul" (v. 1). "My eyes are ever on the LORD, for only he will release my feet from the snare" (v. 15). "My hope is in you" (v. 21).

"Keep looking up."

Sir James Simpson, the Scottish physician who discovered the anesthetic properties of chloroform, freed his world from much pain. But his own heart was anguished by the death of a little daughter. When she was buried in a lonely Edinburgh cemetery, Simpson had a single word carved on the headstone: Nevertheless. And in that small act of devotion, he placed his grief in the hands of God.

"Keep looking up."

Large Consolation

Bertrand Russell once said, "The only adequate way to endure large stresses is to find large consolation." David knew that. So did Paul in the New Testament when he wrote this stirring testimony: "Praise be to the God and Father of our Lord Jesus Christ, the Father of compassion and the God of all comfort, who comforts us in all our troubles, so that we can comfort those in any trouble with the comfort we ourselves have received from God" (2 Cor. 1:3-4).

Large consolation indeed. For in the anguish of life "you are God my Savior, and my hope is in you all day long" (v. 5).

Uncompromising Devotion

I have led a blameless life; I have trusted in the LORD
without wavering.
—*Psalm 26:1*

Fred Craddock, who teaches preachers at Emory University, says we all have this glorious image of ourselves when we first stand up and confess Jesus Christ. He says it's as if we have a brand-new starched and stiff $1,000 bill. We take it to Jesus and shout, "Here! Here's my life! Here's my wealth! Here's all of my being! Take me, Jesus! I give myself to you!"

Jesus takes our bright and shiny and crinkly $1,000 bill. But then he hands it back to us. "Go to the bank," he says. "Cash it in for nickels and dimes."

When we do that, coming home with buckets and baskets and wheelbarrows of coins, he says to us, "Now give me fifteen cents a day for the rest of your life."

All excited, we start out with a flourish. A nickel and a dime, set aside each morning. But there are always so many other things to buy, so many other toys to play with, and soon the nickels and dimes are gone. So is our faith. And so is our uncompromising devotion. Like the beggars on the street, we walk around with limp hands and feeble hearts.

Quitting Halfway Through

It's easy to love your spouse on the day of your wedding. It's easy to make commitments for a lifetime in the heat of passion. It's easy to soar on a blazing glory star of faith when you join the church. But the world around says: "You'll never make it. You'll never keep your vows. You'll never last."

When Jesus asks us for a slow and steady devotion rather than a martyr's burst of passion, we often die inch by inch, a nickel and a dime at a time.

One mother tells this story about her son. He earned a little spending money every winter by shoveling snow from people's driveways and walks up and down their street. One morning, after a heavy snowfall, he seemed awfully slow in leaving the house. She asked him if there was anything wrong. "No," he said, "I'm just waiting till people get started. I get most of my jobs from people who want to quit halfway through."

A Magnificent Obsession

Somehow, David claims he's going for the goal in Psalm 26. He's not about to drop out of the race. He's been knocked down by his own pride and passions, and sometimes by the storms of others. But he's up and running again, a nickel and dime each morning, and heading for the finish line of God's glory.

How does that happen? "I love the house where you live, O LORD," he sings (v. 8), "the place where your glory dwells." He's gained the kind of "magnificent obsession" that author Lloyd Douglas writes about in his novel of that name. The book is about a fellow named Robert Merrick. He's young. He's rich. He's drunk. Life is a game for him, a game of using people and tossing them aside. A game of playing with his toys in his self-centered world.

And then it happens: he's out on his yacht; the wind catches the sail and throws the boom at him; he falls into the water, unconscious, and is rescued, barely alive.

At the same moment, a world-famous doctor, dedicated, devoted, a saver of lives, drowns in a freak accident just down the beach. Young Merrick lies in the hospital. His eyes are closed, and everybody thinks he's unconscious. Two nurses stand over him, and one shakes her head.

"What a tragedy . . . " she says. "A great man who saves lives [is] lost, and this fellow, who never did any good for anybody, [is] saved!"

Merrick knows it's true. He's alive, but he's never really lived. He was pulled from the water, but for no good reason. And in that moment, in that instant of judgment, Merrick gains his "magnificent obsession." He'll go to university. He'll get a degree in medicine. He'll take the doctor's place. He'll save lives and begin to truly live himself.

A magnificent obsession! A purpose for which to live and a cause for which to die. That's the atmosphere that pervades Psalm 26. God! My God! The glory of God! "Your love is ever before me" shouts David (v. 3). That's why "I lead a blameless life" (v. 11).

And his magnificent obsession carries him on from glory to glory (2 Cor. 3:18).

Light

The LORD is my light and my salvation.
—Psalm 27:1

It was a night to remember! Five school buddies at a friend's home overnight. Pizza and popcorn (more than I had ever before stuffed into myself), a late movie on television, and then the stories. Who could tell the scariest tale? We outdid one another with false bravado.

Was it just my imagination? Sure, it was night outside, but wasn't the darkness creeping closer? What lurked in the shadows just beyond the weakening glimmer of the lamps? Our bodies were tired but our minds raced with fear.

Dark Night of the Soul
We've all been there. Dark nights. Ghostly fears. Terrifying images.

And even when we "grow up," something haunting often lingers at the edges of our brightest days. Francis Bacon said, "Men fear death as children fear to go in the dark; and as that natural fear in children is increased with tales, so is the other!"

When the German poet Goethe lay dying, his last words were a terrified shout: "Light! Light! I need more light!" The final fears of short story writer O. Henry (William Sidney Porter) came out this way: "Turn up the lights! I don't want to go home in the dark!" And those who have faced death and loneliness nod silently with F. Scott Fitzgerald's lament: "In the real dark night of the soul it is always 3 o'clock in the morning."

A Lantern in the Night
There is much in Psalm 27 that dances in delight. David's bravado in the face of enemies (vv. 2-3), his enjoyment of worship at the temple (v. 4), and his confident trust in God (vv. 5-6) are ringing examples of faith at its finest.

But the psalm is edged by fear: fear of loneliness (v. 9), fear of rumors (v. 12), fear of alienation from family (v. 10), fear of crime and violence (v. 12), fear even that his religion is useless and faulty (vv. 7, 9). And in the dark night of his soul, David shares with us the tales that have kept us awake too: "Why don't my children call or visit anymore?" "How will I cope with this divorce?" "I don't know how I'll make ends meet till my next unemployment check." "Why did God allow this to happen to us?"

Where is God? "Don't hide your face from me!" cries David (v. 9). In the blackness, in the bleakness, we need to sense God's presence. We need to know that he is there, even if, like Job, we don't understand what's happening around us and inside of us. "The restless millions wait for the Light," says George Bernanos, "Whose dawning maketh all things new."

Voyage of the *Dawntreader*

Caught in a Darkness at sea, too terrifying for words, a Darkness that crawled and oozed and grabbed and stuck, the children of C. S. Lewis's Narnia world sailed their ship, the *Dawntreader,* in circles of fear. "If you've ever loved us at all," cries Lucy to the skies, "send us help now!"

And in a growing speck of light that seemed, Lucy thought, to look a lot like a cross, the battle of the powers whirled around them, till Darkness and fear melted before his Brightness.

"God is Light," said the apostle John, echoing David's song. And no Darkness in this world has ever held back his Dawning!

Lifted Hands

*Hear my cry for mercy as I call to you for help, as I lift up my
hands toward your Most Holy Place.*
—Psalm 28:2

Sometimes two hands aren't enough. One writer tells of the morning
her son came in from play begging for something to eat. They finally settled on a slice of bread smothered in peanut butter. "But," she said, "you
have to eat it outside."

He was only three. Most doors he could open by wrapping one hand
around the knob and sort of dropping his body till turning and pulling became part of the same motion.

But the outside door was different. It needed two hands. And here was
that slice of bread filling one! What to do? His was a creative little mind.
He slapped the bread against the wall, peanut butter first. It stuck while
he grabbed at the knob with both hands. And once the door was open, it
peeled away from the wall, nearly good as new!

Amazing Tools

Our hands are amazing tools. The bones of our hands have thirty different joints, and movements are controlled by more than fifty muscles. Researchers estimate that a typical hand can assume approximately three
hundred million different useful positions while doing the average of a
thousand separate functions that we assign to it in a day. One third of the
sense organs of our bodies are located in our hands. John Webster called
them "curious engines," and Immanuel Kant said they were "the outside
brain of man."

Helen Keller, blind and deaf from early childhood, describes the incredible sensation of "listening" with her hands. She tells of the time
when the cover was removed from phonograph speakers, and her hand
was placed against the vibrating membrane itself. It was Beethoven's
Ninth Symphony. "I could sense . . . the passion of the rhythm, the pulsa-
tion and swell of music," she said. "And the great choir beat sharply
against my fingers with its waves and pulses!"

What a feeling!

Can't Slow Down

The great pianist Sergey Rachmaninoff was in the middle of a concert tour when he took ill and doctors found cancer. Rachmaninoff knew he was dying. He held up his hands, those marvelous producers of magnificent music, and he said, "My dear hands. Farewell, my poor hands."

What would we do without hands? I think of that as I type these words. Latham Sholes, who first put together a working model of the typewriter in the mid-1800s, found that the keys would jam if the typist went too fast. So he deliberately figured out a configuration for the keys that would slow us down. It's the standard keyboard on all English typewriters and computers keyboards, an arrangement called QWERTY. And still our fingers learn, and our hands produce.

Sensitive Expressions

Our hands speak. The grasp of friendship. The touch of healing. The caress of love. Elizabeth Barrett Browning wrote:

> First time he kissed me, he but only kissed
> The fingers of this hand wherewith I write;
> And, ever since, it grew more clean and white.

Our hands create. John Heming said of Shakespeare, "His mind and hand went together." What a productive combination! And who can fail to be amazed at the wonders that leaped from the hands of Michelangelo?

Our hands can destroy as well. Pilate washed his hands of Jesus' blood, but pointed the way to his death. Lady Macbeth couldn't cleanse her hands of murderous designs with all the water of earth's oceans. And poet Dylan Thomas speaks in ghastly wonder of "the hand that signed the paper," "five sovereign fingers" that condemned a society to death.

But most of all, our hands pray. From the depths of his sorrow, from the tragedy of his circumstances, David lifts his hands toward heaven. When the voice is gone, when the eyes grow dim, when the tongue thickens, our hands still speak. Lifted hands. Pleading hands. Needy hands.

And five fingers of love, scarred by the print of nails, grasp us in the never-failing handshake of grace.

> Here a little child I stand,
> Heaving up my either hand;
> Cold as paddocks though they be,
> Here I lift them up to Thee.

> —*"Grace for a Child," Robert Herrick (1591-1674)*

Glory

The God of glory thunders . . .
and in his temple all cry, "Glory!"
—*Psalm 29:3, 9*

William Beebe, the naturalist, used to visit fellow nature-lover Theodore Roosevelt. Often, after an evening of good conversation at Roosevelt's Sagamore Hill home, they would walk across the lawn in the darkness. They would look up at the stars, point out the constellations, and carry on a conversation something like this: "There's the spiral galaxy of Andromeda! Did you know it was as large as our own Milky Way? Over a hundred billion stars. And every one of them is larger than the sun. 750,000 light-years away. And there are a hundred million more galaxies like it out there!"

The numbers would get larger, the facts and figures more spectacular. And eventually they would shuffle on in silence, lost in wonder. Finally Teddy Roosevelt would say, "Now I think we are small enough. Let's go to bed!"

Piercing the Veneer
"Creation was the greatest of all revolutions," said Chesterton. When young Anne Frank was hidden in an Amsterdam attic during World War II, fearful of the dreaded Nazi revolution and longing for a day in the park with her friends, she wrote this note in her diary: "The best remedy for those who are afraid, lonely, or unhappy is to go outside, somewhere where they can be quite alone with the heavens, nature, and God. Because only then does one feel that all is as it should be."

Even in the harshest of storms, as David notes in Psalm 29, the magnificent power of God is displayed. After Sir Ernest Shackleton returned from one of his Antarctic expeditions, he told of the intense suffering he and his two partners had endured: extreme pain, numbing cold, haunting starvation, consuming exhaustion. When rescued, barely alive, all they had left were two axes and a logbook.

"But in memories we were rich," said Shackleton. "We had pierced the veneer of outside things. We have seen God in His glory!"

A Great Word

There are only a handful of truly *great* words in the English language, says one scholar. They are the words without synonyms, the words that can't be explained, the words that sound like what they mean. And one of those words is *glory*.

Only the hushed whisper of that word can describe God, says David. Only the thundering roar of that term can tell what happens when God passes by. And only the shout of that cry fits the emotions that erupt in God's presence: "In his temple all cry Glory! Glory!"

Eyes to See

But bright lights can dim eyesight, and the constant bombardment of God's glory can turn our timid spirits toward the dark places.

One person has put it this way. Imagine a family of mice who lived all their lives in a large piano. Music filled their piano-world, swelling all the dark spaces with sound and harmony. At first the mice were impressed by it. They drew comfort and wonder from the thought that there was some-one close to them—though invisible to them—who made the music. They loved to think of the great player whom they could not see.

Then one day a daring mouse climbed up part of the piano and re-turned very thoughtful. He had found out how the music was made. Wires were the secret; tightly stretched wires of graduated lengths that trembled and vibrated. The mice had to revise all their old beliefs: none but the most conservative could any longer believe in the unseen player.

Later, another explorer carried the explanation further. Now the secret was hammers, numbers of hammers dancing and leaping on the wires. This was a more complicated theory, and it showed that the mice lived in a purely mechanical and mathematical world. The unseen player came to be thought of by the mice as a myth.

But the pianist continued to play. And those who hear the music cry, "Glory!"

Sing!

Sing to the LORD, you saints of his; praise his holy name. You turned my wailing into dancing; you removed my sackcloth and clothed me with joy, that my heart may sing to you and not be silent.
—*Psalm 30:4, 11–12*

When the Ayatollah Khomeini returned to power in Iran some years ago, one of his first decrees was to ban music from the airwaves. No music on the radio, none on television.

"Music," he said, "makes the brain inactive."

Can you imagine that?

"No Singing!"
It's no wonder that the Ayatollah was no friend to Christianity. Music grows naturally in the heart of the child of God. "Speak to one another with psalms, hymns and spiritual songs," says the apostle Paul. "Sing and make music in your heart to the Lord" (Eph. 5:19). And the Old Testament heritage of faith is filled with the majestic splendor of choral celebration.

"Without music life would be a mistake," said Friedrich Nietzsche. And for some, that may summarize all too well their tragic existence. Take the thought of another philosopher, the American George Santayana. "Music is essentially *useless*," he said, "as life is!"

Maybe that's what Robert Ingersoll had in mind as he lay dying. He had spent his life caustically denying God and defying God's power. After he died, the funeral invitations went out according to his instructions. They carried this pathetic line: "There will be no singing."

Can you imagine that?

Heart of Joy
Tom Prideaux, then entertainment editor of *Life* magazine, once wrote about hearing Irving Berlin perform. A vast host of vocalists had sung Berlin's music over the years, but here was the great one bringing his own tunes to life as no other could. "It wasn't a man singing a song," said Prideaux. "It was a man singing his autobiography!"

And that's true of the Christian too. A friend once asked Franz Joseph Haydn why his church music was always so full of gladness. "I cannot make it otherwise," he replied. "I write according to the thoughts I feel. When I think upon my God, my heart is so full of joy that the notes dance and leap from my pen!"

A New Song

In one congregation where I served for a time, a young woman used to come with her friends. She was a nursing student, full of zest, the life of every party. But she was bored at our worship services. She would settle in at the edge of the bench and yawn through the whole message. When everybody stood to sing, she'd stand and look around, just waiting for it all to be finished.

But I'll never forget one Sunday morning. It was Easter. When we started singing, she *beamed!* Her face shone as she made music as energetically as anyone else. I made sure I found her after worship.

"What happened, Chris?" I said. "You're different today!"

Then she told me about her family. Her parents had been divorced years before. Things were bad between her mom and dad. They hurt each other a lot. And they never forgave each other.

Then her dad got cancer. He had died the week before. Chris and her mom had flown out to see him just before the end. He told them he was a Christian. He told them he was sorry for all the grief he had put them through. He told them about how Jesus had forgiven him. He told them about the cross of Good Friday. And when they started to cry together, he told them about Easter Sunday.

And suddenly it all made sense to Chris. That's why she was singing today! Jesus touched her father's life, and now Chris knew his love too.

Ira Sankey was another singer who knew the touch of Christ. He loved the music of David. And David would probably have liked Sankey's testimony too, the one he wrote as a song:

> My life flows on in endless song; above earth's lamentation
> I hear the sweet, not far-off hymn that hails the new creation.
> Through all the tumult and the strife I hear the music ringing;
> It finds an echo in my soul—how can I keep from singing?

In His Hands

My times are in your hands. . . .
—Psalm 31:15

One of the most amazing stories to come out of World War II is told by a chaplain with the U.S. Air Force. A bombing mission in the South Pacific turned into a grueling night of terror for one B-52 crew. The fuel tanks began leaking when hit by enemy fire, and the plane barely managed an emergency landing on the beach of a small island. In the darkness their location was hidden from the Japanese soldiers who held the island. But dawn would make them prisoners of war.

"Chaplain," said the flight leader, "you've been telling us for months about the power of prayer. We're out of fuel! We're surrounded by the enemy! If you've ever prayed, pray now!"

While the rest of the crew patched the fuel tanks, the chaplain knelt in the sands to pray. Even when they knocked off for a couple hours' rest, the chaplain kept to his post.

About 2 A.M., a sentry heard something scrape against the sand at the water's edge. A cautious investigation revealed a large metal floating object. A barge. Piled high with barrels. And each contained gasoline. High octane gasoline. Airplane fuel. In a matter of minutes, the crew was roused, the tanks filled, and they were in the air again, bound for home!

But where had the fuel come from? Later investigations told the story. A supply ship captain, surrounded by enemy submarines six hundred miles and several weeks away, had set his cargo of aircraft fuel afloat in hopes of saving lives. And it landed fifty feet away from the bomber crew *exactly* when they needed it. What an answer to prayer!

Providence
"As luck would have it, providence was on my side!" wrote Samuel Butler. A bit more reverent is David's statement: My times are in your hands.

But what does that mean? Is it a good luck charm? Will it get you out of any scrape, even those of your own foolish doing?

Hardly. We know of too many tragedies and cruelties and unrequited injustices even in the Christian community to believe that. A young Christian girl whose sister was sick and whose family was troubled by a long list of difficulties, once wrote to me: "I am angry with God right now. . . . Sometimes I even think our family is cursed. When something goes wrong I think 'Oh no! *Another* curse!'"

Fatalism

Nor can David's trust in God be mere fatalism. The message of the Bible is not compatible with the idea that evil forces are either God's delight or his intent. No one can thank God for his providential leading when a drunk driver crushes the body of a child. No one can praise God for his providential direction when an airplane crashes or a mine collapses. These are not the things that providence is made of.

And thus it is difficult to read the times we live in or to easily identify the exact way God is moving with power or shaping destinies. The dangers are all too evident when we read the statement signed by six hundred German pastors and fourteen theology professors in 1934: "We are thankful to God that He, as Lord of history, has given us Adolf Hitler, our leader and savior from our difficult lot." Such a statement seems demonic now!

Confession

In a sense, David's testimony is more a confession than a theological treatise. I *believe* God exists. I *know* that God can control the destinies of peoples and nations. I am *confident* that God has a direction, a purpose for this world, and I *want* to be a part of that leading.

Even when things go "wrong" (from my own point of view). Even when tragedy strikes. Even when no miracles happen. *My times are in your hand.* That's the confession of faith! That's the confidence of trust!

A young schoolteacher named Ray Palmer thought about that one night in 1830. He sat at his desk in the darkness and wrote a little poem to God. It was a prayer of trust, a statement of faith.

One day he met Dr. Lowell Mason, a brilliant musician. Looking for verses to set to hymn tunes, Dr. Mason scanned Ray's poetry. It was all quite good but one poem moved him to tears. It was the nighttime prayer. And with a melody of simple majesty, Mason published the hymn that spoke with the convictions of David.

It still grabs hearts. It still brings tears. And it still echoes the testimony of those who know what Psalm 31 is all about. Its opening line goes like this: My faith looks up to thee!

Forgiven!

Blessed is he whose transgressions are forgiven,
whose sins are covered.
—*Psalm 32:1*

The Black Angel. That's what Michael Christopher calls Herman Engel in his play. Herman Engel is a cruel man, an "angel" by name, but darkest black in his Nazi soul. During World War II he led his army in a horrible massacre of French villages. And after the war, justice catches up with him at the Nuremberg trials. He is sent to jail.

A Plot
But not long enough, according to Morrieaux. Morrieaux is a French journalist whose family lived in one of those villages. Only he survived the hand of the Black Angel. After thirty years in prison, Engel is released from prison. Morrieaux says that's too good for him. He begins his plotting.

Engel rejoins his wife. They buy a little cottage in the mountains near Alsace and try to get away from it all for their few remaining years.

But they can't get away from Morrieaux. He searches for survivors of other families slaughtered by Engel's army. He tells them of Engel's release and stirs within them the burning of revenge. He organizes them into a lynch mob. They plan to await the cover of darkness before they shoot and burn the horrid man who lives in the mountains.

But vengeance from a distance is not enough for Morrieaux. He must see the horror and pain in Engel's eyes. He will go to the general under the guise of friendship. He will get the old fellow to talk about the war. He will open up all the crimes of the past and then turn on Engel as his comrades join him in balancing the scales of justice more equitably. They will dance around the Black Angel together as they send him to hell!

Soured Vengeance
When Engel invites Morrieaux in, Morrieaux is a bit shaken. This is no monster, no demon from the dark side! This is an old man, confused about the past, lonely and heartbroken by the years of prison, wanting only to spend a short while with his wife and then die in peace. Mor-

rieaux's revenge begins to turn sour in his stomach. He came for the Black Angel of death, but meets only a troubled man, a human like himself.

Dusk catches them still deep in conversation. And then they hear the sounds of the mob, circling for the kill. Morrieaux hesitates. What should he do? Vengeance tastes bitter. So he opens himself up. He tells Engel of his plan, of the lynching plot, of the death that waits outside the door.

"Let me help you!" he begs. "Let me get you away from here! Let me save your life!"

But now Engel hesitates. Yes, he says, I will let you save me. But on one condition. Will you forgive me? Will you release me from the burden of guilt that weighs me down, that floods my soul, that overwhelms my sleepless nights? Will you forgive me?

Trapped in Hell

Save a life? That Morrieaux can do. That he wants to do. That he *has* to do. But release a soul? Let go of the bitterness, the burning hatred, the consuming passion for vengeance? Forgive Engel? *Never!*

Morrieaux leaves. Engel dies. And everyone loses.

Life without forgiveness is hell. Hell is the place where justice is never tempered by mercy, where relationships are never mended, where grudges grow and grace has taken a holiday. Hell is eternity apart from God's forgiving love. And hell is the prison of unforgiveness into which we lock our enemies with no parole.

Hell. Unforgiveness. They're both the same thing. That's why David sings with such energy: "Blessed is he whose transgressions are forgiven, whose sins are covered!"

Says George Herbert: "He who cannot forgive others destroys the bridge over which he himself must pass!" You can see it in David's lament. He's made a mess of things with others around him, and now the bridge to God's grace is gone. Like Morrieaux, his attitudes and actions have turned sour. Like Engel, he withers in a prison that traps his soul.

And only some power bigger than himself can put it all right again. Only some grace from outside, some compassion that goes beyond justice can open the door and let him live again. Only God.

"For God so loved the world . . . "

Joy!

Shout for joy.
—Psalm 33:3

In the East, the story is told of an extremely wealthy king who ruled a vast domain from magnificent palaces. He had the respect of his citizens and peace within his borders.

But for some perplexing reason he was very, very unhappy. The king's doctors could find no medical problem. Neither could psychiatrists figure it out. But one old wise man, an advisor to the king's late father, had this advice: "There is but a single cure for the king. Your Majesty must sleep one night in the shirt of a happy man!"

Strange advice, to be sure! But the desperate king needed only a hint of finding release from his malady to command that the search begin. So his messengers scoured the land, looking for one truly happy person.

The messengers could find no one. Not one happy person! Everyone had experienced days of sorrow and times of mourning. Many could laugh for a moment, but sooner or later each person would settle back to reflect on the pain in his or her life.

Finally, the messengers happened upon a beggar next to the road leading back to the palace. He wore a smile. He giggled uncontrollably. He laughed at life as it surrounded him. Here was a truly happy man!

"Give us your shirt," the messengers demanded. "The King has need of it!"

But the fellow only doubled over with spasms of hilarity. "I'm sorry!" he gasped, between fits of laughter. "You see, I have no shirt."

Starts in the Heart

The English language has a number of similar words that relate to good feelings inside. *Pleasure,* for instance, reflects our delighted response to sensations that stimulate us. *Happiness* surrounds us because of certain happenings in our lives. And then there's *joy.*

In a sense, *pleasure* is an "it" word; it mostly has to do with *things* that touch our senses. And *happiness* is a "me" word; its primary focus is *my* response to events that come and go in my life. But *joy* is really a "we" word;

it usually reflects what happens between persons, between me and you, between me and God.

Joy starts in the heart. It's a relational word. Robert Rainy, one-time head of New College in Edinburgh, Scotland, used to say that "joy is the flag which is flown from the castle of the heart when the King is in residence there!"

The composer of Psalm 33 would agree.

Refined in the Mind

If joy starts in the heart, it is refined in the mind. It is more than an emotion that comes and goes. It is deeper than a reflexive response that needs the right kind of stimulation. It is an act of the will. "Sing joyfully to the LORD!" commands the psalmist. Joy grows from heartfelt relationships. But it is also a choice of the mind.

Someone once attributed to the Christian church "the haunting fear that someone, somewhere may be happy!" How sad! And in 1769, Alexander Cruden, who was one of the most meticulous Bible students of his day, wrote: "To laugh is to be merry in a sinful manner." How tedious and tasteless!

John Wesley was more on track with Psalm 33 when he said, "Sour godliness is the devil's religion." Such an attitude doesn't belong in a heart responsive to God's love. It has no place in a mind that hears the psalmist's command.

Out of the Mouth

Every language reflects the culture that produces it. Some Eskimo languages have more than thirty different words for "snow." Some African tribal tongues have no word for "ocean." And Hebrew, the language of the Psalms, has twenty-seven different words for "joy" and "rejoicing." Can you imagine that? Joy was as much a part of the Israelite culture as life itself!

That's the heritage of the Christian church. What other religion in the world has such a tradition of music and singing and joyful worship? Last Sunday a woman came to our church for the very first time. She'd *never* been to a Christian worship service before in her life. What struck her most? "You sing so much!" she said.

Right!

Check It Out!

Taste and see that the LORD is good.
—*Psalm 34:8*

The great Wagnerian tenor Lauritz Melchoir tells of his younger days when he was studying music at Munich. One afternoon he was in the garden of his boardinghouse, practicing an aria. Just as he finished the lines, "Come to me, my love, on the wings of light!" a young woman dropped out of the sky and landed right in front of him.

They were both rather startled, but soon they laughed at the comedy of it all. Her name was Maria Hacker, and she was working as a stunt artist with a Bavarian movie company. She had just parachuted from an airplane when a gust of wind blew her off course.

And here she was, miraculously answering his call! The plot was too good to waste, so they decided to get married.

Spurned Invitations

Not all invitations are as dramatic as the one Melchoir sung. Nor do people always respond so delightfully to them. Earlier this century, a newly wealthy couple moved into a beautiful mansion in an exclusive section of Newport, Rhode Island. They wanted to be a part of high society. So they planned a gala housewarming event and sent invitations to all the names on the social register. Then they waited for the guests to arrive.

And waited. And waited. And waited . . .

Local high society had decided to ignore these newcomers, and no one showed up at the party. The wife was furious. She shouted curses at her neighbors, and then she made a vow: "This house will rot before I open it again to anyone!"

The woman kept her word. She and her husband moved to New York City and took rooms at the Astor House Hotel. The beautiful mansion was left boarded up and uncared for, an eyesore to remind the community of an invitation spurned.

Never Invited

Sometimes, though, people don't attend functions because they're not invited. Not long ago, a woman began coming to our worship services. She had never been in a Christian church before. Why? "No one ever invited me," she said. This woman lived in a city dotted with churches; Christians walked on every street. But she could state with simple honesty: "No one ever invited me before."

David wrote Psalm 34 after some narrow escapes from his enemies. These enemies were after David's life, some because they saw him as a threat, and others because they were suspicious of his religion. David thought: If they only knew. If they only understood what my religion is all about. If they only felt the power and the love and the care of my God.

Psalm 34 is David's invitation. "Check it out!" says David. "Taste and see."

"Pass It On"

There was a new song written while I was in high school. It was one of the first that spoke to us teens about the things that David says in Psalm 34. We used to sing it around campfires at night. And I remember the light going on in some eyes when the singers "saw" and "tasted" and "felt" the love of God for the first time. The song went like this:

> It only takes a spark to get a fire going,
> But soon all those around are warmed up in its glowing.
> That's how it is with God's love, once you've experienced it:
> You spread his love to everyone. You want to pass it on!

> —*Words and music: Kurt Kaiser, ©1969 Communiqué Music*

I remember one fellow was in tears. He looked at the friend who brought him along. "Thanks for inviting me," he said.

Has anyone said that to you recently?

Dark Thoughts

May those who seek my life be disgraced and put to shame.
—Psalm 35:4

Peter the Great, eighteenth-century czar of Russia, was very interested in medicine. He often assisted surgeons and dentists in their operations.

So it was no great surprise when one of his valets came to him one morning and asked if the czar would help his wife. She was suffering from a horrible toothache, he said, but refused to have the tooth pulled. In fact, whenever she went to see the dentist, she pretended to have no pain at all.

Peter collected his dental instruments and went with the valet. Though the woman struggled and protested, Peter was finally able to yank the tooth. But a few days later he learned the truth. The valet and his wife had had a terrible quarrel. Her teeth were perfectly fine. The valet had gotten his revenge in tricking his master to perform the extraction!

Hitting Back

We all try to get even, don't we? We may not strike out with the cruelty of the czar's valet at those who hurt us, but we all want revenge. We cut off an irritating driver on the road or lash out with our tongues in the middle of an argument or drop bits of nasty gossip to tear down someone who's done us wrong.

Regardless of our beliefs, revenge is often sweet. Michelangelo painted the face of someone he disliked intensely into the hell section of his *Last Judgment* fresco. Cornelius Vanderbilt sent this letter to two friends, Charles Morgan and C. K. Garrison, who had abused their power of attorney for their own interests: "Gentlemen: You have undertaken to cheat me. I won't sue you, for the law is too slow. I'll ruin you!" And Ramon Maria Narvaez, the great Spanish general and prime minister of the nineteenth century, gave this dying testimony to a priest: "I do not have to forgive my enemies; I have had them all shot!"

Tempered Judgment

Still, when we know the forgiving grace of God, and we hear Jesus' call to love our enemies, we begin to grow uneasy with Psalm 35. Obviously David is hurting. Certainly he's endured more than he should have to from a cruel bunch of ruffians. There's no question that his patience and love and forgiving grace have been taxed beyond the limit.

But does the child of God *ever* have a right to make statements like David's? "May those who seek my life be disgraced and put to shame. . . . May they be like chaff before the wind, with the angel of the LORD driving them away. . . . may ruin overtake them by surprise—may the net they hid entangle them, may they fall into the pit, to their ruin" (vv. 4-8). Was David's bloodthirsty call for vengeance a cancerous growth of sin?

Certainly David was human, as we are. And we are not without our times of ungodly violence. But in the end, David leaves judgment to the Lord. And his focus is not ultimately on the hellfire that might surround his enemies. In verse 27, he grins with those who share his struggles and he ends with this song: "My tongue will speak of your righteousness and of your praises all day long" (v. 28).

Not a bad thing to do when dark thoughts cloud our vengeful minds.

Do You Know What You're Missing?

*An oracle is within my heart concerning the sinfulness of the
wicked. . . . For in his own eyes he flatters himself
too much to detect or hate his sin. . . .
He has ceased to be wise. . . .*
—Psalm 36:1-3

One of the classic tales in *Aesop's Fables* is about an elderly woman who
has very poor eyesight. A doctor offers to cure her for a certain fee. Each
week he comes to her house, pours a healing balm on her eyes, and tells
her to keep them closed for an hour.

During that time, he steals her possessions, one by one. Each week the
woman's eyes gets better, but her house gets barer.

After a lengthy treatment, the doctor declares her cured and demands
his fee. But the woman refuses to pay. When the doctor takes her to court
over the matter, her defense is simple. "I promised to pay only if my sight
got better," she says. "Before the doctor came, I could see everything in
my house, if only blurred and faint. But now I can't see anything!"

A Wise Fool

I thought of that story when I heard about what happened to a young
woman in Chicago a few years back. She was taking an introductory philosophy course at the University of Chicago. Her professor was the
world-renowned scholar Morris Cohen. He had an extremely keen mind
and his lectures were brilliant. But after the final class session, she met
him at the door.

"Professor Cohen," she said, obviously quite agitated, "you've knocked
a hole in everything I've ever believed in, and you've given me nothing to
take its place!"

What a tragedy! To gain insights, to grow in perspective, to have your
eyes opened to the world around, but then to find your most prized possessions stolen! In the Greek language they would call such a person a
"sophomore," a "wise fool!"

Theft of Faith

In his *Introductory Lectures in Psychoanalysis*, Sigmund Freud wrote: "Dar-
win has banished God from nature, Marx has banished him from history,

and I have banished him from man's inner life!" Great accomplishment. But who is the better for it? The ancient Cretan philosopher Epimenedes, often quoted by the apostle Paul, put it this way: "They fashioned a tomb for you, O holy and high one. . . . But you art not dead! You live and abide forever!"

And that's David's theme in Psalm 36. "Your love, O LORD, reaches to the heavens, your faithfulness to the skies!" (v. 5). Still there are many who walk around as "sophomores"—wise in the ways of the world, but fools who say there is no God. And they are the worst off in this grand enterprise of life!

Coming Home

London is a fairly big city, one of the ten largest in Canada. Big cities attract people who are running away from home. You can get out of the confinement, away from the rules and regulations, and quit that foolish business of religion. When we lived there, we regularly used to get letters or telephone calls from parents and pastors about so-and-so who's gone to live in London. Could you look her up? Could you talk to him for us?

So we did. The results of our contacts were rarely exciting, but once in a while we would experience that greatest joy in ministry. A young woman, after a decade of fast times, finds God and in doing so finds herself. A middle-aged fellow, shocked into a rude awareness of the depravity in his own soul, comes crying for the love of the Father. A successful business-man regains his soul when he comes to church. Every one of them says the same thing. "I didn't realize what I was missing!"

Do you?

The Power to See It Through

Wait for the LORD. . . .
—Psalm 37:34

Psychiatrist Viktor Frankl often wrote about the meaninglessness of his patients' lives. He was able to sympathize with them in a powerful way, since he spent part of World War II in a concentration camp. He remembered the dark weeks of 1944 vividly. The numbness of the gray days, the cold sameness of every dreary morning.

And then, suddenly, like a bolt of bright colors, came the stunning whisper that the Allies had landed at Normandy. The push was on. The Germans were running. The tide of the war had turned. "By Christmas we'll be released!" they told each other.

Promises, Promises
Frankl recalls the changes that took place in the camp: every day the workers went out to their same jobs but their hearts were lighter, and the work seemed a bit easier. Each mealtime they peered into the same cauldron of slop but somehow it seemed less difficult to swallow since every bite was a countdown to freedom. The stress in each barracks community was the same: people fighting for a little privacy; jealousies and dislikes aired in spicy retorts. Yet forgiveness came a little easier these days, for the ups and downs of the present dimmed as the future became a closer and closer reality.

It was interesting, says Frankl. Fewer people died in those months. Even the weakest ones began to cling tenaciously to life.

But Christmas 1944 passed, and the Allied troops never came. There were setbacks and defeats, and the bits of news smuggled into the camp made no more promises.

And then, says Frankl, then the people began to die. No new diseases came into the camp. Rations remained the same. There was no change in working conditions. But the people began to die one after the other, as if some terrible plague had struck.

The Plague of Hopelessness
And, indeed, it had. It was the plague of hopelessness, the epidemic of despair.

Studies show that we can live forty to sixty days without food, eight to twelve days without water, and maybe three minutes without oxygen. But without hope we can't survive even a moment. Without hope we die. Without hope there's no reason to wake up in the morning.

David knows that. It's the theme of Psalm 37. There are times when hope is gone, when life is cruel, when the future is a blank wall. Then, says David, there's only one way to carry on. "Wait for the Lord!" he cries. "Be still . . . and wait. . . . "

Testimony

Not easy to do, of course, especially when God seems distant and silent. But it is precisely in those moments that we need the testimony of others, like David, who have waited and regained their hope.

Years ago, Dr. Arthur Gossip preached a sermon entitled: "When Life Tumbles In, What Then?" He preached it the day after his beloved wife had suddenly died. And no one could bring more powerfully than he the challenge of the closing lines:

> Our hearts are very frail, and there are places where the road is very steep and very lonely. Standing in the roaring Jordan, cold with its dreadful chill and very conscious of its terror, of its rushing, I . . . call back to you who one day will have your turn to cross it, "Be of good cheer, my brother, for I feel the bottom and it is sound!"

> That's where David stands when he calls to us from Psalm 37. Do you hear his voice? "Wait for the LORD. . . . "

Discipline

Your arrows have pierced me, and your hand has come down upon me.
—Psalm 38:2

A British nobleman once commissioned William Hogarth to paint his portrait. Hogarth was the kind of artist who believed in realism: "Paint it the way you see it!" That was his motto. And, unfortunately, the nobleman was rather ugly. So when he saw his likeness in the portrait, he was rather upset. He refused to pay Hogarth even a single pound for all his efforts!

But Hogarth needed the money. And for him, a deal was a deal. So he sent a letter to the man, telling him that a circus master had seen the painting, and he had liked it very much. If the nobleman no longer wanted the painting, Hogarth would just add a tail and some horns and sell it to the showman for public display at a carnival.

The very next day Hogarth's commission arrived. The nobleman took delivery of the offensive painting and promptly burned it to ashes!

Deep Darkness
That's the way it is with ugly things. We don't want to look at them. We don't want to wake up to their reflection. At best, ugly things are for a circus sideshow. At worst, we'd like to destroy them and erase their memory from the earth.

Particularly if the ugly things are us. A man named Parker once came up with this "law": Beauty is only skin deep, but ugliness goes clear to the bone. And though we're quick to see that ugliness in people around us, its frightening when we face ourselves and find the worms and decay within. I will do almost *anything* to make excuses about myself rather than admit that I might have done something *sinful* or *evil.*

Part of the problem is that most evil is too sinister to seem sinister. Most sin is too nice to seem "sinful." Gossip starts out as genuine concern for somebody else. Extramarital affairs begin with good friendships. Workaholism originates with the joy of using the talents God gives us.

But they become sin. That's what they are. We can call them anything we'd like: temporary indiscretions; pressures of circumstance; mistakes of judgment. But they're still sin. And they have a thousand thousand brothers and sisters.

In his powerful novel *Heart of Darkness*, Joseph Conrad tells the story of Marlow, a riverboat captain in the Congo. He hears of a man named Kurtz who lives out in the jungle and runs a kingdom of his own.

Kurtz started out as just an ordinary trader. He visited the villages. He bought and sold in the markets. He actually fell in love with Africa and its people. He was a good man, with good intentions.

But somehow, along the way, a web of little things trapped him into a kingdom of evil. When Marlow finds him, right and wrong have no more meaning for him. And his dying words are: "The horror! The horror!"

A multitude of good intentions, innocent deeds, simple choices, and in the end, a horrible web of evil.

"Pain-Love"

And that's why we all need discipline. Sometimes we see it as an ugly word, a torture, a bitter pill to swallow. But in Psalm 38 David sees discipline as a sign of God's love. It hurts. It puts him in agony. It cuts like a knife. But the surgery is one of love.

The Chinese have several characters to express the concept of love. Some are simple. Some are complex. But the most profound of all is the symbol that fuses together two characters, the one for ordinary love and the one for pain.

"Pain-love," it's called. It's the love of a mother for a child. She disciplines her daughter and feels the ache that cuts her own heart. It's the love of a husband. He stays with a troubled spouse and experiences the trauma of her bitterness. It's the love of God. He empties himself of glory and shares the sufferings of his people.

"Pain-love." Deep love. The kind of thing that makes us "disciples" of Jesus. After all, what is really ugly in this world? Sin is ugly, but so are the wounds and scars and pain that it causes. And there's the key to discipline. As David knows, the discipline he's going through isn't the torture of a sadistic ogre in the heavens. It's the "pain-love" of one who cares, who shares, who knows the ugliness of sin, and who will die making things right again.

That's why he ends his tortured cries with the prayer: "Come quickly to help me, O Lord my Savior" (v. 22).

Sinful Silence

---

*I said, . . . "I will put a muzzle on my mouth as long as the
wicked are in my presence." But when I was silent and still,
not even saying anything good, my anguish increased."*
—Psalm 39:1-2

A closed mouth gathers no feet.

True, isn't it? Often the more we talk, the less we say. And sometimes
the more trouble we get into!

Thomas Macaulay was a Scottish statesman and historian during the
last century. He was also known for his incredible ability to keep talking
constantly about anything and everything and sometimes even nothing.
Everyone knew Macaulay by his tongue.

Late in his life, after some years in government service in India,
Macaulay returned to England. But his friends thought he had changed.
"His enemies might have said before that he talked rather too much," said
Sydney Smith, "but now he has occasional flashes of silence that make his
conversation perfectly delightful."

Hold Your Tongue!

"Silence is golden," says the song. In a noisy world, talk is sometimes too
loud and too cheap.

Once, after a brief break in a lengthy and tedious debate at the annual
meeting of my denomination's Synod, one of the delegates led the devotions. He brought down the house with laughter when he read this
proverb of Solomon: "Even a fool is thought wise if he keeps silent, and
discerning if he holds his tongue" (17:28).

Perhaps there was some wisdom among the ancient Romans who con-
sidered Mercury the god of orators. He was also the deity who presided
over commerce and banking . . . and *thieves!* The words of the wise can be
treasure in the storehouses of the mind. But boring conversation can also
rob us of time and enthusiasm.

Comforting Quiet

Ralph Waldo Emerson and Thomas Carlyle were both great writers.
Each knew the value of delightful speech, and each was a master crafts-
man of words. Yet one evening when Emerson called on Carlyle, he was

merely given a pipe to smoke, and the two sat in perfect silence for an entire evening. When Emerson left, they parted at the door with a handshake and brief compliments on the wonderful hours they had spent together.

There can be comfort in silence, particularly in times of reflection or grief. The story is told of a young girl who lost her playmate Jennifer in a tragic auto accident. The day after the funeral, she disappeared for hours. When she finally came home, her mother asked her where she'd been.

"I went to Jennifer's place and comforted her Mommy."

"What did you say to her to comfort her?" asked the mother quietly.

"Well," she answered, "I didn't know what to say, so I just crawled up into her lap and helped her cry."

Tragic Silence

But sometimes silence can be cruel. Robert Louis Stevenson wrote: "The cruelest lies are often told in silence." And he was right. Martin Niemoller knew how right he was. After surviving Hitler's Dachau death camp during World War II, he hung his head and said:

> First the Nazis came for the communists,
> and I didn't speak up because I wasn't a communist.
> Then they came for the Jews,
> and I didn't speak up because I wasn't a Jew.
> Then they came for the trade unionists,
> and I didn't speak up because I wasn't a trade unionist.
> Then they came for the Catholics,
> and I was a Protestant, so I didn't speak up.
> Then they came for me . . .
> By that time there was no one left to speak up for me.

Silence is not always golden. David learned that. For those who know the ways of God, the ways of life and light, to keep silent in the face of evil is tragic and cruel.

What have you said today?

Pierced Ears

Sacrifice and offering you did not desire,
but my ears you have pierced.
—Psalm 40:6

Fashion in North America demands pierced ears, doesn't it? Our little girls come home from school to report the latest statistics on who got their ears pierced. I smile when I remember that my older sister brought major social and theological debates into our home when she even dared to *think* about getting her ears pierced. She was nearly through high school at the time!

Several years ago some comments were made in our congregation about the suitability of a certain person for teaching church school classes. What was the problem? The person had pierced ears and wore earrings. Actually, I guess, he wore one earring.

I think David would have liked to sit in a classroom with a teacher who wore earrings, especially the pierced-ear kind. But I think, too, that he would have seen a whole lot more in it than just a fashion statement.

Slavery

You see, there's a little word from the Lord in Exodus 21 that throws a lot of light on what pierced ears could mean. Suppose, says God, that one of your neighbors gets into financial difficulty. He's in deep debt and his assets are all gone. He's got nothing left to sell but himself.

So he comes to you. You happen to hold a note from him worth thousands of dollars. And since he can't pay, he becomes your servant, your indentured slave. He's now your property, and you put him to work in a hopeless bid to recover at least some of his incredible debt to you.

But God doesn't delight in slavery. He's written off many a bad debt in his time, and he's given people a chance to start over. So he's built some safeguards into the system. Your neighbor can work for you for six years as a slave. But then he's got to go free. You can't hold him. He needs the dignity of his freedom to survive. And the seventh year is his ticket back to independence.

But maybe things have changed a lot for him in six years. He came to you a crushed man, beaten by life. And even though he knew he owed you his very body for the debt he'd run up, he still resented the idea of now being locked into slavery and bowing to you as master.

Yet, over the years, he's learned to respect you. In fact, you've become good friends. He hasn't gotten paid for his work. But he's been well looked after. And he feels more like a part of the family than he does a disdained slave.

Indeed, when he wanted to get married to one of your other slaves, a beautiful young woman whose father sold her to pay another debt, you were proud that he asked you for a blessing as if you were his father. You gave them a terrific party to celebrate the occasion.

Freedom

But tomorrow the six years are ended. He's free to go. True, his wife and children still belong to you, but you're even willing to let them go free with him. That's how close you've become.

He comes to you and says, "When I came here, I was so shattered that I couldn't look you in the eye. You held my soul in your hands, and I often wished you would have crushed me. But you didn't. You were firm but fair. You made me work, but you gave me everything I ever needed. And now you're like a father to me. I have a hard time thinking of going anywhere else. All I am, I owe to you."

His eyes get a little misty, and you feel the tears pumping behind your own cheeks too. And then he says, "Could I stay on with you? Would it be okay if we just kept things like they are? I've really never been able to make it on my own. You've given me more dignity as your servant than I've ever been able to grab hold of as a free man. Will you let me stay and serve you?"

The tears flow. You hug him as a son. He kisses you as his father. And, in the most touching ceremony of Israelite society, you pierce his earlobe and give him an earring to wear. He's your servant for life, not out of demand or debt or duty any longer, but out of love (Ex. 21:1-6).

Now you understand what David says in Psalm 40: I could have tried to work off my debt to you, Lord. I could have tried to buy your good will. But that wasn't really what you wanted. "Sacrifice and offering you did not desire. . . . " But when I learned what kind of a Master you really were, all that was left was love.

That's why I'm proud to tell others that "my ears you have pierced."

Don't Kick Him When He's Down

Blessed is he who has regard for the weak. . . .
—*Psalm 41:1*

Ibn Saud was the first modern king of Saudi Arabia. He lived during the early half of this century, and people in the East still talk about his wisdom.

One day a widow came to him. It seems that her husband had been walking under a palm tree. Another fellow was up in the tree gathering dates. His foot slipped and he fell right onto the woman's husband. Later her husband died from internal injuries as a result of that incident.

Ibn Saud checked the matter out. It was true! Things had happened just that way! So he said to the widow, "What compensation will you take?" He thought that she'd want a pension in order to care for her family. But the laws of Saudi Arabia did allow the death penalty, and that's what she demanded. She wanted the man from up in the tree to die.

Ibn Saud knew that her family needed support, not revenge. So he tried calmly to talk her out of it. But she was adamant. Her husband was dead, and that man would have to die too.

When he saw that his coaxing was useless, Ibn Saud tried one more thing. He agreed to the death penalty, but he also decreed that it would be carried out in a very specific way. The man who had killed her husband would be bound, he said, and set under a palm tree. And then the widow would climb the tree, and throw herself down on the man, killing him.

Only then did the widow realize that revenge kills everybody. She took the money instead.

Down and Out
David is down and out in Psalm 41. He's done something wrong (v. 4), and now he's experiencing all the pain and trouble that his deeds have caused.

Of course, his enemies are having a field day. Like the widow from Ibn Saud's kingdom, they make the most of the situation. They publish David's crimes in all the papers (vv. 5-6) and spread the rumors through the gossip mills (vv. 7-8). But what hurts the most is that even David's close friends get caught up in the spiteful games (v. 9). They're swept along with the emotional tide and add fuel to the fires of disgust and shame.

David is down and out. And now everyone around him conspires to kick him again and again and again.

Kindness

It's easy, isn't it? We've all done it. Right now each of us can think of someone we used to like and respect but whose presence or character now disgusts us. And we haven't hidden our feelings when we've talked with others. Like the widow, we've been hurt and betrayed. And like her, we take our revenge in spiteful ways.

Only one thing saved David in his awful mess. He had one Friend who chose to respond in a different way. The very One who was hurt the most by what David had done chose not to turn his back, not to strike out in bitterness, not to kick David when he was down.

One Person showed David the kindness that would allow him to pull himself together, regain his shattered pride, and walk again in society with both enemies and friends. That Person was God.

But maybe God is not the only one with a character like that. Says Beth Robertson:

> When I think of the charming people I know,
> It's surprising how often I find
> The chief of the qualities that make them so
> Is just that they are kind!

Is she writing about you?

Tears

My tears have been my food day and night, while men say to
me all day long, "Where is your God?"
—Psalm 42:3

The great radio preacher of a former generation, W. E. Elliott, once attended a concert of piano music. Alfred Cortot was at the keyboard, brilliant as always. His final selection was Chopin's B-Minor Sonata, most famous for its "Funeral March." And Cortot's performance was incredible.

After the concert, Elliott greeted the musician and told him how much he had enjoyed the music, especially the Chopin piece. And tears flooded Cortot's eyes as he said, "You see, I felt it so much. This week I lost a very dear friend."

The Language of the Soul

Tears speak volumes. A young woman I know is going through a divorce. She doesn't know why her husband wants out of their marriage. And generally she's a happy-go-lucky person. She can put up with a lot. She can hide a lot inside behind a mask of smiles.

But if anyone mentions her husband's name, she cries. Her soul speaks. And no one needs an interpreter. "The deeper the sorrow," says the Talmud, "the less tongue it has." But the more it tells through tears.

Walk a Mile with Sorrow

No one really wants to cry. Our society, in fact, observes a weeping person and says that he has "broken down," as if he's lost the essence of his personhood. "Laugh, and the world laughs with you," wrote Ella Wilcox. But, "weep, and you weep alone." And the world looks on from a distance, wondering if you are odd or neurotic.

Still, the Bible talks in pretty positive ways about sorrow. "It is better to go to a house of mourning than to go to a house of feasting," says the Preacher in Ecclesiastes 7:2. "Sorrow is better than laughter," he adds (7:3). Emily Dickinson illustrates what he means in her poem:

> I walked a mile with Pleasure.
> She chatted all the way,

But left me none the wiser
For all she had to say.
I walked a mile with Sorrow,
And never a word said she.
But oh, the things I learned from her
When Sorrow walked with me!

Watered for Growth

There's something cleansing about tears, more than just washing the dust out of our eyes. Researchers claim that our tears are only straight H_2O when we peel an onion. They carry nothing of our souls with them. But when we cry from the heart, our tears carry with them toxins from our bodies. They actually clean us out and help us start over with life again.

In a spiritual sense that's even more true. "Tears are often the telescope by which we see far into heaven," said Henry Ward Beecher. That's also what the writer of Psalm 42 found. A weary life, a burdened heart, a tormented soul, and the tears began to trickle. But crying cleanses his vision, washes away the toxins that made him sick, and waters the seeds of his faith so that they can grow again.

Have you had a good cry lately?

A Light in the Dark

Send forth your light and your truth, let them guide me;
let them bring me to your holy mountain,
to the place where you dwell.
—*Psalm 43:3*

The famous psychiatrist Viktor Frankl remembers a day when he felt like the writer of Psalm 43. It was during World War II. Frankl was on a work gang, just outside the fences that hid the horrors of Hitler's infamous death camp at Dachau. "We were at work in a trench," writes Frankl. "The dawn was gray around us; gray was the sky above; gray the snow in the pale light of dawn; gray rags in which my fellow prisoners were clad, and gray their faces."

Frankl tells how he was ready to die. It was as if the gray bleakness had claws, and each moment they dug deeper and colder into his soul. Why go on? What could be the purpose in "living" if, indeed, he was even still alive at this moment? There was no heaven, no hell, no future, no past. Only the clutching grayness of this miserable moment.

A Violent Protest
Suddenly, to his surprise, Frankl felt "a last violent protest" surging within himself. He sensed that even though his body had given up and his mind had accepted defeat, his inner spirit was taking flight. It was searching. It was looking. It was scanning the eternal horizons for the faintest glimmer that said his fleeting life had some divine purpose. It was looking for God.

In a single instant two things happened, says Frankl, that simply could not be mere coincidence. Within, he heard a powerful cry, piercing the gloom and tearing at the icy claws of death. The voice shouted "yes!" against the "no" of defeat and the gray "I don't know" of the moment.

At that exact second, "a light was lit in a distant farmhouse." Like a beacon it called attention to itself. It spoke of life and warmth and family and love.

Frankl said that in that moment he began to believe. And in that moment he began to live again.

The psalmist has the same need. The grayness of his bleak days is stifling. The loneliness of the moment overwhelms him. Is there a reason to carry on? Is there meaning beyond the drudgery of today's repetitive struggles? Is there hope and is there God?

Groping in the Dark

"Send forth your light and your truth," he shouts. Don't leave me alone. Give me some sign. Light a candle in the window and take me home.

John Greenleaf Whittier puts it this way:

> A tender child of summers three,
> Seeking her little bed at night,
> Paused on the dark stair timidly,
> "O Mother! take my hand," said she,
> "And then the dark will all be light."
>
> We older children grope our way,
> From dark behind to dark before:
> And only when our hands we lay,
> Dear Lord, in Thine, the night is day,
> And there is darkness nevermore.
>
> Reach downward to the sunless days,
> Wherein our guides are blind as we,
> And faith is small and hope delays:
> Take Thou the hands of prayer we raise,
> And let us feel the light of Thee.

Home

The closing verse of Psalm 43 mixes despair with hope. For God never denies us the light we need. As Joyce Kilmer wrote:

> Because the way was steep and long,
> and through a strange and lonely land,
> God placed upon my lips a song
> and put a lantern in my hand.

And suddenly we know the way home.

Wake Up!

Awake, O Lord! Why do you sleep? Rouse yourself!
—Psalm 44:23

Recently British researchers discovered that 42 percent of the church-goers in the country fall asleep during the sermon. The numbers may be astounding, but the habit is as old as Eutychus's fatal nap in Acts 20.

Once, when the great eighteenth-century evangelist John Wesley was preaching, he noticed that a number of people in his congregation were fast asleep. Without a warning, he suddenly broke his train of homiletic thought, and yelled out at the top of his voice, "FIRE! FIRE!"

Startled, the sleepers jumped to their feet, now quite awake. "Where's the fire?" they shouted, glancing around the room.

"In hell," replied Wesley, "for those who sleep under the preaching of the Word!"

Sleepyheads

Some people have a hard time waking up. Austrian pianist Artur Schna-bel once performed an entire concert while eyeing an elderly patron of the arts who snoozed in the front row. Only when the music had ended and the crowd burst into a thunderous ovation did the woman wake up with a start.

Schnabel decided to take some pleasure from the incident. He leaned down to apologize, whispering: "It was the applause, madame; I played as softly as I could!"

But the eighth Duke of Devonshire, Spencer Compton Cavendish, was not so easy to arouse. He was renowned for his passion for sleep. It was not unusual to find him asleep at his seat in Parliament. In fact, while he was making his first speech in the House of Lords, he actually yawned at the boring address he was himself giving. And after one particularly fit-ful slumber during a session of the House, he checked the time and an-nounced to his comrades, "Good heavens, what a bore! I shan't be in bed for another seven hours!"

Asleep on the Job

It's amusing when someone falls asleep during a public meeting. But it's quite another thing when people fall asleep at their jobs. A dozing secretary may waste time for himself and his firm. A soldier on watch duty may be court-martialed for snoozing at his post. And a sleepy driver may end up killing herself and possibly others on the road with her. Sleeping on the job is rarely a good thing (unless one is a mattress tester).

But what about God? Does God ever sleep on the job? The writer of Psalm 44 seems to think so. Prayers seem to go unanswered (vv. 9-16) even though God's people meet faithfully for worship and live lives of holiness (vv. 17-18). It's like the tragic scene on Mount Carmel where Elijah accuses Baal of being asleep (1 Kings 18), only this time it's the God of the Bible who seems to have taken sedatives.

Wake-Up Call

We know it's not true, of course. God keeps watch even when our eyelids grow heavy. But each of us has felt the way the psalmist did at times. Each of us has known days when God seemed distant and nights when he seemed to fall asleep right during our agonized prayers. And that's a terrifying feeling.

How do you wake up God? How do you get him back on track when it seems that he's forgotten you?

Russian pianist Anton Rubinstein's wife had a hard time getting her husband out of bed for early appointments. But finally she figured out a way to do it. She would go to the piano and start banging out an incomplete scale or an unresolved chord.

Even in his sleep, Rubinstein couldn't take the tension that caused his senses. He had to get up, find the piano, and complete the scale or resolve the chord. And then he was awake.

In a sense, that's what the psalmist does. Maybe it seems like God is asleep. What will get him going? Only the discord of a world out of harmony. Only the tension of a creation in chaotic dissonance because of sin. Only a prayer that goes beyond personal begging and shouts to high heaven about the scandalous mess of injustice raging in society.

Actually, maybe God is only pretending to sleep until *we* wake up!

A Royal Wedding

At your right hand is the royal bride. . . .
The king is enthralled by your beauty. . . .
—Psalm 45:9, 11

The bride-to-be was obviously nervous. It was only the rehearsal, but already the pastor could see that tomorrow's wedding might be in for problems.

"You're letting it all get to you," he told her gently, as he pulled her aside. "Just take it one little step at a time. When you get to the door with your father tomorrow afternoon, look only at the aisle ahead of you. You've walked it hundreds of times, every Sunday when you come to church. Think only of that.

"Then, when you get to the front, glance toward the altar. Here's where you first received Holy Communion. Let it remind you of your Lord Jesus, who brought you to this special moment. Think only of the altar.

"And then, turn your head to your love. He's your best friend. No one in this world wants to be with you more than he does. Look at him and think of him. And everything will be okay."

Sure enough. Next day the wedding went off like clockwork. Everyone was in place. All the flowers perfumed the air and the music was festive.

But some who stood close to the aisle as the bride entered. wondered a bit at the things she was muttering under her breath: "Aisle . . . altar . . . him . . . Aisle . . . altar . . . him . . . Aisle . . . altar . . . him . . . "

Altered States

It's true that marriage alters us. We don't set out to change the other person when we get married. Still, a living, loving, deepening relationship has its affect on each marriage partner. We live to love and we love to live. And in our living and loving, we grow and change and move and adapt, and somehow become new people. One pop singer calls a good relationship "two hearts beating in just one mind!"

A good marriage is like that. Long ago, A. E. Housman put it this way:

> Oh, when I was in love with you,
> Then I was clean and brave,

And miles around the wonder grew
How well I did behave!

—Poem XVIII, A Shropshire Lad

We don't say: "I'll alter him." But it happens.

Wedding Wishes

Whenever we see the development of a good relationship, we are happy
to join the celebration. Psalm 45 is one of those poems you might write
for a joyful wedding reception. It praises the bridegroom, who just happens to be a powerful king. And it holds the bride up in all her radiant
beauty. What a pair! What a celebration! And what a lot of good wishes!

Throughout the ages, people have sometimes wondered why this wedding song was in the Bible. Why would the Hebrews sing it in the temple? Why would Christians devote a page to it in their Sunday hymnals?

Probably because the king on the throne in Jerusalem was a symbol of
God in heaven. Wishing the king a good marriage was like wishing God
a good relationship with his people. That kind of theme is picked up
again and again in the Bible by Hosea (ch. 2), and Paul (Eph. 5), and
John (Rev. 19).

Commitment

Psalm 45 celebrates commitment and love that goes beyond a passing fad.
It speaks of devotion that is more than just "falling into" a relationship. It
praises energetic, physical, sexual matchmaking that reflects the bonding
of hearts. And it talks of devotion for the duration (vv. 16-17).

It's the kind of thing Yeats wrote about in one of his poems. Maybe
what he says is a good echo of God's Word to us, his bride, today:

When you are old and grey and full of sleep,
And nodding by the fire, take down this book,
And slowly read, and dream of the soft look
Your eyes had once, and of their shadows deep;
How many loved your moments of glad grace,
And loved your beauty with love false or true,
But one man loved the pilgrim soul in you,
And loved the sorrows of your changing face.

—From *The Collected Works of W. B. Yeats*, Richard J. Finneran, ed.,
Macmillan Publishing Co. Used by permission.

Inner Strength

God is within her, she will not fall....
—Psalm 46:5

In Morris West's novel *The Clowns of God,* there's a powerful scene where a father and his daughter are having an argument. She tells him that she's going to go to Paris to live with her boyfriend. He won't let her. Why would she want to do something like that?

Because I'm afraid, she says.

Afraid? Whatever are you afraid of?

She says: I'm "afraid of getting married and having children and trying to make a home, while the whole world could tumble round our ears in a day." She goes on: "You older ones don't understand. You've survived a war. You've built things. You've raised families. . . . But look at the world you've left to us! You've given us everything *except tomorrow.*"

Everything Except Tomorrow

"Everything except tomorrow." And tomorrow is the one thing that we need the most.

One newspaper recently carried this ad in its classified section: Hope chest—brand-new. Half price. Long story.

We've had so many long stories in our lives. And we've had so many broken promises. And we've had so many shattered dreams. We're ready to give up. No more promises. No more commitments. Everything except tomorrow.

Stumbling Feet, Striding Hearts

Psalm 46 is for people without tomorrow. A trembling world. An uncertain future. A host of plagues and troubles. But in the middle of it all stands God and moves God and rests God. "The LORD Almighty is with us; the God of Jacob is our fortress." And those who don't know tomorrow are held in the hand of the One who is forever today.

The old hymn puts it this way:

Thou didst reach forth Thy hand and mine enfold;
I walked and sank not on the storm-vexed sea!

'Twas not so much that I on Thee took hold,
As Thou, dear Lord, on me, on me.

Donna Hoffman, a young Christian mother who battled cancer for a number of years, wrote this little poem in her journal. She was in the hospital at the time. The cancer seemed so strong, and tomorrow seemed like an uncertain dream or a tragic nightmare. She called her poem "Journey":

My soul runs arms outstretched
down the corridor to you.
Ah, my feet may stumble
but how my heart can stride!

No Reserve, No Retreat, and No Regrets

That's the testimony of Psalm 46. Only God's grace can sustain us in a world turned upside down. Even when our feet stumble. Even when the journey seems too long, too troublesome. "My soul runs. How my heart can stride!"

Years ago, young William Borden went to Yale University. He was the wealthy son of a powerful family. He could do anything in life that he chose. And when he graduated, he chose to become a missionary of the gospel of Jesus Christ.

His friends thought he was crazy. "Why throw your life away like that?" they said. "You've got so much to live for here."

But Borden knew who held his tomorrows. He made his choices. And God gave him the inner strength to live his convictions.

He set out on a long journey to China. It took months in those days. And by the time he got to Egypt, some disease managed to make him sick. He was placed in a hospital. And soon it became obvious that he wouldn't recover. William Borden would die a foreigner in Egypt. He never reached his goal. He never went back home.

He could have been troubled by the tragedy of it all. But his last conscious act was to write a little note. Seven words. Seven words that they spoke at his funeral. Seven words that summarized his life, his identity: "No reserve, no retreat, and no regrets!"

Can you say that? Can you sing Psalm 46?

King

How awesome is the LORD Most High,
the great King over all the earth!
—*Psalm 47:2*

Someone has called Christopher Columbus, the fifteenth-century explorer of North America, the "forerunner of modern government." Why? Well, "Columbus didn't know where he was going when he started; he didn't know where he was when he got there; and he did it all on borrowed money." Sound familiar?

Important

Government is always an easy target for criticism. "Being in politics is like being a football coach," said former U.S. Senator Eugene McCarthy. "You have to be smart enough to understand the game and dumb enough to think it's important."

And it is important. No society of anarchy has ever survived its own cruelty. Somehow, somewhere, there must be a personification of law and rule and order that holds in check the evil passions of the collective human heart and fosters a sense of purpose and direction and well-being. In one of the most powerful scenes from Robert Bolt's recreation of the life and times of Sir Thomas More, *A Man For All Seasons,* young Roper views the corruptness of King Henry VIII's government and says he would cut down every law in England to overthrow him.

But More's energies are fired up, and his words come slicing out: "Oh? And when the last law was down, and the Devil turned round on you— where would you hide, Roper, the laws being flat? This country's planted thick with laws from coast to coast . . . and if you cut them down . . . d'you really think you could stand in the winds that would blow?"

Demanding

The Sons of Korah agree, as they sing Psalm 47. The strength, the safety, the blessing of the world comes when God rules on the throne of heaven and directs life on earth. And that's no mean feat. Two little girls were once overheard in conversation while staring up at a portrait of Queen Elizabeth. "What's she doing?" asked one.

"Oh, nothing, really," replied the other. "She's just reigning."

But those who know would agree that reigning is far more than just doing nothing. As the first United Nations General Assembly concluded its sessions, chairman Paul Henri Spaak of Belgium stood to address the body. "The agenda is exhausted," he said. "The Secretary-General is exhausted. You are exhausted. I am exhausted. At last we have reached unanimity."

God might be exhausted too, with the enormous burden of our planet. But something in Psalm 47 speaks of God's reviving strength. It grows with the desires of his people to receive his directing rule. It increases with the delight they know in his protective care. And it expands in the ceremonies of decoration by which they affirm his right to reign.

Worship

In other words, life and health and strength and peace begin with worship. And maybe that's not so surprising. After all, isn't worship a very political thing? It means, in its fundamental sense, the act of ascribing "worth" to some *thing* or some *one* capable of giving meaning to this madness.

Japanese evangelist Toyohiko Kagawa told of the fears that were part of the world he grew up in. And then he spoke of the day that he first understood the message of the gospel. He put it this way: "The good tidings of Jesus lie in the belief that the essence of the universe is an affectionate Creator, however dark the night may be and however fiercely the tempest may roar."

Let the "Pomp and Circumstance" marches roll!

Security

God makes her secure forever.
—Psalm 48:8

A few years ago, *Newsweek* magazine carried a little article about a fortune-tellers' convention in Dublin, Ireland. Palm readers, crystal ball gazers, and astrologers from all around the world got together for a week to compare notes and to make some new predictions.

In the presence of all these people who were supposed to know what tomorrow would bring, a thief got into the building. He stole their crystal balls and tarot cards. When the police came to investigate, they laughed. "Didn't you know this was going to happen?" they asked. "Couldn't you have predicted it?"

Worry

Who can tell what tomorrow will bring? We hope. We dream. We plan. Or we just stumble into it. But our uncertainty about tomorrow sometimes causes more than a little fear.

British wit G. K. Chesterton was once asked by a reporter, "If you were a minister and you had only one sermon to preach, what would it be about?"

Chesterton didn't hesitate for a minute. He shot back, "I'd preach about worry!" He knew his world. He knew the people around him. And, most of all, he knew his own heart.

The story is told of two men on a tandem bicycle traveling across the countryside. The road begins to climb. There's a steep hill ahead. Puffing and panting, they slowly work their way to the top. Finally they reach the summit. They stop for a moment to catch their breath. "Whew!" says one, wiping the sweat off his face. "That was some hard climb!"

"Yeah!" agrees the other. "And if I hadn't kept the brake on, we probably would have slid back to the bottom."

The psalmist knew that kind of fear—fear of falling, fear of failure, fear of factors beyond his control. It's the fear written in the eyes of all who take the changing circumstances of our world seriously. Not that long ago, a young husband told me about his marriage. He enjoyed it very much. But children? Just now? With the way the world was going? He and his wife didn't know if they could even think of bringing a little one into the uncertainty of a world in turmoil.

Put the brakes on!

A Place to Stand

But the psalmist knows more than a shaking world. He knows the security of God. Times may change, kingdoms may totter, Eastern Europe may rock, drug wars may escalate, cancer and toxic groundwater may threaten, but God will still be the strength of the community of faith. He remains the steady rock for those who know where to stand. "This God is our God for ever and ever," shouts the psalmist. "He will be our guide, even to the end" (v. 14).

One writer describes what that means in a very personal way. He attended a business conference some time ago. Awards were being given for the outstanding achievements during the last year. One woman received her company's top honor. She came to the podium, clutched the trophy in her hands, and beamed out at the crowd. There were over three thousand people in the auditorium, but this woman had eyes for only one. She looked down at her supervisor, Joan.

She told of the difficult times that she'd gone through a couple years earlier. She told of the personal problems that she'd experienced. She told of how her work had suffered and how people around her had turned away. They thought she was done for. They thought she couldn't make it. They thought she was a loser.

And she thought so too! She'd called Joan several times, a letter of resignation in hand. She'd decided to quit. She was a failure.

But Joan said, "Let's just wait a little bit longer." And Joan said, "Give it one more try!" And Joan said, "I never would have hired you if I didn't think you could handle it!"

The woman's voice broke, and the tears streamed down her cheeks as she said softly, "Joan believed in me more than I believed in myself."

Isn't that the message of the gospel? Isn't that the story of the Bible? In the middle of a tottering world, with shaky foundations, the Father of all wraps us in his strong arms. And life can begin again.

Riddles

I will turn my ear to a proverb; with the harp I will expound
my riddle: Why should I fear?
—Psalm 49:4-5

"Imponderables!"

That's what David Feldman calls the everyday questions of life that nobody dares ask. He's written three books of answers to strange and peculiar questions people pull from the far reaches of their minds. Some are thought provoking: "Doughnut-shop employees always pick up the doughnuts with a tissue so that their hands never touch the doughnuts. Why do they then put the same tissue in with the doughnuts for the customer to carry home—germs and all?" Or, "Why do people tend to look up when they're thinking deeply about something?"

Some are peculiar: "Why is the color blue associated with boys and the color pink with girls?" And, "Why do clocks run clockwise?" "Why is scoring three goals in hockey called a 'hat trick'?"

Some are just interestingly silly: "Why are the shoes you rent when you go bowling so ugly?" (Did you ever think about that?) "How did Oreo cookies get the name 'oreo'?" (No one really knows, although legends abound.) "Why do our fingernails grow faster than our toenails?" (Would you believe there are at least three possible reasons?)

Mind Games

Riddles have been around since the beginning of human history. In ancient Athens, Socrates taught his students the meaning of life by way of riddles. The question of the Sphinx in Greek mythology—"What walks on four legs in the morning, on two at midday, and on three in the evening?"—stumped all takers, until Oedipus saw in it the picture of a human crawling as a baby, walking as an adult, and hobbling along with a cane in elderly years. And English schoolchildren of an earlier age grew up repeating a rhyming riddle on their playgrounds:

> Little Nancy Etticoat
> In a white petticoat
> And a red nose:
> The longer she stands
> The shorter she grows.

Only the quick of mind would figure out that little Nancy was a white candle with a reddish orange flame on her "nose." And only they would also guess that "what runs about all day, and lies under the bed all night" is not a dog, but a shoe.

Vexing Challenges

But the riddle of Psalm 49 is more than a game. It's a direct challenge to the human heart: "Why am I so afraid of the rich and powerful when they have no control over my destiny?"

The Sons of Korah debate the issue for a while: money talks; power is impressive; the rich seem to live "the good life." The perplexing riddle is that these things, which drive us to distraction, are not supposed to matter. We ought to know the true values of life. We shouldn't be vexed by those who ruthlessly climb over us on the ladder to success.

But we are. And they *do* trouble us. It bothers us that our ethics or morality keeps us poor while the "achievers" flash their disdain across the pages of the supermarket tabloids and entertainment gossip columns. So often we hear people telling us of how God has blessed them while they point to their neighbors' possessions with envious eyes and lusting souls.

One Answer

There's only one answer to the riddle of Psalm 49. Fear of the powerful and envy of the rich die with death. If death robs us all, great or small, is there anything that death can't grab? "Yes!" cries the psalmist. "God will redeem my life from the grave; he will surely take me to himself" (v. 15).

If you know that, the rest of the riddles of life are not quite as troubling. But if you don't know that, then you're only an animal (v. 20). And you die like a dog.

Threats

———

*"Consider this, you who forget God, or I will tear you to
pieces, with none to rescue."*
—Psalm 50:22

"I don't get mad; I get even!" You've seen the bumper stickers. You've
probably even heard people say it.

And when a big, burly fellow with a grim-looking face says something
like that, I'm not one to challenge whether he really means it. A man
who'd tipped the bottle a few times before jumping in his car followed me
into a parking lot one day and stumbled out with a string of curses about
someone cutting him off. He was not a man to be reasoned with. He
spoke threats very colorfully. I didn't doubt that he could act on them.

Poor Motivation Technique

Psychologists say threats aren't the best motivation technique. Company
supervisors who intimidate their workers don't draw out the full potential
of employees' skills or energy. Instead, they tend to create an atmosphere
of hostility and resentment. They breed factions and bitterness, the kind
of thing the apostle Paul calls "the works of the flesh" in Galatians 5:20.

Threats usually challenge us to become more defiant. When the ancient Macedonian king Philip II couldn't win a diplomatic alliance with
Sparta, he sent this note: "You are advised to submit without further delay, for if I bring my army into your land, I will destroy your farms, slay
your people, and raze your city."

The Spartans weren't easily threatened. They sent back a single word
in reply: "If!" And Philip decided to back down.

Hilarious

Some threats are even hilarious. They seem more like cartoons than anything else. A gloomy British clergyman named William Ralph Inge used
to write regular articles for a major newspaper. His columns met with
mixed reviews. But the one that delighted Inge the most came from a
woman who wrote: "I am praying nightly for your death. It may interest
you to know that in two other cases I have had great success!" He laughed
that one off till his death in 1954 at the age of ninety-four.

And then there was Henry Camille, a feisty, pint-size professional hockey star of the 1950s. During one ice battle he lost his temper and lashed out at a big, tough defenseman named Fernie Flaman, who was feared for the cruelty of his fists.

As they pounded each other, the outmatched Henry yelled up at his opponent: "Watch out, Fernie, or I'll bleed all over you!" They both sank to the ice, laughing.

Emergency Measure

If threats have any legitimate place in our communication, it may be in an emergency. Once, when George Frideric Handel had trouble getting a rather temperamental soprano to sing a piece as he had written it, he picked her up, carried her over to an open window, and threatened to throw her out unless she did as she was told. It worked. She sang beautifully!

Psalm 50 is something like that for us. God is love. His wish for us is life and peace and joy. He wants us to find the best that he has to offer. After all, Jesus himself says, "I have come that they may have life, and have it to the full" (John 10:10).

But sometimes we're too blind or ignorant or willful or stupid to know that. Sometimes we're lost in the quick fixes of our drugs or schemes or ladders to success. Sometimes we're drunk with an inflated sense of our own self-importance. And then God's words to us in Psalm 50 are a shocking threat. They demand attention. They force us to reevaluate where we're at and what we're doing.

If it takes those words to keep me from committing spiritual suicide, maybe they'll be the only expression of love I'll be able to hear at the time.

A Broken and Contrite Heart

———

*The sacrifices of God are a broken spirit; a broken and
contrite heart, O God, you will not despise.*
—*Psalm 51:17*

Are you proud?
Robert Louis Stevenson wrote a little poem about pride:

> When I am grown to man's estate
> I shall be very proud and great,
> And tell the other girls and boys
> Not to meddle with my toys!

—*from* A Child's Garden of Verses

We probably all feel that way sometimes, especially when someone
bigger or more haughty than us walks all over our toys or our self-esteem.
And even though we feel like little people many times, we're much too
proud to stay that way.

The opening sentences of Bonamy Dobree's famous biography of John
Wesley capture his struggle with pride: "It is difficult to be humble. Even
if you aim at humility, there is no guarantee that when you have attained
the state you will not be proud of the feat." Isn't that the truth?

Pride is so subtle. In ancient Greece, the philosopher Diogenes came
to Plato's house one day. He already felt that Plato was not as good a
teacher as he, and now he had the proof. On the floor of Plato's house
were several ornate carpets, obviously very exquisite and costly. To show
his contempt for such a waste of money, Diogenes walked all over them
and then wiped his feet in a show of contempt. "Thus do I trample upon
the pride of Plato!" he said.

Plato observed quietly: "With even greater pride, it seems."

"The proud hate pride—in others!" said Benjamin Franklin. And
somehow our pointing fingers have to turn round to our own hearts.

Avoid Comparisons
C. S. Lewis observed that "unchastity, anger, greed, drunkenness and all
that are mere flea bites in comparison with pride."

So how do we come to the humility of David in Psalm 51? And how can we be sure that we aren't proud of our humility when we get there?

Perhaps it demands, first of all, that we take our eyes off ourselves. The truest way to be humble, as Phillips Brooks said, "is not to stoop until you are smaller than yourself, but to stand at your real height against some higher nature that will show you what the real smallness of your greatness is."

Many people in David's day were worse than he, morally, socially, and spiritually. But setting himself up against them would do nothing to challenge the evil in his own heart, nor put him on the road to a higher quality of life. Only a vision of God's glory can do that. And that is the strength of David's humility.

It's Irrelevant

The only way to defeat pride is to make it irrelevant. Once, when conductor Arturo Toscanini was preparing an orchestra and chorus for a performance, he was forced to work with a rather temperamental soprano soloist. His every suggestion was turned aside by her haughty opinions. At one point she loudly proclaimed: "*I* am the star of this performance!"

Toscanini looked at her with quiet pity. "Madam," he said, "in this performance there are no stars."

And in that moment her pride became irrelevant. It was swallowed up in the larger glory of the music. Personal arrogance was like a third left shoe. Who needs it?

So too with David. So too with us. As Isaac Watts put it in his well-known hymn:

> When I survey the wondrous cross
> On which the Prince of Glory died,
> My richest gain I count but loss,
> And pour contempt on all my pride.

Things That Last

He will uproot you from the land of the living. . . . But I am
like an olive tree flourishing in the house of God.
—*Psalm 52:5, 8*

In 1954, Marcelle Maurtette wrote a play called *Anastasia*. It was based on the true story of a woman named Anna Anderson who claimed to be the long-lost daughter of the last emperor of Russia, Tsar Nicholas II, and his wife, Aleksandra.

The Russian tsars believed their kingdom was imperishable. They knew they would rule forever. But at the turn of this century, the groundswell of social and political revolution tossed them aside. The emperor and his family were held hostage in the palace and then executed as the Bolsheviks bathed the countryside with blood.

Rumors persisted that little Anastasia, the youngest of the Romanovs, somehow survived the slaughter. Over the years, a number of women claimed to be her. Some were easily spotted as frauds. Others convinced enough supporters to make a serious claim to fame.

Nobody
And then there was Anna—a nameless, homeless, memoryless wanderer, prone to suicidal fits at the "insane asylum" where she was brought. Nobody knew where she came from. They gave her the name Anna because she had none of her own.

But one day, Anna's doctor came across a picture of the last Russian royal family. Anna bears a striking resemblance to little Anastasia. And she seems to know more about the Russian noble house than one would expect. Anna is hypnotized. She knows even more in her subconscious. There's a real possibility that she could be the only surviving heir of the Romanov family fortune. But who knows for sure? Is there any way to prove it?

Newspapers pick up the story. Is this really Anastasia? By some miracle was her life spared, only to be thrown into this new and dismal tragedy? Or is she only a hoax, a scoundrel, a publicity-seeker? The controversy sells papers. And the press hypes it to the limit.

Somebody

Enter the old empress. She was not in Russia at the time of the murder of her son and his family. And now she lives in exile. If anyone should know if Anna is truly her granddaughter, this woman is the person. And one day she comes to see Anna.

The two women talk together for a long time. When she leaves, the elderly woman tells the world: "Anna is my granddaughter Anastasia!"

Suddenly Anna begins to change. She blossoms as a person. She takes hold of her life. The suicide threats are gone. She washes herself and combs her hair. She looks after herself and dresses in style. She stands up straight in a crowd, and she carries herself with dignity when she walks.

The rumors follow her for the rest of her life. The courts in West Germany debate the issue of her identity for years. But Anna—Anastasia—has a new lease on life. She starts over. She learns to live again. She leaves the past behind and finds herself with a future.

Back to Life

One line in the play carries the heart of the story. How did Anna climb from the pit of her insane asylum and walk again in the land of the living? What transformed Anna the nobody into Anastasia the princess? This is her secret: "You must understand that it never mattered whether or not I was a princess. It only matters that . . . someone, if it be only one, has held out their arms to welcome me back from death!"

Someone gave her a new identity. Someone gave her a reason to live. Someone gave her a vision and a purpose and a hope and a goal. In the unsettling and changing and tumultuous wanderings of her existence, someone gave her something to live for.

The Romanov family lost its royal heritage. The Russian revolution, in turn, is running out of steam. The great powers of the world are shaken. But Anna Anderson came back from the dead. She found something of strength and support in changing times and circumstances. She found someone who believed in her.

And that's what David lays claim to in Psalm 52: "I trust in God's unfailing love for ever and ever" (v. 8).

Surrounded by the ominous and glittering powers of his age, the warty toad becomes a handsome prince!

When . . .

When God restores the fortunes of his people,
let Jacob rejoice and Israel be glad!
—Psalm 53:6

Life was tough for John Currie. He was born in poverty. He never learned to read and write. In 1949, he killed a man and was sentenced to spend the rest of his life in prison.

Some years later his sentence was changed to life at hard labor. But release from the confines of prison did little to change his lot. He was allowed no dialogue in public and no relations with other people. He lived in a drafty trailer that collected dust and insects during the summer and snow in winter. He bathed in a leaky horse trough with a garden hose for plumbing.

Slave Labor

By arrangement with the Tennessee State Corrections Board, a wealthy farmer near Nashville got the use of John's manual labor. The man took John to town a couple of times a year and gave him a few dollars to spend. But that was his only social outlet. It only emphasized more deeply his loneliness and poverty.

In 1968, the State Corrections Department commuted John's sentence. The farmer received a letter spelling out the terms of John's release. But the farmer didn't want to lose his "slave" labor, so he did nothing. And then he died. The letter was lost. John kept on working.

A year passed. Then two. Then five, and ten. Finally, in early 1979, someone learned of John's sad condition. He checked out the situation and finally announced freedom to a broken old man.

A Tragedy

But the saddest chapter of the story was yet to be written. John had nowhere to go. His body was now released, but his spirit remained caged by the years of bondage.

John Currie died recently. And no one really cared. Tragic, isn't it?

The situation in Psalm 53 is almost that hopeless. It's virtually identical to its earlier twin, Psalm 14. David's world is in bondage. There are thieves and robbers and murderers, to be sure. But David's confinement is more powerful than even that—he lives in a society that denies the existence and the validity and the power of God. And so no spirits soar, no minds are challenged, no thoughts are lifted in praise and wonder and glory.

The few who believe in God are like John Currie: trapped in a hard-labor camp with no parole. And they might turn out like him—dull and sour and lonely and defeated.

The Power of Hope

Except for one thing: their jailers have no ultimate authority.

The fools who cry, "There is no God!" are the ones who live in a fantasyland of nightmares. The prison of godlessness is only a temporary skirmish in a larger battle of wills.

John Currie did wrong, was confined, and lost hope. But those who believe in God know that the "sentence" imposed on them by society is itself foolish. And the issue of its being commuted rests in the nail-scarred hands of a higher power.

So they talk about "when . . . " things will change. And hope keeps them alive.

Living in the Future

Surely God is my help . . . for he has delivered me
from all my troubles.
—Psalm 54:4, 7

One of the German army prison camps during World War II was divided into two sections. In order to keep tighter control of captured Allied soldiers, British and Commonwealth internees were segregated from American captives. A fence and out-of-bounds territory on either side marked a no-man's-land where machine-gun fire would kill those who strayed suspiciously close to one another.

A Dull Routine
But one time each day, right at noon, the ranking officer from either group was allowed to approach his counterpart at the fence. Armed soldiers stood close, monitoring every word spoken. After a brief and formal conference, the two leaders would march back to their groups. And the dull routine of prison life would continue.

The situation appeared hopeless. But the ranking officers figured out that they both knew enough of the Gaelic language to use it for passing messages that they didn't want the Germans to hear. They rarely used it, of course, saving it for times of greatest urgency—perhaps an escape attempt.

Good News
Things changed when a recently captured soldier managed to smuggle in the parts of a crystal radio set. Each morning it was hidden by scattering the pieces throughout a variety of secret recesses in the barracks. Each night it was rebuilt and the world outside floated in over the airwaves.

Then came the day that news of the D-Day invasion at Normandy entered the camp. The excitement of the prison soldiers on one side of the fence had to be transmitted to those on the other side. That noon, the ranking officers met for the usual formal interchange. A few words were spoken in Gaelic. Then the officers turned stiffly from one another. With no show of emotion, they marched under guard back to their respective companies.

The Germans were more than a little curious when the barracks on one side of the camp suddenly erupted with cheers and shouting. They themselves knew nothing of the invasion. Hitler's propaganda machine creatively rewrote world events for them.

Inverted Reality

For three more months, the camp carried on a comical inversion of reality. The guards, with their guns and their superior status, were prisoners of ignorance and the coming defeat. Those who cowered in the barracks were certain of their eventual freedom. They wore prison clothes. They ate prison food. They smelled the stench of prison life around them. But because they knew the outcome, their confidence soared. In their hearts they were free!

The former captives who were part of that incredible experience have never stopped telling others of the feelings that filled their spirits during those three months. They were a lot like the thoughts and emotions that drove David as he penned Psalm 54: surrounded by enemies, yet vindicated and released. He experienced the pain of deadly struggles, yet he knew the confidence of God's deliverance. The present demanded all his attention, but he lived in the hope of the future.

Maybe we all live that way, at least once in a while. Have you tuned into the gospel broadcast lately?

Traitor

If an enemy were insulting me, I could endure it; if a foe were
raising himself against me, I could hide from him. But it is
you, a man like myself, my companion, my close friend, with
whom I once enjoyed sweet fellowship as we walked with the
throng at the house of God.
—Psalm 55:12-14

When Canadian missionaries Don and Carol Richardson entered the
world of the Sawi people in Irian Jaya in 1962, they were aware that culture shock awaited them. But the full impact of the tensions they faced
didn't become apparent until one horrible day.

Don had learned enough of the Sawi language to carry on elementary
conversations. He often spent time at the evening communal gathering of
men, telling Bible stories.

Storytellers

The Sawi were great tellers of tales. The best among them could weave
word pictures for hours, captivating and entrancing everyone within
earshot. Don was a novice working under the limitations of a foreign language. Some listened politely as he tried to express himself; most ignored
him and carried on other conversations and activities.

But this night was different. At first, the gathering of men was as restless as usual while Don spoke. The story of Jesus' final days with his disciples before the crucifixion didn't seem to grab them. Then Don told the
story of Judas. And suddenly Don felt a spark of electricity. No one
moved. No one made a noise. All were listening.

Startled and pleased, he carried on. The drama heightened. The room
shivered with anticipation. And when the details of Judas's awful betrayal
danced before them, Don felt a keen sense of involvement in every eye.

Super-Sawi

Then he began to feel uneasy. What was it about the story that drew the
Sawi? Why did this story of treachery draw such enthusiasm? He was
about to find out.

When the last words were spoken, one man whistled in delight. Others chuckled in glee, and some touched their fingertips to their chests in

awe. To them, Judas was a great man. He was a super-Sawi! He was the hero of the story. He had played the greatest trick a Sawi could ever hope to pull off—the "fattening of a friend for the slaughter!"

The Sawi were cannibals. Over generations, their tribe found no excitement that could match eating the flesh of one who had been groomed as a friend. It was the ultimate expression of power, of control, of vindication. To eat the flesh of a friend was the ultimate trip. And Judas was the hero of the gospel.

Torture

Can you imagine it? How could you live in such a society? Think of how Don and Carol Richardson felt. They had been welcomed into the village as guests; now they wondered whether they were to become the next victims of such a value system. Which "friend" in their daily routine would plunge the knife?

Aren't you glad to be living in a "safe" and "sane" culture? Let me tell you of a few people I know.

- There's a young woman whose flush of excitement at marriage has turned to bitter sorrow. Her husband suddenly left her, filed for divorce, and now says the most horrible things to her and about her.
- A man was in business with another member of his church. They sang together on Sunday. But when matters of business ethics forced a wedge between them on Monday, they began to hate each other. They're in different churches now, each telling a vindictive tale about the other to anyone who will listen.
- Two brothers farmed together for years. Now they can't stand the sight of each other. If you want to know the faults of either, just listen to the other brother.
- Four children are waiting for their father to die. Each vows love and tenderness to him. But two plot together against the other two to poison his mind to them.

Can you feel the pain? Have you known the torture? Is your life in the picture somewhere between Jesus and Judas and the Sawi people? Welcome to the real world, the "sane" world, the world of heartache and betrayal and pain that comes not from some distant adversary but from the turncoat treachery of a friend and lover. Welcome to the world of David in Psalm 55.

You know why his heart cries for vindication. And you know what his prayer for hope and comfort is all about. Most of all, you know the urgent emotion of the last line: But as for me, I trust in you.

Courage

In God I trust; I will not be afraid.
—Psalm 56:10

"Screw your courage to the sticking-place," says Lady Macbeth to her doomed husband in Shakespeare's tragedy, "and we'll not fail."

But fail they do, and no amount of courage in the world can save them or turn them into heroes.

Courage is a funny thing. It's a bit like happiness: the more you seek it, the more you demand it, the more you try to call it up, the less it shows its face.

Words can stir us to courage. Who would not rally around the "I have a dream . . ." speech delivered by Martin Luther King, Jr., in 1963, a speech in which he paints the colors of freedom? Who would not feel stronger listening to the dogged determination of Winston Churchill in the dark days of 1940: "Let us . . . brace ourselves to our duty, and so bear ourselves that, if the British Empire and its Commonwealth last for a thousand years, men will still say, 'This was their finest hour!'"

Poetry is the music of courage. Rhythm taps out its marching orders, and rhyme binds many weak hearts into a swelling, confident throng. William Henley's poem "Invictus," written in 1875, catches the essence of what he believes courage to be and gives it a human face:

Out of the night that covers me,
Black as the pit from pole to pole,
I thank whatever gods may be
For my unconquerable soul.

Beyond this place of wrath and
    tears
Looms but the horror of the shade;
And yet the menace of the years
Finds, and shall find, me unafraid.

In the fell clutch of circumstance
I have not winced, nor cried aloud
Under the bludgeoning of chance
My head is bloody, but unbowed.

It matters not how straight the
    gate,
How charged with punishment the
    scroll,
I am the master of my fate;
I am the captain of my soul.

Unfortunately, Henley's strident courage failed him. He spent many of his last years in an insane asylum, and he died in 1903 at the young age of fifty-four.

So where does courage come from, courage that lasts, courage that has heart? It comes from faith in a power, a strength, a force, a person greater than myself. It comes from seeing things in perspective. It comes from a sense of God's overwhelming presence and guiding hand in my affairs. That's what David talks about in Psalm 56. "In God I trust" he says; "I will not be afraid. What can man do to me?"

Well, man can do plenty to him. At the time he wrote this psalm, he was running for his life from King Saul. And his refuge among the Philistines was shattered as they turned on him too. "Man" could do an awful lot to David.

But that wasn't the point. People could not remove him from his relationship with God. They could not get him to compromise his faith. They were powerless to destroy that in David which was essentially right and good and honorable. Courage had little to do with personal strength. Rather, his awareness of God's strength made the difference.

Dorthea Day thought about that when she first read William Henley's poem "Invictus." In response she wrote this stirring amplification of David's cry, called "My Captain":

Out of the light that dazzles me,
Bright as the sun from pole to pole,
I thank the God I know to be
For Christ, the conqueror of my
    soul.

Beyond this place of sin and tears
That life with Him! and His the
    aid,
That, spite the menace of the years,
Keeps, and shall keep, me unafraid.

Since His the sway of circumstance
I will not wince nor cry aloud.
Under the rule which men call
    chance
My head, with joy, is humbly
    bowed.

I have no fear though strait the
    gate;
He cleared from punishment the
    scroll.
Christ is the Master of my fate;
Christ is the Captain of my soul.

The Only Way Out

*Have mercy on me, O God, have mercy on me,
for in you my soul takes refuge.*
—Psalm 57:1

According to an old legend, a wealthy man sent his servant to market one morning on a number of business matters. In just a short while the servant came rushing home, panting and sweating. He glanced back over his shoulder as he ran in.

"Here, here," said the master. "What's wrong?"

The servant told how he'd been at the market, minding his own business, when all at once he bumped against a stranger. They turned and looked at each other, and the servant recognized the other fellow: it was Death himself!

The servant was scared sick. "I'm sure he was looking for me. Please, Master, send me away to my family in Damascus!"

The master had little choice—his servant was beside himself with terror. So he gave the man a horse and sent him on his way.

But the business in the market still had to be done. So the master went himself. While he was there, moving through the crowds, he too bumped against a stranger. When they turned to look at each other, the master saw that it was indeed Death.

He said to Death, "You gave my servant a scare this morning!"

Death replied, "Well, actually, I was surprised to see him here. I'm scheduled to meet him tonight in Damascus."

No Escape

Sometimes it seems there's no getting away from a bad thing. In the mid-1800s, Dutch immigrant pastor and community leader Albertus Van Raalte watched his little colony in western Michigan disintegrate under the ravages of disease and death. One Sunday morning, in the middle of his congregational prayer, he broke down. Sobbing and throwing his hands toward the heavens, he shouted, "Oh God! Must we *all* die?"

Certainly there are times when each of us goes through that agony. It's one thing to experience trouble and torment when you've been living an ungodly existence. You know then that you're getting what you deserve.

But it's quite another thing to be as close to God as David was and still to feel such pain and frustration each day. The specter of Death bumped against him in the marketplace. And if he ran to the land of the Philistines, it followed him right into the caves where he took refuge.

You can almost see him with Van Raalte's tear-stained cheeks and swollen eyes, shouting toward heaven, "Oh God! Is there no relief?"

Amazing Grace

Because we know of the pressures David felt, there is something absolutely amazing about the strength and peace and confidence that come from his lips and pen. "My heart is steadfast, O God. . . . I will sing and make music. . . . great is your love."

David has learned the fundamental secret to living on the edge of cruelty and pain and spite and injury and death. He has learned that only a God who has ultimate control over all these things can make life itself meaningful. Only a God who allows the miseries for a time—as a parent might restrain a helping hand so that a child can grow through the struggles of development—can finally bring all things into his larger plans for peace and joy and harmony.

David's prayer of serenity is like this wise poet's:

> My life is but a weaving between my God and me.
> I do not choose the colours; he worketh steadily.
> Oftimes he weaveth sorrow, and I in foolish pride
> Forget he sees the upper, and I the underside.
> Not till the loom is silent and shuttles cease to fly
> Will God unroll the canvas and explain the reason why
> The dark threads are as needful in the skillful weaver's hand
> As the threads of gold and silver, in the pattern he has planned.

Knockout Punch

Then men will say, "Surely the righteous still are rewarded;
surely there is a God who judges the earth."
—Psalm 58:11

Somewhere today, a family gathers around a meal table in silence. They arrange the plates a little farther apart, so as not to notice the space where one is missing. She was a beautiful, blossoming daughter. She was a sassy, silly sister. But she's gone now, snatched away in a moment by the stupidity of a drunken driver.

They bow their heads and fold their hands and close their eyes. The father prays: "Our Father who art in heaven, Hallowed be thy name. . . . "

But he can't go on. The burden rips open his heart, and he cries out, "It isn't fair!"

Fair Play

We talk about "blind justice." We expect "fair play." We establish laws to guard "gentlemanly conduct." But we know, deep down in our hearts, that this world is not a fair place to live.

A child dies in a riot, simply because he was born in the wrong community. A woman miraculously survives a terrible car crash only to waste away with AIDS, contracted from the blood that saved her life. Bosnia is devastated by war, and any life is game for the sniper's bullet. Ethiopian children starve while corrupt governments battle for wasteful displays of power and wealth and sell stocks of food to purchase weapons.

What's fair about that?

Tragedy

We hurt with our aching world. But the tragedy that stuns us most is the strange set of circumstances that catches our own lives in tangled ways. A family worked long hours to make a passable living. When an opportunity developed in another city, they sold everything and bought a family business there. The economy took a tailspin and they lost everything. Along the way, several family members died through accident or disease in ways beyond their control.

They can smile when they talk with you. But touch that little button of feelings and the tears pour out. It's Naomi's report all over again: "The

Almighty has made my life very bitter. I went away full, but the LORD has brought me back empty. The LORD has afflicted me; the Almighty has brought misfortune upon me" (Ruth 1:20-21).

No fair play here.

Cruelty

Cruelty is the worst form of injustice. If nameless circumstances entangle me in a web of pain, I merely cry out in helplessness. But if people are deliberately sadistic, deliberately mean-spirited, deliberately cruel, then my pain turns to anger and my hurt thirsts for vengeance.

That's where David is in Psalm 58. The words sound like they don't belong in the Bible: "Break the teeth in their mouths, O God" (v. 6); "Like a slug melting away as it moves along, like a stillborn child, may they not see the sun" (v. 8); "The righteous will be glad . . . when they bathe their feet in the blood of the wicked" (v. 10).

These are human words. The Belgic Confession ends with a description of "the last judgment." And we, with our forebears, confess that judgment day will be "very pleasant for us." It will bring us "a great comfort." Why? Because we "will see the terrible vengeance that God will bring on the evil ones who tyrannized, oppressed, and tormented [us] in this world."

Not a pretty thought. But if there is no cosmic justice, no balancing of the books for eternity, no authoritative judgment on those who ruin the lives of others in this world, why should we believe in a "good God?" Why should we believe in a God at all? Might we then not follow the advice of Job's wife after their world ripped apart: "Curse God and die"?

Let people say, at least one day in a future yet to come: "Surely the righteous still are rewarded; surely there is a God who judges the earth." And let those who believe those words work for fair play in these days.

Forgetfulness

Deliver me from my enemies. . . . But do not kill them, O
Lord our shield, or my people will forget.
—Psalm 59:1, 11

Books have a way of disappearing on me. I'll get excited about a new book and tell a few people about it, and then, suddenly, my own copy will be gone. Over the years, through my days as a student, and then in our family travels, I'm sure I've left behind a trail of books that now sit on hundreds of dusty shelves belonging to others.

A few years back, I received a package in the mail from an address I didn't recognize in a place I'd never been. When I opened it, there was a favorite book of mine and a set of college course notes I'd lent to a friend nearly a decade before! A change in jobs, and the packing and unpacking that it required, had brought him to a red-faced encounter with these treasures of mine.

Nineteenth-century novelist Sir Walter Scott feared to lend his coveted books to even the best of friends. He gave each borrower very specific instructions as to when the book had to be returned. "This is necessary," he explained apologetically, "because, although all my friends are bad at arithmetic, they tend to be very excellent at bookkeeping."

Forgetfulness is a very human trait. "Out of sight, out of mind." the old saying goes. Sometimes that can be a good thing. God has blessed us with the ability to remember the best and forget the worst of our troublesome years. Children find the stories of their grandparents so fascinating because the world they tell of seems like a fantasyland far removed from the humdrum existence of today. In the words of one wise person: "Always remember to forget the things that made you sad, but never forget to remember the things that made you glad."

Sometimes forgetfulness can be embarrassing. In his later years, poet Ralph Waldo Emerson had what he called a "naughty memory" that failed him far too often. At a funeral for a dear friend, he remarked, "That gentleman had a sweet, beautiful soul, but I have entirely forgotten his name."

Even the terms for commonplace objects often slipped his memory. Though he had taken walks carrying an umbrella all his life, later he searched in vain for that unique word. Often he shook his head in sad uncertainty and asked for "the thing that strangers take away."

There are times when forgetfulness can be more than embarrassing. It can be downright sinful. Some years ago, William Webb put a sign in the window of his West Worthing, Saskatchewan, butcher shop: "This business has been compelled to close owing to bad debts. A list of the names and amounts owing will shortly be shown." Within hours, the memories of those who had "forgotten" their debts improved, and money began pouring in. The bills were paid, and the butcher shop stayed in business.

In Psalm 59, David prays for God to help him with his forgetfulness. Time after time he has asked for help and deliverance and comfort and strength in the face of his enemies and in difficult circumstances. And so often, he knows, along with deliverance comes amnesia. He forgets the troubles that had bogged him down. And most of all, he forgets the God who delivers him.

Psalm 59 carries an interesting message. "Deliver me!" cries the child of God in the middle of a tough time. "But give me just enough irritation to help me remember from where my help comes."

Generations ago, in his poem "The Pulley," poet George Herbert pictured God creating each of us as individuals, sprinkling our lives with treasures from a jar of gifts standing next to him. Beauty, wisdom, honor, pleasure—all are liberally spread among God's special ones. But at the bottom of the jar lies "Rest." Let's stop now, said God, and not give them that gift.

> Let him be rich and weary, that at least,
> If goodness lead him not, yet weariness
> May toss him to My breast.

Sometimes it's good to forget the pain and toil and problems of the past. But sometimes, as David knows, forgetfulness can be the first step in losing faith.

Rejected

You have rejected us, O God, and burst forth upon us.
—Psalm 60:1

A retired man tells of his "experiment" with the little birds that flock each morning in his backyard. He loves to scatter seeds and other treats for them and watch their "human-like" manners. The doves are more aggressive than the others, probably because of their voracious appetites. He's found that if he waits quietly long enough, they will be the first to eat from his hand.

One morning he tried to play a little game with a certain dove that had become a regular at these feedings. He held out his hand with birdseed in it and silently coaxed the bird to come. Just as the dove reached for the offered grain, the man closed his hand abruptly. The bird stopped, cocked its head in disbelief and uncertainty, and then hopped back a few paces.

The hand opened again. The bird began another bold approach. And once more, the hand clamped shut just before the dove could reach the food. Several more times the pair repeated the little ritual, the man playing "god" and the dove growing in frustration and impatience. Then the bird flew off. It never returned.

Pain
Rejection hurts. Professional writers know only too well the pain of another rejected article or book. English romance novelist Elinor Glyn's first full-length manuscript was rejected by so many publishers that she tried a bolder approach. She sent it to yet another publishing house with this note attached: "Would you please publish the enclosed manuscript or return it without delay, as I have other irons in the fire."

The editor's reply was firm and quick. He returned the pages with this scribbled message: "Put this with your other irons."

Flamboyant British statesman and one-time prime minister of England, Benjamin Disreali, had a similarly witty standard acknowledgment for people who sent him unsolicited manuscripts for his opinion. They received this reply: "Thank you for the manuscript; I shall lose no time in reading it."

Growth

Rejection is a tough business. But when it helps us grow in character it can be a very good thing. Gaston Palewski, aide to former French president Charles DeGaulle, was well-known for his sexual come-ons to the women he encountered. One night after a party he offered to drive a young woman home. She had the firmness of spirit to step on his toes, as hundreds of others had only wished to do. She coldly but very politely responded, "Thank you, but I'm too tired; I think I'll walk." That kind of rejection was what he needed most to grow up.

Diogenes, who founded the ancient Greek philosophic school of the Cynics, knew that rejection could bring strength. Someone once caught him trying to beg for food from a statue. He explained: "I am exercising the art of being rejected." He was preparing himself to cope with life.

Alienation

The midnight hours of history have been dampened by the tears of those whose heartache grows deeper because of rejection. "Sticks and stones may break my bones, but words can never hurt me," we say with bold face in the morning sun. But loneliness returns in the darkness, and every nasty name or spurious glance becomes a taunting reminder that we're not wanted.

That's the pain of David in Psalm 60. He's been well-schooled in rejection. King Saul was a master teacher. So were the Philistines, and so were members of his own family. But one thing always gave him hope: God would never leave him; God would never forsake him.

Now he's not so sure. Even God seems a silent and foreboding foe. Even God seems an enemy warrior. The rejection of the nations is a strain on Israel's resources; the anger of God, for whatever reason, shatters them.

The title notes of the psalm seem to indicate that it was written after the tide had turned, after General Joab had won a decisive battle over the Edomites, after faith and hope glimmered again in David's heart. But the pain of once being rejected, especially by God, is not something from which he can easily retreat.

It would be another thousand years before the world would hear a cry of alienation so bitter that it alone could bring peace to others who felt rejection. For not far from David's palace, one day in the future, a son of his would be rejected by society, condemned by the governing authorities, and displayed in death on a hideous cross, at odds even with God above.

His lips would cry, "My God, my God! Why have you forsaken me?" The answer is the mystery of salvation: "So that we might never again be forsaken by him."

Refuge

Hear my cry, O God; listen to my prayer. From the ends of
the earth I call to you, I call as my heart grows faint; lead me
to the rock that is higher than I. For you have been my refuge.
—Psalm 61:1-3

One day in 1748 the hymn writer Charles Wesley was in a dark and somber frame of mind. He was discouraged at the struggles Christians experience and troubled by his own weak faith.

As he walked in a small garden near his home, he watched an unusual sight in the sky above. A little sparrow was darting madly on the winds in a desperate attempt to escape the clutches of a pursuing hawk. The outcome was certain: in a moment the sparrow would perish.

But in that brief instant something happened. With a last frantic effort, the sparrow angled suddenly toward Wesley. He was wearing a large overcoat, quite bulky and open at the neck, and in a flash the tiny bird dived into the comforting folds. The hawk gave an angry shriek, circled for a moment in hopes of a second chance, and then flew off to find other prey. Wesley could feel the feverish restlessness of his little friend slowly ebb away.

The imagery of the song that came out of this encounter is clear and precise:

> Jesus, lover of my soul, let me to thy bosom fly,
> while the nearer waters roll, while the tempest still is high;
> hide me, O my Savior, hide, till the storm of life is past;
> safe into the haven guide, O receive my soul at last!

Retreat

Everyone needs a refuge, a place of retreat when the going gets rough. Behind the school where I taught in Nigeria was a high mountain. Circling its upper slopes were the remains of a centuries-old stone wall. This landmark was a symbol of hope to the Tiv people from ancient times. When marauding Hausa and Ibo and Udam raiding parties swarmed the Benue River basin, local farmers fled up Mkar Mountain till safety returned below.

The wilderness fortress of Masada served as similar protection for the first-century Jews in their desperate struggle against Rome. The stores and provisions laid up there, combined with the virtually unscalable walls of rock, created a standoff that lasted for years. And in Ireland today, the Irish Round Towers still dot the landscape. They are small stone castles with a single door positioned high off the ground. When the ladder was pulled in and the heavy door bolted shut, everyone inside felt safe from the hostile Scottish scavengers.

Comfort

We know that our religion is more than just a refuge. It should be a shaping influence on all that we do or say or think. After all, that's what our Lord himself said when telling us that we should love God with all our *heart,* our *soul,* our *mind,* and our *strength.*

Over the centuries we've tried to tell Freudians that their limited perception of religious faith is inaccurate. Religion is more than just some complex childhood fixation. We know that Marx was wrong too when he called religion the "opiate of the masses." And a modern "God of the gaps" who takes over only when we can't find the answers through science or technology isn't anything like the personal Creator and Redeemer of the Scriptures either.

Still, as David knows in Psalm 61, if his religion doesn't bring comfort in times of struggle, if it doesn't keep him sane through periods of sore distress, if his God isn't *at least* a "God of the gaps" whose unfailing presence can be counted on when life falls apart, then his religion is worthless.

As Charles Wesley put it:

> Other refuge have I none; hangs my helpless soul on thee;
> leave, ah! leave me not alone, still support and comfort me.
> All my trust on thee is stayed, all my help from thee I bring;
> cover my defenseless head with the shadow of thy wing.

Appearances

*Two things have I heard: that you, O God, are strong, and
that you, O Lord, are loving.*
—Psalm 62:11-12

Appearances can be deceiving. John Wayne acted the part of a full-fledged cowboy in dozens of motion pictures. His last show, "The Shootist," was a movie about an aging western gunslinger. But here's what Wayne had to say about his skills with a firearm: "I couldn't hit a wall with a six-gun, but I can twirl one. It *looks* good!"

Changing Colors

Appearances can be deceiving. Still, we often trust what we see more than what we read or hear. That's why television is so captivating. "Seeing is believing," we say.

Sometimes appearances can change the way we think about things. Consider, for example, the report of Dr. Maxwell Maltz, a former New York cosmetic surgeon, who tells of a magazine contest to find the ugliest young woman in the United States. Cruel as such a contest may seem, the magazine editors actually hoped to change the life of this unfortunate person for the better.

Photos poured in from all over North America. The editors selected a young woman with poor features, terrible grooming, and appalling clothes as the "Ugliest Girl in America."

For her prize, she won a plane ticket to New York City. There a team of specialists went to work on her. Dr. Maltz reshaped her nose and built up her chin. Others gave her a new hairstyle, an elaborate wardrobe of the latest fashions, and grooming instructions. In a modern Cinderella story, the "ugliest" became quite beautiful, almost overnight. Within a few months she was married.

In fact, says Dr. Maltz, her whole attitude toward life changed. Before the cosmetic transformation she had been shy and inhibited. She felt foolish and ignorant and out of place in almost any company. But once she had tasted what she could become, her personality also exploded with new possibilities. She became confident and poised, articulate and informed. She attracted people to herself in any crowd.

Appearances can be deceiving. But who among us would be able to say which appearance was the deceptive one—the young woman whose photos won the "Ugliest Girl" contest, or the young woman who waltzed in beauty?

Trust

Faith is a matter of the unseen, as Hebrews 11:1 says. We don't *need* to see in order to believe. In fact, placing too much emphasis on seeing signs, as some cults have done, can lead people down ungodly paths.

But David senses that faith also has to be a matter of appearances which somehow reveal a little of heaven on this side of the spiritual divide. We cannot believe in a god we know nothing about. Nor can we trust a god whose only qualities are rumored to be cruelty and spite. Certainly, reports of a "90-pound-weakling" god, like the sympathetic hero in Harold Kushner's best-seller *When Bad Things Happen to Good People*, won't bring the world begging for religion.

We need appearances for faith. We need to know the same things that David talks about in Psalm 62: "that you, O God, are strong, and that you, O Lord, are loving." That's, after all, the reason we have the Bible. It gives us a picture of the unseen God in action. It tells us what others have learned about God.

The New Testament gospels present a striking portrait. Didn't Jesus say, "Whoever has seen me has seen the Father"? In Jesus' family photo album are the pictures we need in order to know and to trust and to feel and to gain strength once again.

Eventually, as we're paging through that family album, we'll come to some snapshots of ourselves. There again, appearances can be deceiving. We may believe our picture deserves to win an "Ugliest Person" contest. But after divine surgery, there's sure to be a marriage made in heaven!

Thirsty

O God, you are my God, earnestly I seek you; my soul thirsts
for you, my body longs for you, in a dry and weary land
where there is no water.
—*Psalm 63:1*

Are you thirsty?

If I ask you that question often enough, you'll probably have to get something to drink. Thirst is one of the unconscious demands that shapes our lives. After all, more than 80 percent of our bodies is water. A drink of water now and then is the best thing we can do to keep our bodies running well.

Craving

Thirst, though, is more than just a physical necessity. Thirst is the craving that sets in when an addiction take over. Thirst is the incessant call of the heart for love. Thirst is the emotional overload that demands peace and security in an unsettling world.

Thirst is the word David uses to describe his spiritual needs. A desire for God's presence and blessing is one thing; our *need* for God's attention and care is quite another. The first is a conscious choice. The latter is unconscious; it is urgent and overwhelming.

Faith

One writer paints this picture of his spiritual quest. He's like a man stranded alone in the middle of a vast desert. The sun punishes him from above. The horizon shimmers with heat. The hot sand burns blisters onto his toes.

As he stumbles along, he carries in his hand a small canteen, now nearly empty of precious water. Just as he raises it to his mouth for one final drink, his eye is caught by a blur in the distance.

He lowers the canteen, wipes the dust from his eyes with his sweaty sleeve, and blinks several times, squinting to see more clearly. It's real. But a real what?

He caps the canteen and begins to stagger toward the blur. It's an old shack that once was home to another human being. Winds and weather have stripped the outside, and rodents have licked the inside clean. There's nothing here to keep him alive. But at least it's a place to die.

Once more he lifts the canteen to his lips. But now he stops again. Fifteen meters away is a rusty cast-iron pump. With surprising strength he pushes himself toward it. He pumps the handle feverishly, but no water comes. After years without use, the rod scrapes and screams.

But what's this? Down by the spout is a small sign, lettered in the fine hand of another generation. Friend, it says, there is a river of water flowing beneath these sands. Drink your fill at this pump. But to start the flow, you must prime the pump. Empty your canteen in the hole above.

What should he do? The pump hasn't been used in years. Maybe the water dried up long ago. If he empties his canteen and the pump gives no water, he'll surely die. If he drinks the last swallow, perhaps he'll live long enough for rescuers to find him.

What should he do? What would you do?

Then faith takes hold. Faith in words written by an unknown friend. Faith in words of hope and life. He tips his canteen over the hole; he pours out the precious drops of his future; he empties what he has brought with him in hopes of finding a gift that is greater than himself.

He pushes down on the handle and feels the gentle resistance of the water below. He pushes again, and again, and again. . . . And streams of living water burst from the spout!

Refreshed
That parable could have been written by David, wandering one day in the Desert of Judah. Faith doesn't drink anything or everything. It chooses its refreshment carefully. As the addict knows, it's not how much you drink but what you drink that makes the difference.

Complaint

Hear me, O God, as I voice my complaint. . . .
—Psalm 64:1

Last week our neighbor jumped up on the high wooden fence that he built to protect his private world and yelled at me for mowing the lawn while he was trying to sleep. It was the middle of the day, but he had stayed out late the night before and was trying to make up for lost time. He complains about a lot of things, and I thought his request more than a little unreasonable. Even so, I turned off the mower and gave him another hour and a half.

We don't like complainers. "Nagging isn't horse sense!" says one proverb. "When you feel dog-tired at night," accuses another, "it may be because you growled all day!"

Grumblers

Complaining seems to be an essential element of the human condition. One of Bishop Berkeley's "Principles of Human Knowledge" is this: "We have first raised a dust and then complain we cannot see." Sound familiar?

In 1770 Edmund Burke published a little treatise called *Thoughts on the Cause of the Present Discontents.* I'm not sure what was bugging the world of his day, but his perception sounds quite contemporary: "To complain of the age we live in, to murmur at the present possessors of power, to lament the past, to conceive extravagant hopes of the future, are the common dispositions of the greatest part of mankind."

I've always enjoyed the lines of another English writer who recorded the state of affairs in his community and called it *The Parish Register.* Here's one observation:

> Our farmers round, well pleased with constant gain,
> like other farmers, flourish and complain.

The man's name, ironically, was George Crabbe. Maybe it reflected his own attitudes and feelings.

Proper Complaint

Some complaining seems justified. Take the situation of a weary traveler at a New York City hotel. World-famous violinist Jascha Heifetz was in town for a Carnegie Hall recital. Heifetz's musical perfection owed much to constant practice. At midnight on the eve of his concert, he was still sawing away in his hotel room.

The telephone rang. It was another guest, whose musical appreciation stopped much earlier in the evening. She demanded a little quiet.

"But I am Jascha Heifetz," said the violinist.

"I don't care if you're Lawrence Welk," came the sharp reply. "I want to get some sleep!"

We've probably all made that phone call at one time or another. Or wished we had.

Excessive

Sometimes our complaints seem excessive. British poet Matthew Arnold was neither kind nor gracious. He was known for his overly-critical eye. One time he stayed at the home of an American family while on a speaking tour. His hostess offered him pancakes for breakfast. Arnold took one, tasted it, and then passed the plate to his wife. "Do try one, my dear," he said. "They're not as nasty as they look!"

When he died, one of his neighbors said of him, "Poor Matthew; he won't like God."

Perhaps you're tempted to say that about David when reading Psalm 64: David doesn't seem to like God either. After all, he opens his prayer by telling God he's got a complaint. Is it right to complain to God? Isn't that a bit sacrilegious?

Probably much of our mean-spirited whining is. But consider this: our excessive complaining is actually a reflection of the excessive evil that surrounds us and even spills out from our own hearts. Perhaps if we ever stop complaining about that, we won't have a prayer left.

The Trickle-Down Theory

We are filled with the good things of your house,
of your holy temple.
—Psalm 65:4

You see them almost every day: children wearing tops that boldly proclaim: My folks went to Florida and all I got was this dumb sweatshirt! Or, on the plastic frame around a license plate: We're Spending Our Children's Inheritance.

These testimonies share a common assumption: We have a right to share in the blessings experienced by those over us in society. My parents *must* share their goodies with me. My employer *must* give me a raise if he makes more money himself. The rich in a society *must* distribute their wealth among the poor.

Robin Hood
Remember the story of Robin Hood? Robin Hood was no common thief; he was a distinguished social savior serving as an agent of the proper redistribution of wealth. "I take from the rich and give to the poor," he said. Robin Hood believed Nottinghamshire should be one big, happy family, and he patrolled the highways and byways to make it so for the children and the peasants.

Economists talk about something they call the "trickle-down" theory. It assumes that growing wealth at the top of a social system will "trickle down" through the ranks, till even the neediest beggar rejoices in increased abundance. It's like rain falling on a mountaintop. Moisture feeds the timber and brush up there. But it does more. Water trickles down in rivulets and streams till every part of the valley below is fed.

A Little Help from My Friends
Systems tend to work best in theory, though. Most of us realize that without some assistance, the wealth of the wealthy often stays right there on top of the mountain. Usually it fails to relieve the poverty of the poor. There will always be a need for Robin Hoods in our cruel world to patrol the financial highways and byways. I remember a musical version of "Jack and the Beanstalk" that had the same message. Jack had climbed up to the Giant's glittering castle in the clouds. Everyone cheered when he man-

aged to sneak off with the giant's goose that laid golden eggs. Jack left with this parting shot: "I'll take much more before I'm through! You took it from my daddy, so I'll take it back from you."

The audience was supposed to be pleased.

A Working Model

Psalm 65 is a working model of the "trickle-down" theory at its best. It's a picture of ancient Jerusalem, world-size. Mount Zion is the high point of the city, and its crowning glory is the temple of God.

Somehow, says David, whatever goodness and blessing finds its way around Temple Square eventually trickles down through Jerusalem, refreshing folks along the way.

We ought to pray that praise and thanksgiving fill those courts and richness of grace explodes through those hallways. If that happens, says David, "we are [all] filled with the good things of your house, of your holy temple" (v. 4).

Our human economic theory, based on market-driven supply and demand, is often oiled with greed. It tends to leave us suspicious and jealous. We despise Robin Hood if we're wealthy; we revere him if we're poor. And we drop a few dollars at the lottery booth in a long shot at beating the system.

Kingdom economic theory doesn't necessarily change the system in dramatic ways. Nor does it significantly alter our needs. But it does defuse our greed. After all, remember what Jesus said? "Seek first the kingdom and his righteousness, and all these things shall be yours as well."

Love Talk

Come and listen, all you who fear God; let me tell you what
he has done for me.
—Psalm 66:16

Love has a way of writing itself all over us, doesn't it? We'll do things for love that we never thought we'd be able to do. Take Edward VIII, for instance. He was King of England in the early decades of this century. What a position to hold! But he gave it up in order to marry the woman who captured his heart.

True love begs to be told. At least we'd like to think that's true. But isn't our faith in God really a love relationship too? Yet so often it seems that we want to hide it. William Barclay tells a story about a time when his father led a Christmas worship service in a hospital. It was a delightful hour, he says. They sang about the baby Jesus. They heard the story of God's love. The children laughed and laughed at the good news, and at the jolly way his father told it. One little girl was so excited that her face beamed with the thrill of it all.

After the service, a nurse took her back to the ward. This nurse was known for her sharp and critical personality. The little girl looked up at her and asked, "Did you ever hear that story about Jesus before?"

"Sure," said the nurse. "Many times."

"Well," replied the child innocently, "you certainly don't look like it!"

Do you know that nurse? Have you ever seen her face in your bathroom mirror? Was she hiding her love relationship with God?

Unashamed

Psalm 66 is a lover's testimony. It overflows with the passion of a relationship that is more than right theology. It bubbles with excitement. And it shares the feelings of the heart with all who will listen. There's no holding back.

In his autobiography, *Donahue,* Phil Donahue tells of a mining disaster in Holden, West Virginia. Thirty-eight miners were trapped deep in the earth. Rescue workers struggled day and night to release them. The Red Cross was on hand to offer its aid.

In the middle of it all, a pastor called the trapped miners' relatives together around an open fire on the cold snow. He led them in a prayer for
the men below. Then they held hands and sang, "What a Friend We
Have in Jesus."

"It was beautiful!" says Donahue. He couldn't remember anything ever
moving him so deeply in his spirit. He wanted to broadcast it to the
world; he knew it would make great film.

Honest Expressions
But when he turned to the cameramen, he found that the equipment had
frozen. They had been unable to record any of the service. It wasn't until
2:30 A.M. that the cameras were thawed and ready to roll again. The pastor was still there. Donahue thought he had a second chance. "Would you
run through that service again?" he asked. "We have 206 television sta-
tions across the country who will hear you pray for these miners."

It was a great offer, a real challenge, a fantastic opportunity to speak
nationwide about the Lord. Still, the pastor knew that his testimony
could come out only one way: genuinely.

"No sir," he said, "I just can't do it."

Love talk is that kind of thing. When you try to force it or stage it, you
kill it. But when it jumps out of the heart, as it does in Psalm 66, it's the
most wonderful thing in the world.

What do people know of your love life?

Selfish Prayer

May God be gracious to us and bless us and
make his face shine upon us.
—Psalm 67:1

Sometimes people irritate us with their self-importance. Mohammed Ali, the champion heavyweight boxer, turned every interview into a promotional ad for himself. "I'm the greatest!" he said, till everyone knew his trademark.

One professional golfer thought he could get the upper hand on Ali. He said, "Sure, you're the greatest in the boxing ring; but what're you like on the golf course?"

"I'm the best!" said Ali. "I just haven't had a chance to play yet!"

Self-Centered

Ali got carried away with his boasting at other times too. He was on a plane ready for takeoff when a stewardess noticed his seat belt wasn't buckled. With a gentle reminder she pointed this out. But Ali strutted his stuff. "Superman don't need no seat belt!" he shouted.

"No," said the stewardess, "but Superman don't need no airplane either."

There's probably more than enough self-centered boasting going on in the world, isn't there? And we probably assume that there's one place we can get away from it all, it's the church. Right?

What about Psalm 67? It seems to take that sense of self-importance right into the worship service: "May God be gracious to us and bless us and make his face shine upon us" (v. 1). "God, *our* God, will bless us" (v. 6).

Don't you hear overtones of Ali's boasting in there? "We're the greatest! God shines on us!"

Listen to the Tone

But things are not always as they seem. And the prayer of Psalm 67 is no proud soapbox self-promotion. It has depth and breadth and dignity.

It's really a love song. You can tell that by the tone. Ali's boast "I'm the greatest!" has a different ring than a lover who says, "When I'm with her, I'm the greatest."

The focus is different. The first finds greatness in himself. The second finds greatness in the relationship with someone else that makes him more than he could be on his own. The first may or may not be a lie. The second is always the truth.

Praise That Grows

C. S. Lewis included a little chapter called "A Word about Praising" in his *Reflections on the Psalms*. He had some trouble with Christianity when he first encountered it, he said, because it seemed that God was so self-centered and Christians were so self-important. God wants praise, he thought. In fact, God *demands* praise. And if that's what God is all about, why should anybody want to worship him? Isn't it a little like falling at the feet of Mohammed Ali?

And Christians too: all this business of asking God to bless them! Rather self-important, isn't it? Do I really want to mix with this crowd? he wondered.

But then, says Lewis, he remembered what it was like to be in love. Love demands praise, not because it makes love grow, but because love itself must be spoken in that language. To love is to praise. To care for someone is to seek that person's blessing. Praise is the language of love.

But the praise and blessings of love are never merely self-serving. They are, in fact, self-giving. They reach beyond themselves and seek to touch the lives of others with their fun and fellowship. They seek to broaden and expand the extent of their joy like the rippling waves on a pond. The relationship that results in cries of praise and pleas for blessing spreads beyond itself. It calls to others: "See what we have. Feel what we experience. Share the delights we know!"

Love can never be self-important. And when Psalm 67 bubbles out of lovers' lips, it's a wonderful song.

Processional

*Your procession has come into view, O God, the procession of
my God and King into the sanctuary.*
—*Psalm 68:24*

If you capture a number of caterpillars and place them on the rim of a
small clay pot so that they are all facing the same direction, they will keep
marching around in parade formation until at least one falls off, exhausted
or famished. If there are no significant gaps between the caterpillars, each
assumes the one ahead knows where to go, and none has the will to break
the chain voluntarily. So they keep in step, always following a nonexistent
leader.

Sometimes human beings are like that too. Fad and fashion, the latest
and the newest, tomorrow's trends today . . . We have a great desire to be
part of the crowd, to go with the flow, in tune with the times and in step
with the styles. Mob action often dictates our taste for entertainment,
clothing, food selection, and even "acceptable" social concerns.

Parades

Sometimes the mob gets too maddening, and then we're ready for a more
dignified movement. We're ready for a parade. A parade has structure. It
has direction and purpose. It's a carefully selected slice of life on display.

What town or city worth its salt doesn't have a summertime parade? A
parade lets us show off or view the brightest and the best and the finest we
have to offer: finely groomed horses in precision maneuvers; floats that
turn flowers into a paradise of colors; bands making music that is "moving" indeed; and classic convertibles that serve as thrones on wheels for
the hometown queens.

If mob action fires us up with frenzied emotion, parades dignify our
pride by marching out our best.

Procession of the Nobles

But there is still a higher form of human movement, and that is the pro-
cessional. Processionals happen at the most significant moments of our
lives. The bride in white moves slowly down the aisle as a profound statement of the highest virtues among us: beauty, purity, love, commitment.

The graduate is robed for commencement in all the pomp and ceremony that befits the occasion. He makes us stop and stare and think and dream and hope.

A royal procession can do that too. We feel nobler for the experience of hearing Rimsky-Korsakov's "The Procession of the Nobles." Moussorgsky's tone-poem "Pictures at an Exhibition," which captured the essence of his recently deceased friend's paintings, makes us see the glories of a grand company passing through the mythical "Great Gate of Kiev" in dignified splendor.

Isn't that really one of the Bible's profound messages as well? The mob madness of sinful Babels and the self-important parades of the nations pale in significance as the royal procession of God marches through our times.

In Psalm 68 David describes a picture of the Ark of the Covenant entering Jerusalem. But this procession is symbolic of a far grander one. The march of God through human history is a "procession of the nobles" whom God reclaims from slavery, entering finally through "the great gate" of Paradise into the awesome splendor of God's kingdom.

No wonder David ends the Psalm the way he does: "Praise be to God!"

Scorn

Scorn has broken my heart and has left me helpless;
I looked for sympathy, but there was none, for comforters,
but there was none.
—*Psalm 69:20*

German writer F. Weiskopf tells about a rich Dutch grocer who prided himself on his art collection. It was his crowning ambition to obtain a personal audience with the renowned painter Pablo Picasso. At last he received the opportunity to examine the works in Picasso's studio, with the artist in attendance.

Picasso didn't like the man, and he didn't try hard to hide the fact. After a self-important assessment of each canvas, the grocer finally had this to say: "Master, I understand every one of your productions except one."

"And that is?"

"Your dove. It seems to me so simple, so primitive that I am afraid I am too intelligent for it."

"Sir," asked Picasso, "do you understand Chinese?"

"No," came the reply.

"Well," said the artist, "six million people do!" Then Picasso showed him to the door.

Bigotry
Like Picasso, most of us have a hard time with certain kinds of people. They may be cruel or cunning or mean-spirited. Or their ego is too large or they take themselves too seriously. Rare is the person who can truly claim, along with homespun comedian Will Rogers, "I never met a man I didn't like." We'd like to think we're able to enjoy the company of everyone we meet. But too many people disappoint us.

Much of our antipathy toward others makes sense to us. We can always justify, at least to ourselves, the dislike we feel for someone. But sometimes our displeasure becomes bigger than that and begins to take on a life of its own. Then it becomes bigotry—a dislike and disdain and hatred that feeds on itself and requires no justification from anyone.

One Chicago woman spent her summers in Bar Harbor, Maine. She found that area more than a little colored with prejudice. As she drove her pony-cart down a country lane, something spooked the horse and she was dumped to the ground. Two rich matrons soon came along and saw her lying there in a daze. They got out of their vehicle and approached her. Then one said to the other, "Who is she? We don't know her, do we?"

The other woman shook her head. So they got back in their car and left. If she's not one of *us*, we certainly have no use for *her!*

Isolation and Pain

Bigotry and prejudice isolate us from other people and keep us "safe" in our sheltered communities. In 1905, Winston Churchill's election campaign took him through a slum. Churchill, used to wealth and comfort, looked at the rows and rows of dilapidated little houses with horror. "Can you imagine living here?" he asked his secretary, Edward Marsh. "Never seeing anything beautiful, never eating anything savory, never saying anything clever?"

Prejudice becomes wicked when we believe that people who aren't up to our standards aren't even human. We may not use those words, but the meaning is clear. One man I used to talk with frequently filled every conversation with a stream of bigoted judgments about others. He was a good man in many ways, but he had a very unkind heart. Recently at a meeting, one person spoke at length about another person's unmarried state, assuming that it implied something about that person's sexual preferences. The other single people present left the room quickly, cut and angered by such stupid insensitivity.

A Friend Who Stays

Scorn hurts. It is cruel and mean-spirited. Given full reign, it leads to Hitler-like "final solutions."

David finds himself the object of scorn in Psalm 69. He's lonely. He's tired. He's anguished by the prejudice of others that threatens his sanity and his life. He cries out to heaven for friendship and vindication and hope; for his thirst, he has been given only vinegar (v. 21).

David survived that particular crisis in his life. A distant son of David's made heaven's help possible for all of us. For one day he too would experience the scorn that David felt. In the most prejudicial of all deaths, he would be displayed on a cross in official disdain. Tortured by the hot sun, all he would be given to drink was vinegar.

In that moment, the world would grow ashamed of its bigotry. Creation would hold its breath in astonishment at the lengths to which God would go to stand next to those who feel the pain of prejudice.

Hurry Up!

Hasten, O God, to save me; O LORD, come quickly to help me.
—Psalm 70:1

Now that Germany is one nation again, former East Germans are trading in their "Wartburg" automobiles for the more reliable cars produced by Western European nations. According to *Esquire* magazine, East Germans have a nickname for the poorly produced three-cylinder vehicles. They call them "Martin Luther cars."

If Luther had had one of the cars, they say, he probably would have been so frustrated by all the breakdowns that his famous theological cry— "Here I stand. I can do no other. God help me!"—would have been uttered for another reason.

A "Now" World

We don't like to stand still for long, do we? Years ago people encouraged one another by saying, "All good things come to those who wait." But these days, who wants to wait anymore? We have instant foods and microwave ovens to cook them in seconds. We have instant access to news and information from around the world. We have painkillers to take away our headaches right away, so we don't even have to deal with why we hurt. And if we see something we like, instant credit puts it in our hands immediately.

Who needs patience? Life rushes at us. A friend of mine used to say, "Some people like to see the world. Others like to smear it across their windshields."

There's little time for sightseeing these days. Our world smears itself against us rather rapidly.

Impatience

We think we have a right to be impatient. You've heard of those "laws" people figure out about life in our world. One that's a sure child of our times is this: "The checkout line at the supermarket that moves the slowest is invariably the one you are in."

We know that's not consistently true. But it does reflect our conviction that we have a right to be served quickly. We ought to be in the fastest line. We deserve to be among those who are not slowed down in the mad dash of life.

Back in 1911, Ambrose Bierce published his *Devil's Dictionary*. He defined "patience" this way: "A minor form of despair, disguised as a virtue." He knew us impatient people rather well.

Urgency

In that context David's impatient prayer in Psalm 70 seems right with the times. "Hasten . . . " he says. "Come quickly . . . " (v. 1). "Come quickly to me . . . do not delay" (v. 5).

We may be tempted to picture David in a business suit, carrying a briefcase, striding along a busy corridor, eyes on his wristwatch, saying to his associates along the way: "Come on. Let's get going! We've got a deadline to meet. Hurry up!"

But David's concern is not meeting deadlines or keeping up with the clock or racing with his "day-timer" schedule. Instead, David is experiencing a crisis of meaning. In the crush of his life he's demanding two things: that God prove himself faithful to his loving promises by rescuing David from a premature end before he's fulfilled the commission God promised him; and that God forestall the sacrilegious taunts of those who interpret his absence or distance as license to speed up their own devilish games.

Generally, our impatience tends to be self-serving. But when evil events threaten our world in ever-hastening tempo, there's nothing wrong with telling God to "hurry up!" God knows the crisis already. It's important that we recognize it too.

Throw-Away People

Do not cast me away when I am old; do not forsake me when
my strength is gone.
—Psalm 71:9

An ancient legend tells of a remote mountain village where people used to send their senior citizens out into the woods to die. The villagers had an eye to the future; they felt that those beyond a certain age would only slow down progress or use up valuable resources to no economically profitable end. Those who reached a certain age weren't "put out to pasture" or "put out of their misery"; they were simply put out of other people's way.

The legend has a wonderful ending, though. At one point the villagers decided to build a huge meeting hall. Only the tallest and straightest of trees could be used to construct its main supports. There was a problem, though: the logs were so long and straight that it was virtually impossible to tell top from bottom once they were cut. And if the posts were installed upside down, the building would be in danger of collapse.

One young man claimed to have the solution. He struck a bargain with the community: he would tell them how to solve their problem if they would agree to stop sending the older folks of the village off to die.

Their immediate needs forced the villagers to give in to his terms. But instead of giving them the needed information, the young man led his grandfather from a secret hiding place. The elderly gentleman had been a woodsman all his life, and now he provided the wisdom and insight that can only be gained through years of experience. In that moment the villagers realized how foolish they had been. And from that day on, the elderly were given an honored place in the village.

Out of Sight, Out of Mind?

"Yes," we say, "that's the way it should be. Senior citizens have so much to contribute, so much to offer, so much to tell us. Our society would be poorer without them."

But is that really the way we live? Maybe we look to a few of our elders who have some indispensable wisdom we need, like the grandfather in the legend. But what of those who have little to offer in terms of "profitable" knowledge or skills? I know too many lonely elderly people who feel like "throw-away people." They are tolerated at best, forgotten at worst, and unquestionably bypassed in the fast track of mainstream society.

Even in Japan, which has historically revered it older members, things are changing. Some time ago Ronald Yates wrote an article for the *Chicago Tribune*. He interviewed a seventy-six-year-old former gardener in a tiny Tokyo apartment. "I don't like this new Japan," he said. "It is a lonely, cold place. . . . Everything is electronic, nothing human. Even my two daughters are more concerned with their kitchen appliances than with their father."

No wonder Lord Byron penned these lines:

> My days are in the yellow leaf;
> The flowers and fruits of love are gone;
> The worm, the canker, and the grief,
> Are mine alone.

"Yuppie" Christianity?

It can be that way in the church too. The focus of our faith is a Man in his "prime," a Jesus who lives on forever as a robust young fellow in his early thirties.

In Robertson Davies's novel *The Fifth Business*, an elderly priest speaks of his disillusionment with the Christian faith:

> I am an old man and my life has been spent as a soldier of Christ, and I tell you that the older I grow, the less Christ's teaching says to me. I am very conscious I am following the path of a leader who died when he was less than half as old as I am now. I see and feel things that he never saw or felt. I know things he never seems to have known. . . . Am I at fault for wanting a Christ who will show me how to be an old man? All Christ's teaching is put forward with the dogmatism, the certainty, and the strength of youth.

If life is for the young, is religion too? That's the question that haunts the psalmist when he cries to God: "Do not forsake me when I am old!"

Somehow he gets beyond his doubts to a renewal of his faith. But that doesn't make the pain of his struggles any less real. Or the alienation he feels in a youth-focused society.

Long Live the King!

Long may he live! . . . May his name endure forever; may it
continue as long as the sun. All nations will be blessed
through him, and they will call him blessed.
—Psalm 72:15, 17

Being the leader of a community isn't easy. A cartoon shows a man near death lying on a hospital bed. Two visitors sit next to him, and one hands him a card. "The good news, Pastor," she says, "is that the Women's Club at the church decided to get this 'Get Well' card for you. The bad news is that the vote was 23 to 22!"

That could be the picture of any of a hundred different leaders in our world today. A prime minister skates at the bottom of the popularity polls. A president wins a Nobel Peace Prize from those outside of his country and buckets of complaints from those within it. Another world leader seems intent on courting the disfavor of the whole world.

If one of them were to be taken to hospital, Hallmark Card company stock wouldn't go up a penny! The ancient Greek philosopher was right: "Authority is never without hate."

Led Where?
A few years back, Jim Lundy wrote a book called *Lead, Follow, or Get Out of the Way*. According to Lundy, the most common message circulating in many organizations is this lament: We the uninformed, working for the inaccessible, are doing the impossible for the ungrateful.

To put it another way, he says, most people feel like the mushrooms being grown in one of those long, low barns: We feel we're being kept in the dark. Every once in a while someone comes around and spreads manure on us. When our heads pop up, they're chopped off. And then we're canned! Do you ever feel like that?

High Marks
Psalm 72 is a song of royal leadership. It has no hint of the tired frustration we so often feel about heads of state and leaders of corporations. Enthusiasm builds, till it seems as if the sun rises and sets on the king. He's given high marks all around:

Vision (vv. 2-4): A+
Personal Integrity (vv. 5-7): A+
Prophetic Voice (vv. 8-11): A+
Compassionate Heart (vv. 12-14): A+
Accountability (vv. 15-17): A+

The person who originally received this chorus of praise must have been quite a man. Was it David? Was it Solomon himself? Or did Solomon write it for a son he hoped would be even wiser than his father?

Probably we'll never know. But the New Testament church had no problem identifying a Son of David and Solomon who lived up to the glories shouted in Psalm 72. Isaac Watts's well-known hymn paraphrases the psalm this way:

> Jesus shall reign where'er the sun
> does its successive journeys run,
> his kingdom stretch from shore to shore,
> till moons shall wax and wane no more.

In His Steps

If Psalm 72 stirs in us noble thoughts about David or Solomon, it does well. And if it points us to King Jesus, so much the better. But if it fills us with a desire to actively participate in such a kingdom ourselves, then the Word of God is doing its best work. For every child of God is a king or queen who shares the possibilities of restoring righteousness and dignity to relationships on earth.

In the words of Ted Engstrom:

> The world needs men [and women] . . .
> who cannot be bought; whose word is their bond;
> who put character above wealth; who possess opinions and a will;
> who are larger than their vocation;
> who will not lose their individuality in a crowd;
> who will be as honest in small things as in great things;
> who will make no compromise with wrong;
> whose ambitions are not confined to their own selfish desires;
> who are true to their friends through good report and evil;
> who are not ashamed or afraid to stand for the truth. . . .
> Are you counted in that number?

Drifters

*My flesh and my heart may fail, but God is the strength of
my heart and my portion forever.*
—Psalm 73:26

I was sitting at a cafeteria table at a large university last summer.
Crowds of hungry people swept by, none that I knew or ought to have
known.

But then a face. Hadn't I seen that face before? And that smile. She
knows me. But how? From when? Who is she?

Memories of the Way We Were
And then her voice as she greeted me. Sure, I knew her! It was Lynn. Ex-
actly one decade ago she was a young member of a SWIM (Summer
Workshop in Ministries) team for which I had served as leader.

We chatted excitedly. It's hard to catch up on ten years in ten minutes.
What are you doing here? Are you married? Children? Career? Ever see
any of the "old" team members?

Lynn's eyes were bright, but her spirit was much more guarded than it
had been a decade before. When I knew her, she had recently made public profession of faith and life before her was an open door of Christian
service. She had goals ("college") and plans ("work with disadvantaged
children, maybe") and enthusiasm ("Who knows where God might lead
me?"). If any one of the SWIM team members was going to make a difference in the world for Christ, it would be Lynn.

Somehow it didn't all work out the way she planned. A whirlwind relationship with a guy others had cautioned her against. Pregnancy. Forced
marriage. Verbal and physical abuse. Substance dependence. Withdrawal
from the church. Divorce. Shame. Pain.

How did it happen, Lynn? To you, of all people?!

It Just Happened
"That's just it . . . I don't really know. I wanted to experience life like
others did. One thing led to the next. There was never any real turning
point, or decision to drop my faith. It just happened."

It just happened. . . .

A mother calls me about two daughters. Neither denies the faith. But they've drifted into other lifestyles, and the church really isn't that important anymore. It just happened. . . .

A businessman succeeds while others fail. He doesn't really need the church or God, although he would be the last to deny their validity. But that's not where he's at. It just happened. . . .

Reginald Bibby of the University of Lethbridge writes about what he calls a "religionless Christianity." "It's not a matter that they've done a serious examination of the faith and decided it doesn't make intellectual sense," he says. "The biggest problem is just one of apathy." People drift through the circumstances of life, and along the way become simply somewhat indifferent.

Like Lynn. Like a host of people we know. And like Asaph in Psalm 73. He directs the choirs at temple worship in Jerusalem. He goes to practices on Wednesday night. He composes a new song each month. He participates in the staff meetings at the temple. But his heart and flesh fail. He's even thinking that he's doing the wrong thing by maintaining this facade of faith for his family (v. 15).

Somehow other things have stolen his heart and his religion. Maybe it's the sense of frustration that religion doesn't make a difference in his life. Maybe it's a lack of spiritual integrity on the part of those around him. Maybe it's just the silence of God. But the drift of life swirls him into a current of doubt, apathy, indifference. "Religionless churchianity."

Snagged by Grace

Then grace enters. Asaph goes back to church. Lynn tells me she asked her church council if she could stand and apologize to the congregation where she once stood to make public profession of faith. Drifters find a new current and hearts regain strength. Why?

Perhaps because life in the other currents isn't as satisfying as the travel brochures promise. Perhaps because rude circumstances wake us up to deeper needs. But perhaps, most of all, because God never lets us go.

When you're drifting along in the water of life, a snag can be an annoying thing. But if the water is pulling you toward Niagara Falls, the snag may be the most refreshing sense of grace you could ever imagine!

Covenant

Have regard for your covenant. . . .
—Psalm 74:20

A certain baker made the finest bread in town. He prided himself on his loaves and also on his business savvy. He bought his butter for baking directly from a local farmer in order to save middleman costs. And because he knew the farmer wasn't too bright, he offered loaves of bread in payment for the butter.

Things went along fine for a while. The baker chuckled to himself at the deal he had made. He even figured out how he could do better for himself: he began to make the farmer's loaves of bread a little bit smaller. When that worked well, he made them smaller still.

But then something happened that really inflamed his temper. The pound cakes of butter he got from the farmer began to shrink as well. How dare the man cheat him like that! When he stomped into the milk parlor one day, demanding an explanation, the farmer was flustered. He was sorry, he said. He had no idea that his cakes of butter were getting smaller. "You see," he said, "I always measure out a pound of butter by the weight of one of your pound loaves of bread."

Handshake Honesty

One could wish that our actions were as good as our words, and that our words were always as good as gold. Wouldn't it be nice if the leaders of warring countries could walk up to each other, decide there's been too much rattling of war sabers, agree to an honorable peace, and then shake hands, knowing the deed would be done?

Our world isn't like that. Too many promises are broken. Too many loaves of bread weigh less than they should. And too many times we've been taken for a ride. "Trust" is only for con-artists and charlatans. The rest of us need legal contracts.

Suspicious Fingers

God knows that. He can't trust us anymore, even if he would like to. He knows enough of the fickleness of the human heart. And he knows that we don't have it in us to really trust him either. We're suspicious of our government leaders. We're suspicious of people with a different color of skin. And, if you press us far enough, we're even suspicious of ourselves. We cover our suspicions up by pointing the finger elsewhere. Even at God.

Asaph does that in Psalm 74. "Why have you rejected us forever, O God? Why . . . ? How long . . . ? Why do you . . . ?" (vv. 1, 10-11).

You know what he's thinking, don't you? I've been there. I'll probably be there again. And so will you. Just this week a woman talked with me at length. "God doesn't care," she said.

Crutches

But remember the idea of "covenant." That words appears more than 267 times in the Old Testament and thirty-three times in the New Testament. What does it mean? Why is it such a big deal in the Bible?

In the world of ancient Israel, the Hittite nation had created the covenant formulary that structured relationships between kings and their subjects. A covenant spelled out the relationship's identity: For better or worse, this is who we are. It established its history: Do you remember how we got together? It stated the framework of that relationship: These are the limits within which we agree to walk together. It made promises: Here's what we can make out of our relationship. And it offered a challenge: If you want to live life to the fullest, make this relationship work.

Of course, a covenant relationship went both ways. God constantly reminded Israel to find herself within their covenant relationship. But Israel could also make demands of God: "Have regard for your covenant," says Asaph. "Live up to your promises. Take care of your people."

From God's perspective, the covenant shaped Israel's life. But from Israel's perspective, the covenant gave them a grip on God. Maybe it was faith's crutch for them, as Asaph says here.

But don't tell a person whose legs have given out that crutches aren't important.

Horns

*I will cut off the horns of all the wicked, but the horns of the
righteous will be lifted up.*
—Psalm 75:10

I grew up on a farm, but that doesn't mean I learned how to milk a
cow. We were into other kinds of livestock—our "cow" was big and white
and had four tires and only one horn. It was the rural delivery truck for
"Quality Check" dairies.

We did see other horns around though. Every now and again Dad
would buy a load of beef cattle that hadn't been dehorned. They'd have to
be herded one by one into the squeeze pen to be held motionless while a
brave soul with a saw hacked away at their horns. Usually when the horn
fell to the ground, a small spray of blood shot out of the beast's head for a
few minutes and then coagulated in a smelly mess down the sides of its
face.

What a difference dehorning made in an animal's bearing! A steer with
horns was a wild and haughty ruler. It had rage in its eyes and a steamy
temper that could flare in an instant. At least that's how I saw it from my
position of frail safety, staring through the cracks in the fence boards.

A dehorned animal, however, could become a friend, a pet, a member
of the family. You could reason with an animal without horns. You could
hug it and hold it by the neck. And removing the horns from an animal
didn't mean that it became weak or cowardly. A better term would be
"meek." Someone defined meekness as power under control, and that's a
good picture of the animals I knew. Animals with horns could flail about
in anger or fun, hurting themselves and others in the process. Dehorned
animals could be just as rambunctious, but their expenditure of energy
didn't have to become bloody or vicious.

Power Play
Asaph uses the imagery of horns in Psalm 75 as a way of describing people. The arrogant, he says, blow their own horns (v. 4). And they wear
their horns in a wicked power play against others (v. 5). That's why there
is so much bloodiness in our world.

Asaph calls on God to dehorn "the wicked" and to balance the scales of justice for the hurting and oppressed. In fact, the act of dehorning the wicked becomes an opportunity for "the righteous" to make music. As the horns of power and evil fall to the ground, those who trust the Lord pick them up and turn them into musical instruments to sound praises to heaven (v. 10). A bloody horn of depravity is turned into a shining trumpet of grace!

Asaph's prayer in Psalm 75 is one that needs to be raised often in our troubled world. Canadian musician Murray McLaughlin wrote a song at year's end in 1989. He wrote it because he was tired of all the news reports that kept telling how evil and corruption and criminal activity seemed so strong. He wrote it because he wanted life to give the little guy the break for once. He wrote it with the hope that whatever powers there are in the universe to balance the scales of justice might lean in the direction of those who love peace and joy and goodness.

"May the Good Guys Win!"

> May I get what I want, not what I deserve.
> May the coming year not throw a single curve.
> May I hurt nobody, may I tell no lies.
> If I can't go on give me the strength to try.
> Ring the Old Year out! Ring the New Year in!
> Bring us all good luck; may the good guys win!
> May the times to come be the best you've had.
> May peace rule the world; let it make us glad.
> When you see something wrong, try to make it right:
> Put a shadowed world into the bright sunlight.
> Ring the Old Year out! Ring the New Year in!
> Bring us all good luck; may the good guys win!

Maybe Murray McLaughlin doesn't know who he's praying to. But there's no doubt in Asaph's mind about who listens to a song like that. Nor does Asaph question the outcome of life's battles. Just wait to see who blows the last horn.

Warrior

Make vows to the LORD your God and fulfill them; let all the
neighboring lands bring gifts to the One to be feared. He
breaks the spirit of rulers; he is feared by the kings of the earth.
—Psalm 76:11-12

Oliver Cromwell was a mighty soldier and a mighty churchman. Leading his troops into England's seventeenth-century civil conflicts, he spoke these words just before they forded a river: "Put your trust in God, but mind you keep your powder dry!"

Enigma

War and military power are an enigma for Christians. On the one hand, power, might, and domination are themes of Old Testament theology. Here is God, the greatest warrior marching across the earth. He is praised for his bloody victories. He is commended for his "scorched-earth" tactics. He is lauded for his wrath and vengeance. The vehicle God uses is the army of Israel.

At the same time, New Testament theology gives every impression of demanding conscientious objection to war of any kind. It is hard to reconcile military action of any sort with the teachings of Jesus. In fact, for the first two centuries of its existence, the Christian church was avowedly pacifist. Kenneth Scott Latourette, the dean of church historians, tells of a Christian young man who was killed because he refused to take up arms as a soldier as late as A.D. 295. And many other stories recorded in the early pages of church history commend nonviolent response to belligerence of any kind.

Pacifism

For instance, a centurion named Vespasian, one of Nero's cohorts, reported sadly that forty of his men had become Christians. The soldiers were given several opportunities to recant but stalwartly held to their confession of faith. At last they were stripped naked and placed on the middle of a frozen lake. Vespasian and the others took up positions around warm fires on the shore. Out on the lake, the chant continued all night: "Forty wrestlers, wrestling for you, O Christ, to win for you the victory and from you, the victor's crown!"

The chant weakened, but lingered on through the nighttime hours. As dawn approached, though, a new note was added. The number changed to thirty-nine as one poor wretch crawled across the ice to salvation at the fire.

In that decisive moment, reports an early church historian, Vespasian himself stripped off his warrior's arms and clothes and ran naked across the frozen hell to join the others in a chant of Christian testimony. Such was the commitment to peace of the early church.

But what do we do with the warrior's cries of the Old Testament? What do we do with the battles of Israel? What do we do with the military tactics of righteous King David, who lined up captives from war on the ground, measured them off by lengths of cord, and killed two groups of Moabites for every group he allowed to live (2 Samuel 8)?

Awkward Humility

There are no easy answers. Peter Craigie, a former professor of religious studies at the University of Calgary, wrote a little book called *The Problem of War in the Old Testament.* He had served in the British Armed Forces and thought strenuously about his involvement as a Christian. In the end, the best he could say was this: War is a product of a sinful world; Israel fought under God's direction partly as an independent political unit and partly in response to God's preliminary notes of cosmic judgment; Jesus brought an end to the collaboration between God and a *specific* human political entity; spiritual warfare continues till eternity, but must now rarely, if ever, employ the means of human military combat.

So what do we say about the sword-rattling that is taking place in various parts of the globe? It's very hard to know, except for this: No one can lay claim to divine right. Nor ought any Christian delight in conflict. The casualties of armed engagements are early warning tremors of the awful day when God will be known as Warrior by all who now ignore him.

Troubled

---

*You kept my eyes from closing; I was too troubled to speak. I
thought about the former days, the years of long ago; I
remembered my songs in the night. My heart mused and my
spirit inquired. . . .*
—Psalm 77:4-6

Charles Gatemouth Brown is one of America's foremost composers
and singers of "blues" music. He's earned a Grammy and other awards for
his songs. A few years ago Brown was asked why he thought his music
spoke to so many people. "Well," he said, "anyone who has brains gets the
blues." That includes most of us.

Thinking Person's Pain

Years ago, one of my high school teachers tried to stimulate our brains by
introducing us to the finer points of English literature. She pushed us,
kicking and screaming, through a condensed version of Shakespeare's
Macbeth. We stumbled over and purposely destroyed most of the dialogue
in our determination not to even remotely like this stuff.

But then came the opening of Act IV—three witches standing around
a cauldron, stirring an evil brew and chanting their mysterious lines. And
finally we found our hearts beating in time with theirs: Double, double,
toil and trouble; fire burn and cauldron bubble.

Here was something we could relate to. Here was life as it was for us in
turbulent times: the generation gap, the Vietnam war, Watergate, a recession, an irrelevant church, the death of God.

How much more could a thinking person drink from the gruesome
cauldron of life? Our classmate Charlie committed suicide. And many of
us didn't sleep well anymore.

Personal Threat

As Asaph writes in Psalm 77, we can take only so much of the "double,
double, toil and trouble" before we find insomnia gripping us and sensory
overload attacking our brains after dark. Threat is always personal. A
thousand evil things may have happened in Asaph's larger world, but a recent event within his family finally got to him. A million wonderful

things could take place around him, but this momentary difficulty wiped out the remembrance of other loves and joys.

Sundown brought Asaph no rest; only another barrage of threats: "Will the Lord reject forever? Will he never show his favor again? Has his unfailing love vanished forever? Has his promise failed for all time? Has God forgotten to be merciful? Has he in anger withheld his compassion?" (vv. 7-9).

There aren't enough words in the English language to catch all the ways that Asaph's pain surrounds him.

Turnaround

A few years ago, a fellow named Sean Coxe came to an impasse in his life. A relationship had died. A business had soured. Religion left him cold. Now he was angry with life. He was angry with the people who'd let him down. He was angry with himself for being such a sucker. Most of all, he was angry with God.

Sean was at the end of his rope, helpless and alone. He could think of doing only one thing. So he took his last three hundred dollars and flew to Florida to see his aging father. Sean's father had been the one solid rock in his life during his younger years. Now he needed to see his dad again and try to put his life back together.

That night they stood out on a dock watching a glorious sunset over the Gulf of Mexico. It was beautiful. But Sean was bitter. He said to his dad, "You know . . . if we could take every great moment like this that we've ever experienced in our entire lives, and put them all back-to-back, they probably wouldn't last twenty minutes!"

He expected his dad to object to that. He expected his dad to tell him to grow up, to quit complaining, to pull himself together. But all his dad said was: "You're probably right, Son."

Then his father looked at him, and he continued: "But they're precious minutes, aren't they?"

And that's how Asaph finally finds his sleep. In the middle of all his distress and anxiety, he chooses to call to mind moments when he sensed the power and the love and the compassion of God. Maybe they're few and far between. Maybe God's footprints can't be seen (v. 19). But remembering those moments convinces him that these momentary troubles cannot erase the eternal power of God's providential care.

Parables

O my people, hear my teaching; listen to the words of my
mouth. I will open my mouth in parables. . . .
—Psalm 78:1-2

Anyone who's read Herman Melville's novels knows he was a great storyteller. But those who knew him personally felt the full impact of his storytelling skills. One evening Melville was visiting Nathaniel Hawthorne and his wife. As the evening progressed, Melville stole the show. He told the tale of a fight he had witnessed on a South Seas voyage. A magnificent Polynesian warrior, he said, had wielded his club in a desperate battle struggle.

As he poured out his passionate story, Melville marched about the room and flung his arms in the motions of attack. The Hawthornes were captivated and speechless.

The evening wore on, and finally Melville made his way to the door. After he was gone, the Hawthornes suddenly realized he had left without his club. They spent the better part of an hour searching their home for it. In fact, when they next saw Melville, they asked him what had become of the club. Only by repeated oaths was Melville able to convince them that there hadn't been a club in his hands!

Now *that's* storytelling!

Communication at Its Best

Storytelling is a great art. Civilizations without written languages pass along their identities from one generation to the next by way of storytelling. Even in literate cultures, stories carry message and meaning long after propositions and arguments have become tedious. The prophets of the Old Testament were great storytellers. If you removed all of the stories and images from the Old Testament, what you'd have left would be a Bible condensed further than *Reader's Digest* editors could ever manage!

It's the same in the New Testament. Our Lord was a consummate storyteller. We're told that he never spoke publicly after the start of his ministry except in parables. And the crowds couldn't get enough. Here, finally, was someone who spoke their language. Here was someone who made doctrine live. Here was someone who brought them in touch with God.

Asaph does that in Psalm 78. He wants to give a gift to the next generation. He wants his children to share the grace and the beauty and the power of God. He wants them to live stronger and purer lives than he did. And he wants to share with them the deepest mysteries of God's care and love. So does he write a book of doctrine? Organize a code of ethics? Slate a list of theological propositions?

No. He tells a few stories. He describes some events from the past. He dances about the room with an engaging tale. And when he's done with the storytelling, it's all been said. The mystery has been passed; the next generation shares the riches of grace.

A Teacher's Best Friend

Storytelling is still the best way to teach the young. We all know that. Our daughters can't wait to climb on our laps and have us read a story to them. Every night they need another chapter from the Chronicles of Narnia or the *Little House* books or *Winnie-the-Pooh* before they can go to bed.

But sometimes we seem to lose that thrill as we get older. We turn faith into doctrine and our relationship with God into a theological argument. Not long ago someone in my congregation wondered if storytelling really had any place in sermons. You might guess from reading these meditations that storytelling is a way of life for me, and that it spills over into my Sunday sermons. Not everybody appreciates that, perhaps because it's not terribly well done or because it's quite unusual. But sometimes we find stories threatening because they demand involvement and response, and we'd rather not have our religion get to us that way.

Still, God comes to us by way of a story. Not in just the parables of Jesus or the narratives of the Bible. Jesus himself is the story of God. After all, John opens his gospel by saying that the "Word" of God was made flesh for us. Jesus is the complete story of God's love for us.

"To write a mighty novel you need a mighty theme!" said Herman Melville. And when you've got that mighty theme, you can't help but tell stories!

Reproach

We are objects of reproach to our neighbors, of scorn and derision to those around us.
—Psalm 79:4

Dr. James Dobson tells a story about his son when he was just a little fellow. Ryan had a knack for getting into trouble. If there was something to break, chances are he smashed it. If there was something to get into, he was like a weasel. If there was something to mess up, he was the devil's whirlwind.

After a while, the Dobsons got rather exasperated. Shirley Dobson would shake her head and say to her husband: "Somebody better do something about that boy!"

One day they were working around the house. Suddenly both had the same feeling of uneasiness. They looked around for Ryan, but they couldn't find him. Then they got scared: what had he gotten himself into now?

Somebody Better Do Something!

Finally Dr. Dobson looked out the kitchen window. There was Ryan. Somehow he'd climbed onto the back of a big truck that was parked out on the street. Before he knew it, he'd managed to get high enough to scare himself. When he tried to find his way down, his shirt got caught. He was swaying back and forth, hanging from the rear of the truck.

Dr. Dobson was in a bit of a panic. He wasn't quite sure how to help Ryan. He was afraid that if he shouted or ran up to him suddenly, the boy might be startled and fall to the pavement and hurt himself.

So, very quietly but very quickly, he sneaked up to Ryan from the side of the truck. He thought it was a little strange that Ryan wasn't crying or calling out for help. But as he got closer, he heard his son muttering very emphatically to himself: "Somebody better do something about that boy! Somebody better do something about that boy!"

If you can see that picture in your mind, then you've got a good feeling for the background behind Psalm 79. Like a boy who's been playing where he shouldn't, the nation of Israel was messing with fire. Like a person who's pushed her luck just a little too far, the Israelites were hung up on a situation they couldn't escape. And like the child in each of us, the only thing they could think about was this: "Somebody better do something!"

Beyond Prayer

Power politics was the name of the game in Israel's world. It wasn't much different from today, actually. First the Assyrians, legendary for their cruelty, swept through the ancient Near East with their armies. More recently the Babylonians conquered and ruled. Today, the territory of both kingdoms falls largely within the boundaries of Iraq.

In any case, the Israelites had made a number of stupid political alliances. Now they were paying the price: Jerusalem was destroyed, the temple was a wasted pile of rubble, and littered streets reeked with death. Survivors walked through the dust in a daze, and the captives who had been stolen away as slaves gave up hope.

If there was any prayer left, it was the kind that Ryan muttered that day: "Somebody better do something about that boy!" They certainly couldn't help themselves.

They were really beyond prayer, in a sense. They had lost their religion. For a long time now, they'd pretended that God didn't exist, that he didn't really have a place in their world. And so, when they needed him most, they couldn't find him.

Hide-and-Seek

A father came home one day and found his nine-year-old daughter crying her heart out. When he asked what was wrong, she managed to blurt out between sobs that she and her friend had been playing hide-and-seek. When it was her turn to hide, she'd hidden so well that her friend had finally given up and gone off to play another game. When she came out of her hiding place, she was all alone.

The stories in the Old Testament are a lot like that. First Israel would hide from God. Then God would hide from Israel. And somewhere along the way, they both started playing different games.

That's the tragedy of Psalm 79. That's why reproach hangs over the land. There, swinging on the hook of judgment, sways little Israel. One can almost hear the mutter: "Somebody better do something!"

But here's grace. In the end, Asaph knows God won't let them hang there forever. Even the cry "somebody better do something!" is more a testimony of hope than the anguish of despair. For one day Somebody did take Israel off the hook, even allowing himself to be caught in the process.

Restore Us

Restore us, O God; make your face shine upon us,
that we may be saved.
—*Psalm 80:3, 7, 19*

Gabriel Garcia Marquez wrote a classic novel called *One Hundred Years of Solitude*. It's the story of a village where the people had become infected with a very strange disease. From the outside everything seemed normal: they remained strong and healthy, they continued to function in the usual ways. To all appearances, there was nothing wrong with them.

Forgetting

But an invisible affliction began inside their minds. Slowly they started to lose their memory. After a while, they couldn't remember the names of simple, ordinary objects around them. Then they forgot the names of their friends. And soon they had trouble recalling the names of their husbands and their wives and their children.

At first it happened so gradually that nobody paid much attention. After a while, though, it touched everyone's lives. Their world started falling apart.

One young man saw what was happening. He knew it wouldn't be long before he lost his memory too. But in the meantime he did the only thing he could do: he acted as the memory for the whole village. He started posting little signs all over the place: "This is a table"; "This is a window"; "This is a cow—it has to be milked every morning."

On the road leading to the village he put up two large signs. The first read: "The name of our village is Macondo." And the second, "God exists."

Remembering

In some ways, the prophets and the songwriters of the Old Testament were like that young man. In a world that was stricken with the disease of forgetfulness, in a world that suffered from collective amnesia, in a world that seemed unable to function anymore because of a kind of Alzheimer's disease, the prophets and songwriters remembered names. They remembered Jacob and Joseph. They remembered Egypt and Sinai. They remembered something called "the covenant."

And on the roads where the people walked about in a daze, they posted the signs: "This way to Jerusalem"; "Don't forget the temple"; "God exists."

When Asaph penned Psalm 80, he left instructions with the director of music: "Have the choir sing this anthem to the tune of 'The Lilies of the Covenant.'" There was good reason for him to pick that tune, for Psalm 80 is a memory song, a signpost song, a picture song describing the most important scenes from Israel's history. In a few words Asaph sketches a portrait of the relationship God and Israel shared. That relationship has given identity to both of them, he says.

But now it seems like everyone is losing their memories. Does God remember Israel? Does Israel remember God? "Covenant" is the best song that Asaph could request right now.

Lost

The Desert Fathers told of a father and a son who were traveling together. They came to the edge of a forest. Some of the bushes were loaded with berries. They looked so delicious that the son asked if they could stop for a while and pick berries.

The father was anxious to be on his way, but he saw the desire in his son's eyes and agreed to stay there for a short while. The son was delighted. Together they searched the bushes for the biggest, plumpest, juiciest berries.

Then the father knew it was time to move on. He simply couldn't delay any longer. "Son," he said, "we *must* continue our journey."

But the boy begged and pleaded, till there seemed no reasoning with him. What could the father do?

He told his son, "You may stay and pick berries a while longer, but I will begin slowly to move down the road. Be sure that you are able to find me, though. While you work, call out to me, 'Father! Father!' and I will answer you. As long as you hear my voice, you will know where I am. But as soon as you can no longer hear me, know that you are lost, and run with all your strength, calling out my name."

That might be the story behind Psalm 80. And it might be the story of your life right now too. How's your memory? Are you calling out for God?

Party Time

---

*Sing for joy. . . . Begin the music. . . . Sound the ram's horn at
the New Moon, and when the moon is full,
on the day of our Feast. . . .*
—*Psalm 81:1-3*

During the Middle Ages, parts of Europe had a wonderfully unusual annual celebration called the Feast of Fools. It didn't occur, as you might expect, on April 1; most often it was celebrated at the turn of the year, the same time as our modern New Year's Eve parties.

At the Feast of Fools, everyone put on masks, sang outrageous songs, and made as much noise as possible. Society was turned upside down: those of low social position put on the clothing of rulers; they were in charge of church and state for a few brief hours. Every "normal" convention of serious life was mocked and lampooned.

Modern Need

Modern theologian Harvey Cox writes about the Feast of Fools in a book by that title, calling people in our serious world to find time to celebrate life and love and God again. The pace of our workaday world is a killer, he says. Often the only thing we know how to do is take rushed "vacations" from it all in a mad dash for rest that never comes. What we need, he claims, is a sense of fun and celebration in our lives that keeps us from taking ourselves too seriously and that reminds us on a regular basis of grace and freedom.

You only have to read Psalm 81 to know that's good theology. In fact, when God introduced himself to Israel at Mount Sinai, he not only gave them a code of behavior to shape society; he also mandated a regular routine of parties—weekly sabbaths, seasonal celebrations, and special events that might occur only once in a lifetime. For some, life is a burden. For others, life is putting in time. But for Israel, life was meant to be a party, a festival, a celebration of the grand things an intimate relationship with God could mean.

A Fitting Description

The idea of life as a celebration is constant throughout Scripture. Jesus often compared the kingdom of God to a banquet. He instituted a fellowship meal as the identifying feature of his community. And no picture of eternity could fully describe the visions of glory seen by John from the island of Patmos as well as that of a wedding reception. Those who know God's love and care say often, "It's party time!" in the best sense of the term.

Of course, sometimes we distort what it means to party. Trimalchio's banquet, staged for the Emperor Nero in A.D. 60, was outlandish in its overabundance of food—guests were required to regurgitate what they'd eaten in between each of the four courses in order to be able to go back to the table and gorge themselves again. In like manner, the overwhelming proportions of a feast celebrating the installation of the Archbishop of York, England, in 1470 (10 fat oxen, 6 wild bulls, 300 pigs, 300 hogs, 3,000 calves, plus approximately 25,000 deer, birds, and rabbits, just to mention the meat dishes) led to a later prohibition guarding against clerical excess at the table. Obviously food isn't the primary focus of the party Asaph describes in Psalm 81.

Nor does that party focus on one's own accomplishments. When the hostess noticed George Bernard Shaw standing alone in a corner at her celebration, she worriedly asked him if he was enjoying himself. "Certainly," he replied. "There's nothing else here to enjoy!"

Framework Around the Routine

The Bible's idea of a party involves keeping our eyes on life as God's gift and love as God's treat. It doesn't take away all the inconveniences and hurts we experience from day to day. Nor does it keep us from being drained, at times, by the dullness of some of our routines. It does put a framework around life that calls for joy in living, hope in expectation, and delight in salvation.

And that may be the best reason of all to go to church next Sunday morning.

Here Comes the Judge

How long will you defend the unjust and
show partiality to the wicked?
—*Psalm 82:2*

Years ago, a third-rate Shakespeare repertory company in Denver, Colorado, gave one of the most abysmal performances of *Hamlet* ever seen. The critic of the *Denver Post* wrote a biting review: "There has always been an argument whether Shakespeare wrote all the plays with which he is credited, or whether the real author was the English philosopher Francis Bacon. After this evening's performance, the way to discover the truth about the so-called Baconian theory is to dig up the graves of both Shakespeare and Bacon; the one who turned over in the night is the real author."

I'm sure that theater troupe wished they were out of town before that review hit the streets. We don't relish the idea of critics judging our actions or words negatively, even if they might be right. In her book *Female Friends*, Fay Weldon tells of a daughter expressing relief at her mother's death. "Now," she says, "there's one less pair of eyes to judge me." Over the years, I've known that woman behind a hundred faces in the tortured souls that have crossed the threshold of my study.

Justice

Even when justice is on our side, we tend to quail at its power. A man once waited at a distance from the scene of a trial while the jury deliberated the evidence. Finally the verdict came in: not guilty. The lawyer relayed the news to his client by way of a two-word telegram: "Justice prevails." Immediately the man wired back: "Appeal at once!"

Perhaps the idea of justice threatens us, especially when we think about God. "How can God be loving, if you talk about his terrifying justice?" we ask. We prefer the attitude of Henry Ford, who wrote in his personal diary one day: "Don't find fault; find a remedy."

A Remedy

Why can't God be more like Henry Ford? Well, he is, in a way. Or perhaps we should say that, at his best, Henry Ford was something like God.

For in the grand sweep of things, God chose to find a remedy that was stronger than any fault troubling the universe.

But does that wipe out justice? Does that take the gavel out of God's hand and throw his law book out the window?

Asaph doesn't think so. God doesn't delight in the judgment that might fall on those who tremble at heaven's fury. In fact, as we well know from the pages of the New Testament, God delays judgment as much as possible, encouraging people and nations to find his remedy (2 Peter 3). Yet, at the same time, Asaph rejoices in the justice of God, which sometimes brings judgment. For where would "the weak and fatherless . . . the poor and oppressed . . . the weak and needy" (vv. 3-4) go to find help if there were no courts of justice in the universe to hear their pleas?

C. S. Lewis once said that he didn't become a Christian until he thought about the judgment a doctor has to make between cancerous and noncancerous tissues as he wields his scalpel. Both tissues are living. Both demand food and water. Both form part of the body mass. But, said Lewis, even from our limited vantage point, we praise the doctor for dealing with the cancerous tissues in a destructive way so that the other tissues might find life and strength.

So too in the universe. Strangely enough, no matter how evil we are, a secret knowledge within us delights in the judgment of God. Short-story writer O. Henry illustrates that pointedly in one of his tales. A ruthless thief sits in a city park, smoking a large cigar. That morning he had swindled a child out of a dollar for his breakfast. Later he tricked a simple-hearted old man out of his savings for the fun of it. He sits there, eyes sparkling in mischievous delight, until a young woman hurries by.

The thief recognizes this woman in her simple white dress. Years ago she was his friend at school; they'd even sat together on this very bench as young lovers. But her virtues and his vices had quickly parted their paths. And now, in the evening glow, the full judgment of his filthy life collapses in on him. He jumps to his feet, rushes down a dark alley, pounds his burning face against the cool iron of a lamppost, and dully declares: "God, I wish I could die!"

Someday, says Asaph, that will be the one prayer escaping from the lips of those who flaunt justice now. For the grace of redemption experienced by the poor and oppressed arrives on the day when all the world's newspapers carry the same bold headline: HERE COMES THE JUDGE!

Out of the Lunatic Asylum

With one mind they plot together;
they form an alliance against you.
—Psalm 83:5

Henrik Ibsen's drama *Peer Gynt*, a tale of Norse folklore, is a fascinating look at the pride and vanity and self-centeredness in every human heart. Peer spends his life in a variety of amazing adventures, always living up to his creed that he will be himself.

Emperor in the Kingdom of Self

Once he visits a "lunatic asylum" where, he assumes, people are much different than he. After all, with their fears and paranoia, these people obviously live "outside themselves," as he puts it.

Begriffenfeldt, the director of the institution, corrects him:

> Outside themselves? Oh no, you're wrong.
> It's here that men are most themselves—
> Themselves and nothing but themselves—
> Sailing with outspread sails of self.
> Each shuts himself in a cask of self,
> The cask stopped with a bung of self
> And seasoned in a well of self.
> None has a tear for others' woes
> Or cares what any other thinks.
> We are ourselves in thought and voice—
> Ourselves up to the very limit. . . .

In fact, Begriffenfeldt tells Peer Gynt, he's not so different from the residents of the asylum as he might think. For in his reckless pursuit of self, Peer has become much more a lunatic than they. Says Begriffenfeldt:

> And consequently, if we want
> An Emperor, it's very clear
> That *you're* the man!

Plot and Counterplot

Peer's life of shameless self-seeking might be summarized from a global perspective in Psalm 83. Asaph documents the cunning plots and counterplots of the nations, now forming this political alliance, now buying that international influence, all in a mad dash at the loot of the world.

Obviously Asaph has a legitimate complaint against the egotistical values and cruel imperialism of the nations around him. Who in his right mind would praise Hitler for his land grabs prior to World War II? Who condones the United States' eighteenth- and nineteenth-century vision of "Manifest Destiny" as a reason to wrench land and livelihood and even life itself from North American native peoples? Who can appreciate the vicious expansionism of Hirohito's Japan or Stalin's Soviet Union?

That's an easy question to ask. But the truth of the matter is this—citizens of each of those countries praised the events of their times. The boy who brags to his friend, "My dog is bigger than your dog!" grows into a man who shouts redneck slogans or marches under the glorious shadow of a world leader's rhetoric.

Beyond Redneck Rhetoric

Asaph's prayers to God in this psalm might seem to be more of the same. Listen to his desire for divine action against Israel's enemies: "Make them like tumbleweed, O my God, like chaff before the wind. As fire consumes the forest or a flame sets the mountains ablaze, so pursue them with your tempest and terrify them with your storm. Cover their faces with shame" (vv. 13-16). Those words sound a lot like the propaganda surrounding modern conflicts.

Except for one thing. Hear Asaph's closing prayer. Do this all, he says "so that men will see your name, O LORD" (v. 16). Act on our behalf, he pleads, so that all in this world will know "that you alone are the Most High over all the earth" (v. 18).

That's the only exit from the lunatic asylum of international politics. And those words are the key to unlocking us from the prisons of self-centered propaganda.

Worship: Focus Restored

Blessed are those whose strength is in you, who have set their
hearts on pilgrimage. . . . They go from strength to strength,
till each appears before God in Zion.
—*Psalm 84:5, 7*

English author Osbert Sitwell once wrote a novel about a private detective on the trail of a man in Paris. The detective began to think that his subject might be staying at a particular hotel. But how could he find out for sure without arousing unnecessary suspicion?

He hit upon this plan: he would go up to the front desk and ask the clerk if a man by the name of—here he would give his own name—was staying at that hotel. While the clerk looked through the guest register, he would be able to see if the name of his quarry was listed there.

A Startling Encounter

The plan was brilliant. Except for one thing. When he asked the clerk if a man by his own name was staying at the hotel, the clerk immediately replied, "Yes, sir! And he has been waiting for you. He's in Room 40. I'll have you shown right up."

Imagine his shock at finding that someone else with his own name was staying at that hotel! And because the clerk had already called for another staff member to show him to Room 40, all he could do was follow on where he was led.

So he came to Room 40. There, to his surprise, was a man who looked exactly like himself, only twenty years older.

What would you do if one day you ran into yourself as you will be twenty years from now? What would you ask yourself? What would you most like to know?

Lost in the Woods

So often we wander around as if we were in a forest. We go as we're pushed or drag along as we're pulled. There's a story about a Lock in one of Lewis Caroll's children's tales. It's a big padlock, just like the one you might use to lock your bike or the door on your garden shed. Only this Lock is alive. It has legs and arm and a face on its side. And it's always running around in a hurry.

"What's the matter?" someone shouts, as the Lock runs by.

The Lock replies: "I'm seeking something to unlock me!"

Is that you? Is that a picture of your mad scramble from day to day, caught up in the moment, blinded by the pressures, trapped by circumstances?

Wouldn't it be nice to stop for a while and climb a tree that gets you above the forest? Wouldn't it be nice to have a kind of radar that would pierce the fog of the future?

Another Source of Direction

It would be wonderful, sometimes, to be able to see ourselves twenty years from now. In a sense it would lift us above the dense undergrowth of our daily meandering and point us in a direction that we can and will walk with confidence.

Unless we become characters in one of Osbert Sitwell's novels, that privilege will escape us. But the worship of God can do something like that for us and do it even better.

The pilgrimage of Psalm 84 is a description of lives with purpose. Those "who have set their hearts on pilgrimage" may not be able to see themselves in the future, but they do see God. And that vision gives shape to the daily course they follow.

In the New Testament, the apostle Paul put it this way: "Set your hearts on things above, where Christ is seated at the right hand of God" (Col. 3:1).

From that vantage point the track through the forest of our lives becomes far more apparent.

Can you see yourself twenty years from now? And more important, can you see the face of God?

The Kiss of Life

Love and faithfulness meet together;
righteousness and peace kiss each other.
—Psalm 85:10

One of the few true "winners" in the Persian Gulf War was CNN. Maybe you didn't know what CNN stands for before then, but it would be hard to find anyone today who doesn't know what Cable News Network is all about. When all eyes turned toward Iraq at the start of the conflict, there was CNN broadcasting live from Baghdad. It was a case of the little guy on the street teaching the old boys of broadcasting a thing or two.

News King
Cable News Network is the brainchild of Ted Turner. Speaking at the National Newspaper Association Convention some years ago, Turner described himself rather immodestly as the "News King." The title probably fits.

But what really got the crowds going as Mr. Turner spoke was when he said that the Ten Commandments are obsolete. He said that they didn't relate any more to the global problems of our world. "I bet nobody here even pays much attention to them," he said. He speculated that if Moses were to come down from the mountain today with a copy of the Ten Commandments in his hand "they wouldn't go over" at all. "Nobody likes to be commanded! Commandments are out!"

What do you think? Is Mr. Turner right? How would you answer him?

God Is Out
Before you get too far with that, let me tell you one more thing about Ted Turner. Some time ago he was the guest of honor at an awards banquet in Orlando, Florida. He received a prize that proclaimed him "Humanist of the Year."

After he took the trophy into his hands, he gave a little speech. He told the people there how he had become a self-made man. He said that he was raised in a very "religious" home. His family attended worship each Sunday and prayed at the meal table. He'd even said prayers each night at his bedside. He'd always assumed there was a God. And he always believed that God heard and answered his prayers. Until one day.

Ted's sister got sick. The disease lingered on in her body. The doctors couldn't seem to do anything about it. So Ted said he decided to do something about it: he prayed for his sister. He begged God in heaven to make her better. He pleaded with God to spare her life and give her health again.

But it didn't happen. His sister got worse and worse, and finally she died. That was the day, Ted Turner told his audience, that he knew there's no God up there! What kind of God would have allowed his sister to suffer like that and then to die? It didn't make sense to him. He couldn't understand it. And right then, he said, he decided that he would have to live the rest of his life depending only on himself. He was done with this God of the church, this God of the Bible, this unfeeling phantom.

At that moment, Ted Turner, the great "News King," broke down. He couldn't go on. With tears in his eyes, he backed away from the podium.

Can you guess what happened next? After a moment of deathly silence, the crowd jumped to its feet and erupted in wild applause. "Right on! At last somebody had the guts to say it. There's no God! And even if there is, we don't need him anymore."

This is the great problem of faith, isn't it? None of us deserves good fortune, at least not from the perspective of cosmic evil. Still, if there is a kind and loving God, why are we so often tossed to the whims of the seemingly random and chaotic clutches of blessing or disaster? Why not feel the fires of hell we truly merit, or otherwise experience some benefits from our fairly decent existences? Why must pain and pleasure run such an odd three-legged race through our lives?

The sons of Korah ask that question too in Psalm 85. And they know there are no real answers for them, at least none that will take away the hurt of the suffering heart or the agony of their struggling kinfolk.

Their only hope is a kiss. A kiss in which "righteousness and peace" meet and embrace. A kiss in which suffering is not removed by surgery but healed with love. A kiss in which the drama of heaven and hell is played out to its final conclusion.

Theology isn't enough to explain what they're looking for. Neither is philosophy. That's probably why God didn't drop a textbook of psychological explanations from heaven in answer to their questions. He dropped himself instead.

Ted Turner still hurts. So did the sons of Korah. But sometimes we need a kiss more than an answer.

Back to School

Teach me your way, O LORD, and I will walk in your truth;
give me an undivided heart, that I may fear your name.
—*Psalm 86:11*

Children's menus are sometimes the most interesting thing about a restaurant. Here's a riddle I found on one: Why did the teacher wear dark glasses?

The answer: Because her class was so bright. Of course!

Probably more teachers wish they had her problem. Take, for instance, Charles Eliot. He was president of Harvard University at the turn of the century. After he had devoted forty years to his position, a group of Harvard professors gave a dinner in his honor. Each outdid the last in toasting his accomplishments and praising his virtues. One fellow even said, "Since you became president, Harvard has become a storehouse of knowledge."

"What you say is true," replied Eliot, "but I can claim little credit for it. It is simply that the first-year students bring so much, and the graduates take so little away."

"Let Me Out!"

I imagine there are others who think that way as well. Former Amherst College president George Harris greeted the new arrivals one term with his usual speech about the challenges ahead. But after only a few lines he stopped. "Ah," he sighed, "I intended to give you some advice, but now I remember how much is left over from last year unused."

Most of us can't wait to get out of school. Maybe it's the springtime weather. Maybe it's our feelings of self-importance or our frustration with plodding along together when we want to run free by ourselves. In any case, we often leave our formal education behind with much that still could be learned. We'll pick things up along the way, we say. We'll get the rest of our education from the streets, or in the College of Hard Knocks.

The Toughest Lesson

Maybe so. But life isn't always a very kind teacher. Helen Steiner found that out. She was raised in Ohio, along the shores of Lake Erie. She planned to attend Ohio Wesleyan College and get a degree in law. But the flu epidemic of 1918 killed her father, and she was forced to support the family financially. For a decade she worked at an electrical utility company, hoping, dreaming, wondering about the future.

Then, suddenly, the future walked her way. She met and fell in love with Franklin Rice, a dashing young banker. They were married in 1928, full of anticipation and excitement. Who could have known that the stock market would crash the next year and dissolve young Franklin's career in an instant? He couldn't stand the torment, and he committed suicide.

A deceased father, a lost career, a vanished fortune, and a dead husband. What should a young widow learn from all of this?

There was no time for learning, at least not then. Helen had to eke out a living. The only job she could find was a poor-paying contract for editing greeting cards. She wrote a few verses like the ones in the cards. A couple were published by the Gibson Card Company, but not enough to make her either rich or famous.

The Beginning of Wisdom

But then someone read one of Helen's poems on the Lawrence Welk Show one evening. And within a few years, Helen Steiner Rice became one of North America's best known "folk poets."

It was then that she shared with others the one poem that expressed her greatest lesson from life. It seems to parallel David's prayer in Psalm 86, perhaps because it speaks about the one thing we all need to learn, regardless of which school we attend:

> So together we stand at life's crossroads
> And view what we think is the end.
> But God has a much bigger vision
> And he tells us it's only a bend.
> For the road goes on and is smoother,
> And the pause in the song is a rest.
> And the part that's unsung and unfinished
> Is the sweetest and richest and best.
> So rest and relax and grow stronger.
> Let go and let God share your load,
> Your work is not finished or ended;
> You've just come to a bend in the road.

A New Humanity

*The LORD will write in the register of the peoples: "This one
was born in Zion."*
—*Psalm 87:6*

Here's a parable: a man is convicted of a criminal act. But before he is
sentenced to life in prison, the governing authorities issue a pardon. This
convicted criminal is permitted to live in society like a law-abiding citizen. How do you think he'll be treated? Probably few people will accept
him—children will be told to stay away from him; employers won't hire
him; banks won't give him a loan; landlords will refuse him as a tenant.
He'll most likely be the butt of jokes, jokes that cut him down as inferior,
jokes that ring with self-righteous pride.

Finally, in desperation, the man finds a home among a small community of women, men, and children who take him in because they, like him,
are convicted criminals. They, like him, have received the pardon of grace.
It's the present pardon that gives them unity, not the sin of the past. It's
the grace of forgiveness that makes them one, not the successes or failures
of other times.

Society of the Forgiven
In a sense, that's a picture of the church of Jesus Christ. Each person has
been convicted of sin, yet each lives in the grace of God's pardoning love.
What good would a pardon be if each of us were forced to live in isolation
at the edges of communities that rejected us, joked about us, and refused
to let us in?

To be pardoned and yet to be alone would be the worst of all punishments God could inflict on us. Instead God has created a new humanity,
a society of the forgiven who no longer see each other with the scarlet letter of adultery, or the neon sign of pride, or the sticky fingers of materialism, or the bloody hands of murder. Each person is welcome, not because
he or she is a sinner in a club of rogues, but because each has received the
kiss of forgiveness from the great Governor of the Universe.

Psalm 87 anticipates that society. Can you imagine God bringing people from each of the great pagan and often beastly civilization of ancient

Israel's world together in a family he calls his own, a society in which he writes each name with love in the register? That's the theme of this song.

An Amazing Song

It's an amazing theme to sing. Our participation in the present humanity of this world drives us often toward distinctions, separations, bigotry, and racism—even in the church. That was powerfully brought home to me during our time as missionaries in Nigeria. We were received with openness and love by our friends in the Church of Christ in the Sudan among the Tiv.

But one of their practices really bothered us: on Communion Sunday, everyone was expected to wear white. Now, in itself, wearing white to symbolize purity before God isn't a bad idea.

But if a person didn't wear white, regardless of her spiritual condition, she was physically directed to the back of the church building. And when the elements of communion were passed, those whose shirts were yellow, or whose skirts had pink designs on otherwise white backgrounds, or who were too poor to buy a white blouse—these were served the bread and wine last, as if they were second-class citizens in the kingdom or inferior members of the church.

As a bit of a protest, we never wore white on Communion Sunday, and we always sat at the back and received communion last. Even though we were treated nicely enough, we felt the pressures of racism and the horrors of pride and judgment.

"I Got Shoes"

That experience taught me the meaning of that old spiritual, "I Got Shoes." While the richly dressed white folks in the old South of the United States marched off to their churches wearing their polished Sunday shoes, the black slaves, with their bare feet, were left to gather for worship as they could. And while white folks were singing about the worldwide church of Christ, black folks were singing:

> I got shoes! You got shoes! All God's chillun got shoes!
> And when de angel Gabriel calls us home, Gonna walk all over God's heaven!

For they knew that God takes care of his children, and when he brought them finally to glory, he wouldn't check to see the color of their skin, or the whiteness of their clothes, or even the place where they were born. Instead, he'd simply ask them if Jesus was their brother. And then, like the only begotten Son, they too would receive a pair of shoes, the sign of people who were no longer barefoot slaves of others but cared-for children of God.

When God Lets Us Down

Why, O LORD, do you reject me and hide your face from me?
. . . The darkness is my closest friend.
—Psalm 88:14, 18

Pain and suffering are a way of life for us. One Spanish philosopher asked the question, "What is this life that begins amidst the cries of the infant and the screams of the mother?" We come into this world with wails and tears, and that's often how we leave it too. Tears are at least one kind of universal language.

Battered by Betrayal
There are different levels of pain, of course—a cut or bruise annoys us; emotional abuse batters us; major surgery frightens us; the death of a family member can double us over in anguish. But one kind of pain seems worse than the rest, and that is the pain of betrayal. A friend turns her back on me. A spouse walks out on me. A community disowns me. Caesar turns around in the threatening crowd and loses his will to fight when he meets the eye of Brutus: *Et tu, Brute?* Judas meets his friend Jesus with a kiss that means both love and death. Stalin rides to power on the blood of his countrymen. Nothing hurts us more than to be betrayed by the one we counted on, the one we cared for, the one we loved as dearly as ourselves.

Of course, usually we can count on God just then. When all else fails, we can always turn to religion, right? But listen to the cry of Psalm 88: *You* have put me in the lowest pit. . . . *You* have overwhelmed me with all your waves. . . . *You* have taken from me my closest friends and have made me repulsive to them.

Those are words of betrayal, and they're spoken to God. I cry to you for help . . . and you reject me. What do we do with that?

The Divine Enemy
Novelist Peter DeVries grew up in a Christian home in Chicago. He spent his life trying to figure out where God was when he needed him most. His most powerful novel, *The Blood of the Lamb,* is also his most tragic. It's the story of Don Wanderhope (notice the name), born into a family that believes God will always be there for them.

But one tragedy follows another, till Don wishes God wouldn't pay so much attention to him. Don's wife bears a daughter before she herself commits suicide. Little Carol is the one spot of grace in her father's life. Don has struggled with his faith through the years. And when Carol gets sick and is diagnosed with leukemia, he goes back to church. He prays for Carol. He begs God to heal her. He pleads with Jesus to touch her life.

But she dies anyway. Don leaves the hospital, carrying the birthday cake they were going to share. He walks past the church of St. Catharine. Hanging over the door is a life-size statue of Christ on the cross. In his anger, he takes the cake in his hand and throws it at Jesus. Icing drips from the face like blood.

That's the final prayer of Don Wanderhope. That's what he thinks of the God who betrayed him. He's not alone. I hear the refrain over and over again: Why did God let this happen? How could God do this to us? Why doesn't God listen to my prayers?

The Twist of Faith

Where do we turn when God betrays us? That's the question we ask in the nightmares of our tragedies and loneliness. Anyone who tries to answer ought to tread carefully.

A haunting scene comes into focus here, one which Heman, the author of Psalm 88, never would have imagined in his Old Testament world. It's a dark night in Jerusalem. The streets are silent, the marketplace crowds dispersed. A hushed breeze plays with scents of cooking and animals. Through the shadows of an olive grove a small group of men meanders. They stop and settle to sit or sleep, while four figures step further. Then three halt and one moves on alone. In personal agony he wrestles aloud with God, weeping and praying not once, but three times: "Father, take this bitter cup from me!"

From heaven comes only a silent denial. When morning light breaks, this figure will be taunted and tormented, and finally hung on a cross of death. The darkening skies will split with his cry: "My God, my God! Why have you forsaken me?"

This picture of divine betrayal is, in fact, the one sure testimony that for every other child of God, no matter how dark the night, the Father's ears are never deaf; his eyes are never blind; his hands will never lose their grip.

Feelings of betrayal remain. Doubts linger. But the testimony of Scripture reaches beyond Psalm 88 to Romans 8: Nothing will be able to separate us from the love of God in Christ Jesus our Lord.

An Untimely Death

---

*You have cut short the days of his youth; you have covered
him with a mantle of shame.*
—Psalm 89:45

As Moses speaks for the last time to the Israelites, he says a ponderously good word: "The secret things belong to the LORD our God, but the things revealed belong to us and to our children forever, that we may follow all the words of this law" (Deut. 29:29).

That word of advice comes back to me every time I read Psalm 89. It has to do, I suppose, with the circumstances under which I first read these lines with some depth of appreciation.

The Death of a Child
I was a young pastor in my first congregation, and a tiny child, born with his twin brother prematurely, struggled for months before dying. The parents decided to have a funeral. After all, we as a congregation had joined them for most of a year in their uncertain watch over little Bert. Though their parental pain would always be more intense than our shared concern, the loss of this little life was the loss of the community. Only through a public funeral could we acknowledge that together.

"This is the verse we want you to use in your message," they told me. And I read Psalm 89:45. It made sense, of course. It was, indeed, the thought in all our minds.

An Ancient Catastrophe
But how did this message first come to be written in Scripture? There's an ancient painting at Karnak, in upper Egypt, that shows a man of royal bearing, prematurely aged, being led by Pharaoh Sheshonk to the god Amun. The man is humiliated, beaten, conquered. And on his leading hand there is a ring bearing this title: "King of Judah."

The man is Rehoboam, young son of the great King Solomon. His father was the ruler who extended the territories of Israel to their greatest boundaries, the emperor who made gold and silver as abundant in those prosperous times as the stones that paved Jerusalem's streets.

But now, in a short span of time, the walls of Jerusalem have been breached; the gold has been removed from the temple; the boundaries of the land have collapsed; and the young king of Judah is led like a whimpering child to be mocked in front of the austere idols of Egypt.

Where is the sense in all of this? Where is the justice? And where is God?

Ethan is an old man who's lived through a great time in Israel's history. He sits in the choir chambers of the desecrated temple and sings a mournful dirge—Psalm 89. David, the man of God, appointed him choir director many years ago. Solomon kept him there as one of the chief musicians of the holy courts. And during those years he wrote hundreds of paeans of praise, declaring the wonderful things God was doing in the world. But how does this latest turn of events fit in? "You have cut short the days of his youth," says Ethan, "you have covered him with a mantle of shame."

Holy Discontent

Here's the holy discontent of the child of God. Confident, on the one hand, that God is powerful enough to change the course of human history, strong enough to make things right, bold enough, even, to tie Death in knots and send him packing. But disquieted as well by the seemingly senseless whims of fate, the horrifying taunts of misery, the strangely demonic triumph of evil over good.

"How long, O LORD?" (v. 46). Ethan asks the question for himself. He asks the question for the parents of little Bert. And he asks the question for each of our hearts.

Psalm 89 begs us to look again at the dying words of Moses. Indeed, says Moses, there are secret things that will ever trouble us, ever stymie us, ever throw us around in fits of consternation. But, says Moses again, there is enough revealed by our God to give us the will to carry on in faith and hope and life. "The secret things belong to the Lord our God, but the things revealed belong to us and to our children forever, that we may follow all the words of this law."

That's a paraphrase of the whole of Ethan's psalm. And at the death of an infant child, it's probably the most honest reflection we can make. Rev. J. Allan Shantz, one-time pastor in Kitchener, Ontario, had the dubious honor of speaking at the funeral of his eighteen-year-old son. "It is not that God speaks to us in our pain and loss," he said, "but that he confirms his truth to our hearts *in spite of* our pain and suffering."

"I do not understand what God is about," Pastor Shantz went on. "But whatever God is doing with us as a family, and as a church (for it has affected us all), let us remember that God never stands aloof. Through his Son, God participated in this life. Christ himself is going through everything that you and I will have to face as we travel to the city of our God." Do you believe that?

A Portrait of Ourselves

Establish the work of our hands.
—Psalm 90:17

When Ralph Waldo Emerson was just a young child, he spent an afternoon watching a man sawing wood. It was a hot day, and the man was sweating and grunting and groaning. Little Ralph's heart ached for the man, so hard at work. But he didn't know what he could do to help. Finally it dawned on him. "Sir," he said, "may I do the grunting for you?"

Life and Labor

Work is a big part of our lives from our earliest years. One writer put it this way: "Most footprints on the sands of time were left by work shoes." So it's fitting that Moses prays, in Psalm 90, that God allow our work to have some meaning bigger than a forty-hour week, larger than the series of jobs we perform.

Earlier in the psalm, Moses prays that God will take note of our brief lives, bending the values of the universe in our favor. Then he asks for wisdom to choose our work well. But he has one more request. In essence Moses asks God to make us partners with him in the grand creative work he is still accomplishing. "An unfulfilled vocation," says French novelist Balzac, "drains the color from a man's entire existence." Moses' prayer desires a life painted with divine colors, sharing in the energy still radiating from heaven's throne.

Work That Lasts

"To work at the things you love, or for those you love, is to turn work into play and duty into privilege." In Psalm 90, Moses is saying: "We love you, Lord. Let us share in your creative work. Allow the things we do each day to be a small part of your plans for eternity."

Writing to the church at Corinth, the apostle Paul says that some of the things we do from day to day are like wood and stubble and straw and won't withstand the fires of judgment day. But other things we do, he says, are like gold and silver and precious jewels. They will not only survive judgment day but will be a part of the glories of heaven and earth for all the ages to come.

The beautiful thing is this: God allows us to work alongside of him. God make our efforts his effort; he makes our creations a part of the world he is sculpting. Angela Morgan puts it this way:

Work!
Thank God for the swing of it,
For the clamoring hammering ring of it. . . .
Oh, what is so fierce as the flame of it?
And what is so huge as the aim of it?
Thundering on through dearth and doubt
Calling the plan of the Master out.

Something in what we do, says Moses, in what we say, in the relationships we establish, in the children we bear and raise, in the studies we pursue, in the buildings we build, in the pain we ease, in the service we render . . . in all of these is the touch of God in our world, the extension of his mercy into his creation.

May the favor of the Lord our God rest upon us;
establish the work of our hands for us—
yes, establish the work of our hands.

Earth's First and Last Song

When God rested on the seventh day of creation, he handed his toolbox over to Adam and Eve and their descendants, and he said, "Now it's your turn. Be fruitful and multiply. Take care of the world I put you in. Subdue the earth and continue to shape it in the way I've begun."

And all the sons and daughters of Adam and Eve shiver with delight to know that our fingers are God's fingers, our hands are God's hands. When we pray Moses' prayer of Psalm 90, we're reminded that in some mysterious way, God chooses to carry out much of his providential grace through our lives and our work.

If God Is for Us

You will not fear the terror of night. . . .
—Psalm 91:5

License plates in the state of Illinois proudly declare that it is the "Land of Lincoln." It seems that everybody wants to be connected with a famous person if they can. One Illinois teacher in Bloomington informed her students about the great man who once lived in their state. Then she asked, "If you could go back in time and talk with President Lincoln, what important question would you ask him?"

The answers spanned the spectrum of young minds and their creative imaginations. But the one she talked about with a smile for a long time afterward was this: "Mr. Lincoln, were you afraid when you started first grade?"

Butterflies in the Stomach

Probably he was afraid. If not then, at any number of stressful experiences along the eventful course of his life. We know that, because we know he was human. A couple weeks ago our daughters started school again. The day before starting first grade, our youngest flew around the house in a frenzy of nervous activity and then yelled down from her bedroom, "I'm so afraid about tomorrow that I can't sleep!"

She's not the only one. A couple of days before that, I'd officiated at the marriage of my "little" brother. For the two days of the rehearsal and the wedding, I was shaking with anxiety. The bride and groom, on the other hand, were the picture of calm.

Paralyzed

Fear can paralyze. Said Viktor Frankl: "Fear makes come true that which one is afraid of." So often in our experience that happens, doesn't it? Martin Seligman, of the University of California, did a study that showed similar results in test groups of students and insurance salesmen. A student who feared failure generally failed in some big test, and then went on failing till she left school or changed her major. A salesman who didn't sell a policy for a week began to suspect that he was a failure and then rarely sold a policy again. Those who fear, said Seligman, leap from paralysis to incapacity to failure.

Sometimes even to death, we might add. Government records show only six deaths, none by suicide, when the city of London, England, was totally destroyed by fire in 1666. The needs of others and the task of re-building kept people alive. Now jump ahead to 1944. German bombers darken the skies day after day. The explosion of their deadly cargo blows fear into every heart. Records show that some weeks the greatest numbers of deaths were caused not by shrapnel injuries or disease, but by suicide.

Jump ahead again. London, two decades ago. A fog rolls in and lingers for awhile—the kind you can feel, the kind that creeps in and sticks. After one day, the number of suicides in the city goes up slightly. After two days it quadruples. On the third day, the figure doubles again. By the end of the fourth day, there have been more suicides in London than on any day since World War II.

A Bigger Fear

Fear can kill. It must have almost killed the writer of Psalm 91. You can tell that by the way he talks. But something keeps him alive, even when it seems that his world has collapsed, that the fog of fear has rolled round him and seized his very soul.

What turns his heart around? In a sense, a greater fear. Not the fear of terror, but the awe of wonder that a power larger than the waves of spreading war stoops down and scoops up his life in a loving embrace. He hears the voice of God say: "I will rescue him; I will protect him. . . . I will be with him in trouble. . . . I will deliver him" (vv. 14-15). The psalmist knows a power that can meet and turn back any enemy.

So it is with the child of God. Fears come and go, even the "terror of night" (v. 5). But the greater awe at the refuge of the Most High drives back every threat. As the apostle Paul would write centuries later, "If God is for us, who can be against us?" (Rom. 8:31).

Fountain of Youth

[The righteous] will still bear fruit in old age,
they will stay fresh and green, proclaiming,
"The LORD is upright; he is my Rock. . . . "
—Psalm 92:14-15

Here's a parable by a cartoonist named Saxon. It's about a fellow who's just reached retirement. Now he wonders about his place in society. He begins to spend much of his weekend time walking alone in the woods. One day he finds himself on an unfamiliar path that leads him to a small pond. As he stands beside the pond, the water begins to stir and bubble until there is a lovely little fountain. Astonishingly, a voice calls out to him: "Arnold Flagler! This is the Fountain of Youth!"

In the next frame Arnold is hiding behind a tree, distress written all over his face. He shrinks back in fear as the fountain leaps and soars, and a sound of unbelievable music fills the air.

The voice calls to him again: "This is the Fountain of Youth, Arnold Flagler. Drink!"

Arnold isn't quite sure what to do. He peaks around the trunk of the tree and asks, "What will happen to me if I drink?"

Youth will be yours!" cries the happy voice.

Arnold kneels at the water's edge. "I mean," he says, "how does it work? How young will I be?"

The fountain swirls and sings as it dances higher and higher. "Youth will be yours!" it calls again.

But Arnold has more questions. "Will my family know me? What about my pension and the cumulative profit-sharing plan, and all that?"

Once again the reply is the same: "Youth will be yours!"

But the voice is fainter, and the fountain begins to droop and shiver.

"Listen," says Arnold in desperation, "just tell me one thing. Has anybody else ever tried this? Anybody I know?"

By now his nose nearly touches the water, spurting only a bit on the surface. In a slow moment the music fades away and the waters subside until the fountain vanishes entirely and the pond is still.

A despondent Arnold Flagler wanders slowly home, hands in his pockets. That evening, his wife asks him, "What did you do in the woods today?"

"I got lost," he says.

Lost in the Woods

That's the story of too many lives, isn't it? Listen to the psalmist's song "for the Sabbath day," as he titles Psalm 92. He talks about the "senseless man" and the "fool," the ones who seem, somewhere along the pilgrimage of life, to get lost in the woods. They run all their lives in the busyness of business, they walk through the wonders of wondering, they stride through the relatives of relationships, and then, when they get to the other side, they look back and don't have a clue where they've been going all along or where they meant to be. That's when they realize how horrible it is to get old. Neither the old nor young have a staying power for the changing years.

Staying Green

What brings excitement to the psalmist at the thought of growing old? It has to do with a Fountain of Youth he encountered one day in his wanderings through the wilderness. That Fountain was the grace of God, and once those waters refreshed his body and spirit, he could never truly age.

Last year the sharp-minded British writer Malcolm Muggeridge died at the age of eighty-seven. Several years earlier he had written his thoughts on growing old as they related to his Christian faith. He talked about lying awake at night, half here and half in the world to come, and then thinking about what it meant to have a grasp on both worlds at the same time. "What you realize," he says, "with a certainty and a sharpness that I can't convey to you is first of all, how extraordinarily beautiful the world is; how wonderful is the privilege of being allowed to live in it; how beautiful the shapes and sounds and colours of the world are; how beautiful is human love and human work. . . . "

He went on to talk about the greater wonder that dawns on him in those moments, the marvelous purposes of God. "Whatever may happen," he wrote, "whatever men may do or not do, whatever crazy projects they may have and lend themselves to, those purposes of God are loving, are creative, are universal. And in that awareness, great comfort and great joy."

There's a man who's found the true Fountain of Youth!

Foundations

The world is firmly established; it cannot be moved.
—Psalm 93:1

Aristotle has been called the "father of science." He lived in Athens nearly 2,500 years ago, and his powers of observation and his reasoning abilities were as fine as anything Sherlock Holmes displayed under the pen of Sir Arthur Conan Doyle.

Aristotle dissected over fifty animals to find out how they operated from the inside out. He described in great detail the characteristics and habits of over five hundred species living in his corner of the world. Most of the time his accuracy amazes modern scientists.

Of course, Aristotle could also be wrong at times. For instance, he thought that meat left to itself would spontaneously generate maggots. He was also certain that the function of the brain was to cool the body's blood, much like the radiator in a car. And he believed that earthquakes were caused by air trying to escape from the interior of the earth.

Shake, Rattle, and Roll

If Aristotle had been right about earthquakes, then earth would have known some major "blowouts" throughout history. The earthquake that struck Tangshan, China, in 1976, registered 8.3 on the open-ended Richter scale and killed more than 300,000 people. It generated as much energy as a 100-megaton hydrogen bomb. How much energy is that? Well, if the U.S. would have dropped 5,000 atomic bombs on Hiroshima in 1945 instead of just one, a similar amount of power would have been unleashed. Or, if you bought all the dynamite you could, and finally stockpiled 100 million tons of it, you could set off a blast that would equal just that single earthquake in China.

And that one wasn't even the worst. Twice, since recording devices have charted the inner turmoil of the earth, there have been earthquakes measuring 8.9 on the Richter scale, one in Ecuador (1906) and once in Japan (1933). That's like 15,000 Hiroshima bombs or 300,000,000 tons of TNT!

Survival

Communities in earthquake zones would love to have "no fault" insurance. But life isn't that simple. After a 1923 earthquake leveled Tokyo, city planners demanded new structures for buildings and deep foundations that could withstand earth's shudders shifting the surface. Now they're even planning new "low-rises"—huge living and working complexes to be dug into the ground like rabbit dens. Two Japanese corporations already have government financing for developing huge underground cities that would accommodate a hundred thousand people or more with a full range of living quarters, offices, theaters, libraries, sports centers, and the like. These planners are seeking safety from earthquakes by getting down to the "foundations of the earth."

Ancient peoples, of course, didn't have the technology for such a venture. They relied on prayer and superstition to protect themselves. When workers repaired Japan's famous Edo Castle following the 1923 earthquake, they found human skeletons crushed beneath the foundation stones. The Shoguns of former generations believed that buildings constructed on human flesh would never fall, either to enemy or to earthquake. So dozens of slaves knelt in prayer, were showered with gold coins, and then were pressed to death under the weight of large boulders that eventually bore the weight of the castle walls.

The Best Insurance in the World

Earth's foundations still stand, in spite of every shaking and quaking. The psalmist celebrates that fact in Psalm 93. He knows the God who created earth, the God who shelters earth, the God who holds the seas in their places and restrains the winds of the storms.

In the end, says the psalmist, you can be sure that the earth will never shake apart. After all, the One who made the earth is the same One who made a covenant of trust with his people on earth (v. 5). That covenant was confirmed in the death of one who became a servant and slave (Phil. 2:5-11), and was crushed beneath the foundations on which we now rest secure (1 Peter 2:4-8).

The God Who Avenges

O LORD, the God who avenges,
O God who avenges, shine forth.
—Psalm 94:1

The Chinese have a proverb: The fire you kindle for your enemy often burns yourself more than him. It's true, isn't it? In Mary Shelley's classic novel *Frankenstein*, the monster created by the young doctor eventually destroys himself in horrible ways when the evil power of vengeance is unleashed.

One-Liners
On stage, the quick-witted sparring of vengeful actors can bring down the house with laughter. Many television sitcoms depend on sarcastic one-liners for ratings. "The best revenge," says one actor to another in one of those fist-clenching situations, "is to live long enough to be a problem to your children." And the audience roars.

Politicians play the game too. Cheap shots land in every newspaper across the country and become seven-second clips on the evening news. Lady Astor of Britain, earlier this century, carried on a running battle of mind and tongue with Winston Churchill. Once, at a party, she said to him, "If you were my husband, I would poison your tea!" Sir Winston quipped back, "And if I were your husband, I'd drink it!"

No Laughing Matter
Commentator Paul Harvey always includes a light story or two in his broadcasts. One such story is about the Methodists and the Baptists in a small town. It seems that both had church buildings on the same block. Since the Methodist worship services started a half-hour earlier than those in the Baptist church, the Methodists grabbed all the parking spaces and sometimes overflowed into the Baptist parking lot.

Not to be taken on their own territory, the Baptists planned a quiet revenge: they put bumper stickers on the offending Methodist cars that read: I'M PROUD TO BE A BAPTIST.

Religious battlegrounds aren't always so peaceful, though. History is littered with "crusades" and "inquisitions" and "holy wars." Sometimes, in the name of God, communities become tragic wastelands of righteous indignation turned mean and cynical. Arthur Miller's play *The Crucible* shows how the witch-hunts in Salem, Massachusetts, quickly evolved into spiteful orgies of pagan revenge. All done, of course, with the "holiest" of motives, invoking God's name in support and blessing.

An editorial in *Christianity Today* laments the trend in Christian literature that seems bent on turning Christianity into fear and creating sales based on power and vengeance. Denominational squabbles often appear to do the same thing, creating opposing "camps" spitting invectives and building schemes of power-brokering.

Pertinent Prayer

With that in mind, Psalm 94 might be read as adding fuel to unholy fires, deepening the resonance of vengeful tones. God is named as one "who avenges" (v. 1), who "pay[s] back" enemies (v. 2), who "destroy[s]" enemies (v. 23). The prayer carries a sense of revenge, of religious warfare, of reformation by revolution.

To our ears it seems to either play our fickle games or hurt our pious consciences. Can we sing this song in church today? Maybe.

Only if we keep three things in mind, three things that are essential to the psalmist's cry. First, vengeance is left to the Lord; there is no mention of vindicating human terrorist tactics in some kind of "holy war." Second, the instances of evil mentioned are specific and dramatic, making it possible to identify demonic intent (see vv. 4-6). Third, the one who prays acknowledges his or her own imperfections (v. 12).

Prayers like this one are extremely dangerous. In the mouth of a vengeful person looking for a bigger piece of the pie, Psalm 94 can be the worst kind of religious slander. But from the heart of the destitute, the pained and lonely and bruised child of God, this song is a pertinent prayer, unexcelled in its sense of divine dependence.

And when it's prayed in that context, astounding things happen.

Kneeling

Come, let us bow down in worship, let us kneel
before the LORD our maker.
—Psalm 95:6

The Dutch have a term for the pulpit in a church which roughly translates as "wooden pants" in English. More weak knees than one might suppose have been hidden behind such stout trousers!

Knees have an interesting history in the Bible. "Weak knees" are an early indication of fear (Job 4:4; Isa. 35:3; Ezek. 7:17, 21:7; Dan. 5:6; Nahum 2:10; Heb. 12:12). Sometimes they cave in because a devout person has fasted too long (Ps. 109:24). Then again, the joints of the legs might be struck by some kind of illness as a divine warning (Deut. 28:35).

Knees are private, of course. Some of the tenderest language of the Scriptures reflects intimate relations involving knees. Samson came to trust Delilah as his closest friend, finally telling her the secret of his strength as she stroked his head lying on her knees (Judg. 16:19). Of course, he soon fell to his knees in service to her masters.

In the final scene of Isaiah's prophecy, God speaks words of intimate love to his people Israel. He says that some day Jerusalem's fortunes will be reversed: her walls will be rebuilt, her temple resurrected. In that day, Jerusalem will be like a wet nurse to God's people—they will be carried at her breast and "dandled" on her knees (Isa. 66:12). That's quite a picture!

Of course, the idea of children on the knees of grownups has always represented love and commitment (Job 3:12). When Rachel couldn't have children early in her marriage to Jacob, she told him to have intercourse with her maid Bilhah. The child Bilhah bore was placed immediately on Rachel's knees as a sign of adoption and belonging (Gen. 30:3; most modern English translations cover up the exact action mentioned in the Hebrew text). The same sort of thing happened when Jacob received Joseph's sons in an intimate moment (Gen. 48:8-12), and again when Joseph adopted his great-grandchildren as his own flesh and blood by placing them on his knees (Gen. 50:23).

Kneeling is also known in the Bible as a proper posture for prayer and worship. All the earth will worship God on its knees (Isa. 45:23); all creation will one day kneel before the ascended Christ (Phil. 2:10). Daniel knelt in prayer (Dan. 6:10) three times a day, a pattern followed in some measure, at least, by Solomon (1 Kings 8:54), Stephen (Acts 7:60), Peter (Acts 9:40), and Paul (Acts 20:36; Eph. 3:14).

And here's something you may not have known: in the Hebrew language of the Old Testament, the word for "kneeling" and the word for "blessing" are one and the same. Usually we think of people kneeling in royal ceremonies or religious festivals, and our minds connect "kneeling" with "worship." We see the act of kneeling as one in which a lesser person bends low before a greater person to convey homage and respect. All that is certainly true.

Still, the root meaning of the words for kneeling and blessing are the same. Perhaps because no blessing is ever a blessing unless it comes in a form that cannot be bought, earned, or taken by force. The person on his knees is vulnerable—he can't move easily, he can't escape quickly, he can't contribute significantly to the affairs of the person before whom he kneels, at least not in a way of equals. The one kneeling is at the mercy of the one before whom he kneels. A woman who was abused as a child remembers how her father enjoyed forcing her to her knees and then kicking her or molesting her. She was, in those moments, entirely under his control, totally at his mercy.

One who kneels before another is totally at the mercy of the other. But a blessing is a gift that can only be received by those on their knees. People on their knees cannot buy a single thing that they need from others— they can only receive it as unmerited mercy.

That's why the lines above are at the heart of Psalm 95. The earlier verses are the song of those raised up from their knees by God's beautiful blessing. The lines that follow are the torment of those who refuse to kneel and thus refuse to be blessed.

Maybe that's why it is said that the whole world looks different from the perspective of your knees.

Choir Time

Sing to the LORD a new song; sing to the LORD, all the earth.
—Psalm 96:1

A few years back a story circulated among churches in Ontario about something that happened one Sunday morning in a large congregation in the province. It seems that the morning worship service was nearing its conclusion. What a glorious expression of worship it had been! The church was packed, the liturgy was meaningful, the message from the pulpit struck a deeply responsive chord. The congregational singing was at its very best, and the choir beautifully lifted its descants, soaring through the thin veil that separates earth from heaven. A marvelous beginning to the week.

As the congregation stood for the parting hymn, the choir began its descent down the aisle. First in line were the sopranos and altos. Among them was a woman wearing a brand-new pair of shoes. High heels. Very pointed high heels.

Halfway down the aisle there was a metal grate covering a heating duct. That pointed heel slipped right into the space between two bars and stuck tight.

But the woman was a professional. On with the music. On with the march. Without missing a note, she stepped out of her captive shoe and strode confidently toward the back.

The fellow right behind her was just as sharp. He saw what was happening and instinctively reached down to pull her shoe loose. It went like clockwork: he had her shoe in his hand, and he never missed a beat in the song.

But the heel was *very* stuck in the grate, and when he lifted the shoe, the grate came along. He was pretty startled—music in one hand, woman's shoe stuck to the heating duct cover in the other. Professionalism reigned, though, and he just kept marching on. Crisis averted. Not a note missed.

Until the fellow behind him stepped into the open heating duct.

Divine Comedy

That's a wonderful story, isn't it? I wish I could have been there. It brings out the best of what Psalm 96 is all about. Worship is there, to be sure, and singing. Glory and honor and mystical delight. Praise and adoration. The majesty of all that is right and good and noble and beautiful.

Perhaps that makes us think of heaven, or church, or temple worship, and the dignity of stately liturgies and polished choirs. But look again. Psalm 96 is actually more of an "earthy" song, a song for the markets and the fields, a song for the halls of Parliament and Congress, a song for the open road and the expansive sky. Psalm 96 is for real people who dress up in choir robes but who also step into heating ducts. It's for people who notice the difference between justice and injustice because they've been hurt themselves a time or two. It's for people who feel deeply and shout loudly, for folks who cower silently or rumble off-tune, for children and adults who want to make a difference in life but know that too often circumstances have conspired against them.

Psalm 96 is for you and me, in the divine comedy of life, the comedy of activities that "happens" to unfold around us, but which we know has its roots in the sovereign, mighty, glorious, redemptive heart of God. Psalm 96 is for those who can say, whatever is pictured on the nightly news, "The LORD reigns" (v. 10).

The Language of Music

A shout like that has to come out in music, doesn't it? Narrative *tells*, but lyric *lifts*. Story *says*, but chorus *creates*. We *understand* through the preaching of the Word, but we *experience* the great music of the church. That's why music has always been the heart and soul of worship services. The church that sings together stays together.

In another generation young Isaac Watts came home from worship and criticized the service: stale, boring, lifeless. Not that the theology was wrong. Only that the language of worship wasn't the language of the people, either where they were or where they wanted, by the grace of God, to be.

"Then do something about it," challenged his father. Isaac Watts did do something. He wrote new songs to declare the old truths in the language and expressions of the people. And in a short while the whole character of worship changed in his church. Because all around them the saints of God heard the harmony of creation. And when they finally received a part they could sing, it only unleashed within them a chorus that supplemented the grand symphony of the universe:

> Were the whole realm of nature mine,
> that were a present far too small.
> Love so amazing, so divine,
> demands my soul, my life, my all.

Let the Earth Be Glad

The LORD reigns, let the earth be glad;
let the distant shores rejoice.
—Psalm 97:1

Can you imagine the headline? "GOD WINS ELECTION! NATIONS ERUPT IN CELEBRATION!"

Not likely in our lifetime, I suppose, yet it is the essence of Psalm 97 in a nutshell. For now, our world seems quite content to get along without a sense of God's majesty and divinity. A sixty something-year-old woman talked to me about that years ago. She liked church, she said, but she didn't really care much for God. At least the God of the Bible. Always so dark and foreboding. Always overwhelming, overpowering. Always too big to be kept in his place.

God Forgot

Wouldn't it be better, sometimes, if God were less big and grand? If, perhaps, he would be there to create all things, and then again maybe to get us out of trouble when we really need it? If he would win a local election in some small church community, but wouldn't get involved in the global political scene?

Thomas Hardy once wrote a poem about a man who has a complaint and decides to take it to God. Only he has to look hard for God because God has sort of drifted off to the other side of the universe. Finally the man locates God and he asks for a hearing.

Things aren't going well on Earth, he tells God. Couldn't God do something about it all? After all, he *is* God, isn't he?

"Earth?" replies God. "I don't remember it. . . . "

Then the man gets upset. "But God," he shouts, "you've *got* to remember Earth. After all, you created it! How could you forget Earth?"

After a bit of a sigh and a reflective thought, God says to the man, "Oh, now that you mention it, I think I do remember something about Earth. There's some faint recollection that I did something like that. . . . But," he goes on, "it doesn't matter. . . . "

Does that make you shudder a little bit? "It doesn't matter. . . ." And Earth is left to its own devices, its own political games, its own feuding powers. Hardy called his poem, "God Forgot."

Keep Your Distance

Sometimes we wish God might forget us a little bit. But the psalmist seems to think there's a better way. Perhaps the difficulties we face in life are the very reason why God shouldn't forget, and why he shouldn't stay too far away from us. Because it's his very overwhelming presence that brings a measure of perspective to life on Earth.

Without the justice of God, without the norms of his structures for creation, without the righteousness that establishes right and wrong in our consciences and in our hearts, life on Earth would become a battle-ground of powers without mercy and wills without restraint.

What's the Good News?

Listen to the way Lloyd C. Douglas once put it. He's the fellow who wrote those fascinating novels of an earlier generation, *The Robe* and *The Big Fisherman*. When he went to college, he boarded in a large house where the owner lived in the basement, and every room on every floor was converted into an income-generating apartment. For some reason (maybe because the landlord himself was a musician), nearly all the tenants were singers or instrumentalists. The place was always filled with music, some of it grand and good, some of it quite hard to take.

Lloyd Douglas had an ongoing joke with his landlord. They'd meet on the steps, and Douglas would greet him by saying, "Well, what's the good news today?" Invariably, the man would reach into his pocket, pull out a tuning fork, rap it against his heel, and set it against the wall till the whole stairwell echoed with its sound.

"That's middle C!" the landlord would say. "That's the good news to-day. The soprano in the attic may be singing sharp, and the cellist may be off his music, and the tenor may be flat today, but that's middle C. At least you can count on that!"

The psalmist would agree. What's the good news today? "The LORD reigns, let the earth be glad." All the other music in our world may be playing out of tune, but in this be glad: The Lord reigns. And by his middle C all the fiddlers' tunes shall be judged.

A New Song

Sing to the LORD *a new song.*
—Psalm 98:1

I used to greet people by cheerfully calling out to them, "What's new?" That was before a motorcycle-driving friend of mine, a loner by nature and introspective by choice, shared with me his enormous fascination for the popular 1970s best-seller *Zen and the Art of Motorcycle Maintenance.* According to author Robert Pirsig, "'What's new?' is an interesting and broadening eternal question, but one which, if pursued exclusively, results only in an endless parade of trivia and fashion, the silt of tomorrow."

"An endless parade of trivia?" "The silt of tomorrow?" You can see why I changed my habit after a critique like that. Now I greet my friends with the pastoral politeness of "How are you doing?"

Fad

Newness can be trite, I guess. In *Our Mutual Friend* Charles Dickens once described the Veneerings (rather surface people, even by name) this way: "Mr. and Mrs. Veneering were bran-new people in a bran-new house in a bran-new quarter of London. Everything about the Veneerings was spick-and-span new. All their furniture was new, all their friends were new, all their servants were new, their plate was new, their carriage was new, their harness was new, their horses were new, their pictures were new, they themselves were new, they were as newly married as was lawfully compatible with having a bran-new baby. . . . " Apparently Dickens didn't think much of people who specialized in "newness!"

Still, "newness" beckons us every day. The Squire in Chaucer's *Canterbury Tales* said that "Men love . . . newfangledness." That's true, isn't it? Marketing depends on changing styles—every six months there's a new product on supermarket shelves or at least a "new" version of the old. New car models generate new excitement, even if it's all a matter of moving the molding or reshaping the taillights. New fashions mean the old ones are out, and woe be to the person who wears a tie too thin or a collar too wide.

Fascination with the newest and latest is as old as humanity. In the *Odyssey,* Homer says, "It is always the latest song that an audience applauds the most." Dr. Luke says something similar about the ancient

Athenians in Acts 17:21—they "spent their time doing nothing but talking about and listening to the latest ideas." Voltaire's travelers in *Candide* were moderns who constantly moved on, saying, "If we do not find anything pleasant, at least we shall find something new."

Fear

The fad of the new often creates a reactionary fear in those of us who want something deeper in our lives. "Nothing quite new is perfect," said the Roman statesman Cicero, and we're inclined to agree. "Be not the first by whom the new are tried," cautioned Alexander Pope. Again we nod our heads.

Abraham Lincoln once addressed his nation and pulled many heartstrings when he said: "What is conservatism? Is it not adherence to the old and tried, against the new and untried?" We've often used that argument ourselves, haven't we?

The ancient Jewish writer of Ecclesiasticus even applied that fear of the new to human relationships. "Forsake not an old friend," he said, "for the new is not comparable to him; a new friend is as a new wine; when it is old, thou shalt drink it with pleasure" (9:10).

Fulfillment

But the fear of the worst in new things can sometimes blind us to the best that is yet to come. Near the end of Shakespeare's *The Tempest,* Miranda shouts with joy at the beauty of the world that is opening to her. "How beauteous mankind is!" she cries. "O brave new world, That hath such people in't!" Our thoughts immediately take her innocent rapture and recast it in the dark shades of Huxley's stolen title for a horrible *Brave New World* where science and technology and totalitarian government join unholy hands to bind human hearts and kill human spirits. Will the "new" do that to us? We pray it won't while we fear it might.

Still, says the psalmist, not all the new is bad, nor all the future dismal. "Sing to the Lord a *new* song." The old songs won't do. The remnants of another time can't express our feelings today. The melodies of greatness are ever-changing, and only a new song will echo all that we see and sense of the fulfillment of the glory of God at work in our world.

The dialogue of the passionate couple in *Antony and Cleopatra* tests the limits of the love between them. How far will love bear them along? So far, says Antony, that it could carry them even into "a new heaven, a new earth."

Rightly so! God's love, God's care, God's delight fills this world so fully that the ever-new song of his people will flood even a new heaven and a new earth.

Mountaintop

Exalt the LORD our God and worship at his holy mountain.
—Psalm 99:9

British mountain-climber George Mallory tried a number of times to conquer the peak of Mount Everest. In fact, he lost his life in 1924 on those slopes, and debate still rumbles in mountaineering circles about whether or not he reached the pinnacle before he died. He's the one who coined the phrase "because it is there" in response to the question of why anyone would want to climb a mountain.

High Places

"Because it is there" is a pretty fair psychological assessment of human interaction with high places. The ancients set their cities on hilltops to command the advantage in war. Rich folk have always wanted "a room with a view" and are able to buy the higher ground for their palatial homes. Historically "high places" were scenes of religious devotion, probably because of their isolation from the busyness of human society and their proximity to the heavens.

Even little children get in on the act. Who, in northern climates, at least, hasn't played "King of the Mountain" in a winter school-yard, pushing all comers down icy slopes? And who among us doesn't relish "mountain-top experiences": times when we feel "elated" and "elevated" and "ecstatic," times when we are "flying high," "sitting on top of the world," and "on cloud nine" somewhere there in the heavenlies.

Zion

Jerusalem, of course, was located on the slopes of rolling hills in central Judea. When David brought the traveling caravan of God's wilderness home into the city, he pitched the tabernacle in the northern suburbs at the highest elevation. That's where he instructed Solomon to build God's permanent earthly home, the temple, as well. And both David and Solomon, powerful as they were, had their own palaces tucked away slightly down the slopes from God's dwelling. That was a way of declaring to all around them that the true King in Israel was the Lord God stationed at the heights of Zion.

Mountains no longer carry with them the "religious" significance of earlier times. Now they are playgrounds for pleasure-seekers, tamed by skis and snowmobiles. Tunnels and superhighways ease travelers over the rugged places, and airplanes make them vanish altogether. The broad, the easy, the plain, and the simple beckon us. We do our climbing by way of elevators and escalators. Edward Kasner, renowned topologist at Columbia University for many years, knew more about mountains, on paper at least, than nearly anyone else in his day. He vacationed most often in Brussels, claiming that it was a convenient base from which to organize a mountain-climbing expedition to the highest point in Belgium. When people asked him how high that peak was, he replied, "Twelve feet above sea level." That was enough of a climb for him. And he has many compatriots in our age.

Elevated Worship

True worship of God demands mountains and heights and climbs of significance. Worship has an "elevating" dimension—read the apostle Paul's description in 2 Corinthians 12 of being "caught up" in the third heaven. "Flat" worship is boring and insignificant. Even those among us who don't wish the exuberance of hand-clapping, foot-stomping music still need to be drawn out of the "depths" of our difficult times. We need to pray for "higher ground."

Psalm 99 doesn't so much define theology as it declares glory. Strong glory, like the shoulders of the mountains. Majestic glory, like the sweeping pinnacles. Firm glory, like the justice that rolls down from heaven. Beckoning glory, that calls us to bathe in the cascading waterfalls of God's forgiving and cleansing love.

> When I look down from lofty mountain grandeur . . .
> Then sings my soul, my Savior God, to thee:
> how great thou art, how great thou art!

Shout!

Shout for joy to the LORD, all the earth.
—Psalm 100:1

Some years ago Robert Graves wrote a short story called *The Shout*—a strange tale about a man who had learned a secret shout from an isolated African tribe. If he used his vocal cords properly, and if he gave full vent to his lungs, he could bellow a sound that would kill every living animal or human within a certain range.

Even when a person protected his ears by stopping them with wax, there was a danger that he might be driven mad by the shout. All the world around him paused in wonder as he carried in his larynx the shout that could change their lives.

Mob Madness

It sounds too fantastic to be true. Still, there have been shouts throughout history that have caused death and driven men mad. The shout of the Israelites at Jericho, after having marched in solemn silence for seven days, created more than a little stir. It literally shook the foundations of the city. And what of Gideon's little band, surrounding the slumbering hosts of Midian? Their shout turned alien dreams into nightmares and scattered the brave in a military upset of mammoth proportions.

Even today, shouts can be unnerving. During the World Series a few years ago, the Minnesota Twins had an edge over the Atlanta Braves every time a baseball game was played in the domed stadium at Minneapolis. Braves' players said the roar from the shouting of the crowds was so intense that their concentration collapsed and errors mounted.

In Charles Dickens's *Pickwick Papers*, someone asks Mr. Pickwick about what he should do on the streets of London during times of mob unrest. "It's always best to do what the mob does," replies Pickwick.

"But," says the other, "what if there are two mobs?"

In that case, urges the knowledgeable Pickwick, "Shout with the largest!"

Religious Fervor

Shouting isn't always an unnerving and destructive mob activity, though. The poetic report of the creation of the world in Job 38 says that on that day of celebration the morning stars sang together and all the angels of God shouted for joy. That's more like the picture of worship in Psalm 100. "Shout for joy to the LORD, all the earth" says the psalmist.

Other scenes from Scripture describe a similar exuberance when the people of God get together. The dancing and shouting in Exodus, for instance, when God brings his people through the Red Sea. Or the celebrations at the dedication of the temple, raised to a high pitch of religious fervor by Solomon. And again, when Jesus enters Jerusalem on a donkey. Chesterton writes about that occasion from the donkey's perspective:

> There was a shout about my ears,
> And palms before my feet.

Jesus himself affirmed the shouts, telling the quiet-wishers that even the rocks of creation had to explode in praise when heaven passed so near.

Shudder, Shiver, Shout

So too with us. Worship, in many traditions, can become reduced over time when excessively bound by the apostle Paul's admonition to have things done "decently and in good order." Sometimes the good order of the day calls for a shout, one which unnerves and upsets the status quo. For when heaven passes by, earth always shudders with fear or with delight.

Blameless

I will be careful to lead a blameless life. . . .
—Psalm 101:2

In one of Tennessee Williams's plays, there's a preacher who plays the hypocrite. He's smooth. He's cunning. He's as enticing on the outside as he is dark and deceptive on the inside. Williams calls attention to the preacher's hypocrisy by having one of his characters say that the preacher's smile is "as sincere as a bird call blown on a hunter's whistle."

Preachers aren't the only ones prone to hypocrisy. There's a discrepancy in each of our lives between what we portray on the outside and what we live on the inside. I'll never forget the young man who refused to become a member of one of the churches I served because he knew too much about one of our "pillar" saints, a man who often served in leadership roles. Backhanded business deals and troubled family relations made his broad smile about "as sincere as a bird call blown on a hunter's whistle."

Coining the Metal of Our Hearts

In the conscience-searing multiple-valued culture of our day, it's easy to get by with several public faces and different moral standards to use in each of our varying social roles. In fact, it's often expected of us. "Keep your religious beliefs to yourself," we're told. "What does morality have to do with the job you do for us?"

Perhaps more than we'd like to think. When Georg Brandes, the Danish novelist, was a young man, Henrik Ibsen took notice of him. Ibsen was much older than Brandes, and Brandes looked up to him. He asked the famous dramatist for help and encouragement.

So Ibsen wrote Brandes a long letter, overflowing with love and power. If you want to serve your world, said Ibsen, you've got to look inside first. You've got to find out what you're made of. You've got to mine the depths of your own heart. He said, "There is no way in which you can benefit society more than by coining the metal you have in yourself."

He's right, isn't he? In spite of the faces we show, we're never really ourselves till we know our hearts and then live honestly in direct expression of our true value systems.

Habits and Reputations

In fact, in Psalm 101 David seems to think that integrity is directly related to depth of faith. And so it is. Habits of the heart are habits of life. Habits are hard to break, but they're just as hard to make. The habit of a deep faith, a firm belief, a confident relationship with God is a habit that takes a lifetime of practice.

Sometimes people will talk about "sowing wild oats," or of "getting it out of my system" when they laugh off some silly or obnoxious behavior. And perhaps we need to experience some things in order to find our way to the things that truly matter. But we need to be careful. Habits are hard to break, and habits of shallow living are just as hard to break as habits of deep living. A woman once came running up to Artur Rubenstein after he'd finished another brilliant performance. "Oh, Mr. Rubenstein," she cried, "I'd give *anything* to be able to play the piano like you do."

She was shocked by his reply. "No you wouldn't," he said, "because you didn't!"

So it is with us. Did you ever know someone of great faith who didn't have to fight for it, who didn't have to struggle for it, who didn't have to grow it out of the difficulties of her life?

During World War II many German Lutherans lost their faith, seduced into a false religion by Adolph Hitler. But Martin Niemoller could not be seduced. Niemoller was a German military hero from the first World War, but he could not stomach the policies of the Holocaust. For seven years Hitler tossed him from one concentration camp to another. But during his imprisonment Niemoller mined the metal of his heart and he played the truth of his personal faith. When they released him, a gaunt and weathered man, this is what he said: "Christianity is not an ethic, nor is it a system of dogmatics, but a living thing."

Those who saw the fruit of his life knew who he was, where he stood, and how his reputation was built.

Vanishing Act

For my days vanish like smoke. . . .
—*Psalm 102:3*

When theater critic Dorothy Parker was given a small, dingy cubbyhole of an office in the Metropolitan Opera House building in New York City, she seemed to disappear. No one ever came to see her in her out-of-the-way quarters, and she became lonely and depressed. So when the sign writer came to paint her name on the door, she asked him to put "Gentlemen" in place of her own name. She thought that would bring a few men into her office, if only by mistake.

Disappearing People

Loneliness is written all over Psalm 102 too. In fact, its title is so unusual that for centuries scholars have remarked about it and speculated on it: "A prayer of an afflicted man. When he is faint and pours out his lament before the LORD." Who was this man? When did he write? What happened to him that he cried out so forlornly?

The possibilities are endless: a Davidic king in the seventh century? Someone left in Jerusalem after its destruction in 586 B.C.? An heir to the royal throne now in exile in Babylon? We don't know for sure. We probably never will.

But that doesn't take away the power of this prayer. It's a prayer that's been whispered a million times in a billion settings by a trillion lonely people. The words may vary, but the prayer is always the same. Just listen to this poem written by someone who wished to be identified only as "A Lonesome Middle-Ager":

> Do you know what it means to be lonely?
> Do you know how it feels to be blue?
> Do you know what it's like to feel
> No one really cares just how things are with you?
> You can call up your friends, and I do that;
> You can ask them how they are too.
> But you wish that they'd say, "Come on over,
> And help us eat up the leftover stew."
> Most everyone has a son or a daughter,

A husband, a mother or sis.
But when you're alone with no loved ones,
To me, I just merely exist.

Fragmented Society

For the author of Psalm 102, loneliness was the natural by-product of a society without a center. In his world the temple had either been neglected or destroyed, and culture was fragmented and scattered as a result. With no spiritual glue in the central relationship of life, all the other relationships fell apart quickly. The outcome was loneliness and alienation.

We know that ourselves. The church may not be a perfect organization, but where it ceases to exist, or where it becomes something less than the visible earthly dwelling of God, society is cheated and cheapened. Just listen to the cries that erupt from the former Soviet Union these days. And even with its proliferation of church buildings and "christian" organizations, North American society often experiences the same malaise.

One Hope

The "afflicted man" of Psalm 102 saw only a single hope for a change in his condition. That single hope had nothing to do with social programs, at least not on the surface. All he wanted, all he pleaded for, was a return to worship. He asked for a place to worship. He begged for people to worship with. And he pleaded for God to be worthy of the worship directed his way.

Amazing as it sounds, the psalmist honestly believed that a return to true worship would pull his world back together. Maybe that's worth a try for us.

Father

As a father has compassion on his children, so the LORD has compassion on those who fear him.
—Psalm 103:13

In one of the "Peanuts" cartoons, Charlie Brown sits in his father's barber shop and describes his relationship with his dad: "My dad likes me to come down to the barber shop and wait for him. No matter how busy he is, even if the shop is full of customers, he always stops and says 'hi' to me. I sit here on the bench until six o'clock, when he's through, and then we ride home together."

He thinks for a minute, and then he goes on: "Boy! It really doesn't take much to make my dad happy!"

Mysterious Fathers

It's nice to know a father that well. But for many of us, fathers are a lot more mysterious. Some years ago, researchers at Cornell University studied family behavior across North America. They came to the conclusion that the average father spends only 37.7 *seconds* with each child each day. Can you believe it?

Sometimes, it seems, all we know about our fathers comes from observing them from a distance. The late playwright Channing Pollack knew that. He used to tell a devastating little story about something that happened when he was a young boy. His parents took him along to a party one night at a magnificent house on a large estate. There was a little girl there about his age, and they played together till they ran out of ideas.

Then young Channing said to her, "Let's hide behind this curtain, and maybe no one will know we're here!"

Her answer shocked him. He never forgot it. She said, "Maybe no one will care."

Can you imagine it? A young child says about her own parents: "Maybe no one will care." How horrible to grow in a world like that.

Daddy

That's why David's praise and prayer in Psalm 103 is so powerful in the life of the child of God. It's the Old Testament echo of what Jesus told us so beautifully in the New Testament: Our lives have meaning because we are loved. We are loved by a Father. We can sing and dance and play because he cares about us. Jesus even said we could call him "Abba." If you ever go to Israel and see the children darting through the markets, you'll hear them tugging at their fathers' trousers and calling "Abba! Abba!" It's the equivalent of "Daddy" to them.

Daddies can fix anything. Daddies are always there for us. Nothing means more to daddies than our cares and concerns. Of course, that doesn't mean daddies give their children anything they ask for. That wouldn't help them grow in life. But what a child needs, what really matters most to a young person, that a good parent will *always* supply: a sense of worth, the confidence of belonging, a knowledge that someone cares.

Running Home

Ian Maclaren tells the story of a young woman in his book *Beside the Bonnie Briar Bush*. She's raised in a Christian home, but leaves it behind in search of a better life, a freer self. She finds the kind of life she thinks is free, and she gets for herself all that she's ever desired.

But it's never enough, and what she possesses begins to possess her. Finally she doesn't even know what it means to be free.

One day she decides to go home. When she gets near the cottage of her birth, she wants to turn around. Her footsteps falter. She begins to turn her body. But then the dogs in the yard catch scent of her. They haven't forgotten her, even though it's been so long.

Then the light comes on at the door. The door opens. All she can see is her father, bathed in the light. He calls out her name even though he can't see her face. He calls out her name, even though he doesn't have a reason to expect her. He calls out her name, and suddenly her feet come running to him.

Then he takes her into his arms. He sobs out blessings on her head. Later, when she tells her neighbor of that night, she says, "It's a pity, Margaret, that you don't know Gaelic. That's the best of all languages for loving. There are fifty words for 'darling,' and my father called me every one of them that night I came home."

Maybe, when we pray the words of Psalm 103, that's a good picture to have in mind.

—*Spirit Fruit*, by John M. Drescher. Herald Press, 1974

Leviathan

There the ships go to and fro, and the leviathan, which you
formed to frolic there.
—Psalm 104:26

Can God create a stone too big for him to move?

Remember the questions we used to ask the pastor in order to stump him or at least get him off the topic during catechism classes?

Theological absurdity is always a game. Sometimes it keeps people from facing their inner selves by diverting attention. That's what the Pharisees kept doing with Jesus. And the woman at Jacob's well in Sychar (John 4) tried to do the same thing.

God at Play

But what if theological absurdity is sometimes just God having fun? Francis Thompson once wrote a child's prayer, imagining what life in heaven might have been like for Jesus before he was born as Bethlehem's baby. He put these words in the mouth of a youngster at bedtime: "Hadst Thou ever any toys, like us little girls and boys? And did'st Thou play in Heaven with all the angels (that were not too tall) with stars for marbles?"

That's theologically absurd, we say. But might it not reflect the fun God has in heaven and in this universe? Eternity is a long time to while away without a bit of merriment now and again, wouldn't you say?

Somehow the songwriter of Psalm 104 seems to give that impression. The dazzling array of wildlife about him is almost like God's playground, filled with pets and treasures and secret hiding places. That's especially true in verse 26: "There is the sea, vast and spacious, teeming with creatures beyond number . . . and the leviathan, which you have formed to frolic there."

Hollywood Horror

Do you know what a "leviathan" is? If you watch scary thrillers, you probably know Hollywood's version—the mean, mutating, half-human sea creature that terrifies underwater explorers.

Actually, the biblical version of leviathan isn't all that different. Listen to what the prophet Isaiah says about him: "In that day, the LORD will punish with his sword . . . Leviathan the gliding serpent, Leviathan the coiling serpent; he will slay the monster of the sea" (Isa. 27:1). There's almost enough there to cast images for a dozen new movies!

Job hints at something of the same. After enduring all of the blows that rob him of possessions, family, and health, he curses the day he was born. He compares the blackness of his situation to the awful horror awaiting "those who are ready to rouse Leviathan" (Job 3:8). Leviathan is a child's worst nightmare, still lurking in the adult subconscious.

A number of ancient civilizations told legends of Leviathan, the great monster of the deeps, subdued early in history by the gods but biding his time for a great eruption of bloody vengeance. That picture isn't far from Scripture, either in Job's or Isaiah's poetic terrors, or in the images of Revelation 12 and 13 where the Beast from the sea and the horrible Dragon rise in one last vicious attempt to lay waste the kingdom of God.

God's Pet

But here is a picture of Leviathan the pet. God himself expands on this brief theme in his thunderous speech to Job (ch. 41). Leviathan stirs the depths like a boiling cauldron. He snorts fire and belches smoke. His eyes blaze like laser beams and his cry of laughter smashes ships. But Leviathan is tamed by the Lord Almighty, led around on a leash like a pet, and ridden in playful frolic on the waves of the ocean.

Why did God make Leviathan? How fierce a creature, terrorizing every human dreamer in the uneasy world of nightmares! How horrible a picture of Satan and his devilishly destructive powers! And yet, how charming a pet, playing like Flipper the dolphin with the Almighty through the rolling seas.

Why did God make Leviathan? I don't think I would have thought much about this theologically absurd question if I hadn't been camping one cold summer's night high on an Alaskan glacier with an elder of a church in Anchorage. Surrounded by the absurd immensity of the mountains, the boulders too big for anyone but God to lift, the strange and delicate wildlife, and the incredible glacial ice pack, he read Psalm 104 with echoing resonance. And in that high and strange place, creation suddenly became the playground of God. I only wish I had brought my binoculars. I'm sure I could have caught a glimpse of the distant ocean boiling as Leviathan and God frolicked in energetic abandon there on the high seas.

A Room Called Remember

Remember the wonders he has done, his miracles, and the judgments he pronounced.
—Psalm 105:5

A few years ago, a Presbyterian minister named Frederick Buechner wrote about a dream he'd had. He dreamed he was staying in a large hotel with many floors and hundreds of rooms. The room he'd been given was absolutely wonderful. For some reason it made him feel warm and comfortable and happy. He says he can't remember what the room looked like, but he still gets a shiver of delight whenever he thinks about being there.

In his dream, after staying in that room for awhile, he left the hotel on a variety of journeys and adventures. Later, though, his dream brought him back again to that same hotel. Only this time, when they gave him the key to his room, it was a different room than he'd been in before. He says that he could actually *feel* the difference as his dream took him into the new room: it felt cold and clammy, cramped and dark. This room made him shudder with fear.

In his dream, he went down to the front desk again. He told the clerk about the change in rooms and asked if he could have his old room back again. He said that he didn't know the number of the room, but he described it: bright, cheery, homey.

The desk clerk smiled. He knew exactly which room that was. In fact, he said, Buechner could have that room anytime he wanted. All he had to do is ask for it by name.

"Well, then, what's the name of the room?" Buechner asked.

"Simple!" said the clerk. "The name of the room is Remember." A room called Remember!

Religion with Depth

Buechner woke up then. But his dream stayed with him: a room called Remember. A room of peace. A room that made him feel loved and accepted. A room that gave him a sense of coming home. Buechner says the room called Remember is that place in our own hearts where we find our truest selves. It's those times in our lives when we connect the "now" of the present with the reality of the past and the promise of the future, and sense again the pervasive loving hold of God on our souls.

Psalm 105 is a room called Remember. There's only one reason it rehearses the litany of history: to give Israel, standing in the temple at worship, a sense of identity. Experiential religion requires a constant "high," an ever-increasing dose of entertainment, an emotional fix of mind-blowing proportions at every new gathering. But deep religion has a history to it. And even when the moment doesn't excite, the soul runs deep with hope and gratitude (vv. 1-4).

"Keep My Memory Green!"

Charles Dickens once wrote a little story called "The Haunted Man." It is the tale of a chemist who is troubled by his memories. He wants to get rid of them, to be free of them. He wants a fresh start in life without the ghosts of the past whispering in his soul.

Miraculously he discovers the secret to forgetting. He's suddenly able to wipe out the past, to lock the door on the room called Remember.

And what does he find? He finds that it is the worst thing that could ever happen to him. To lose your memory, to lock the door on the room called Remember, is to lose the very essence of your own self.

In the very last line of Dickens' story the man cries out: "Lord! Keep my memory green!"

That's a prayer we all need to pray more often. Because once we lose our memory, we lose our very selves.

A man's real possession, says Alexander Smith, is his memory.

How rich are you today? Why don't you go back to the room called Remember, there in your heart, and find out?

The Dungeon of Forgetfulness

He saved them from the hand of the foe . . . but they soon
forgot what he had done.
—Psalm 106:10, 13

A few years ago, Luis Bunuel wrote about his mother in the *New York Review of Books.* He told how she had come down with Korsakov's syndrome, a disease that attacks those sections of the brain that hold our memory. It wipes the slate clean: all the people she knew, all the things she'd done were gone.

Luis watched this happen to his mother. She didn't know him anymore. She didn't even remember how to tie her shoes. She couldn't function because when her memory left her, so did her identity. Luis wrote: "Memory is what makes our lives. Life without memory is no life at all." He went on: "Our memory is our coherence, our reason, our feeling, even our action. Without it, we are nothing."

Luis welcomed his mother's death when it finally came. He said it was a blessing, actually, because once her memory was gone, her identity was gone too.

When Faith Slips Away

Maybe he overstated his case. But then again, maybe not. The psalmist says much the same thing about ancient Israel in Psalm 106. The people of God have lost their memories, he says. And when that happened to them, they lost their identity as a nation. They died. They ceased to exist.

Some time ago I was talking with a middle-age couple. They used to belong to the church, but over the years they drifted away. "We lost our faith," they said to me.

How did it happen? I asked. Was there a crisis? Did God let them down? Were they taken over by some other religion?

No, they said. It just happened gradually over the years. They got so involved in their business. . . . And then they traveled a lot. . . . And then they were doing this. . . . And then they were doing that. . . . And along the way they just stopped believing.

We talked for awhile. I asked them about God and about the things their parents believed in. I asked them about the songs they learned, years ago, when they were growing up in Holland. They laughed a little at first, because they started to remember things they hadn't thought about in a very long time. Then their eyes began to glow as one memory jogged another, and the stories started tumbling out.

Then came the tears. Do you know why?

These people hadn't really *lost* their faith; they'd just *forgotten* it. When they went back to the vaults of their minds, to the treasures of their inner spirits, to the heritage of their lives, they found again what they had missed for too long.

"Remember Jesus!"

A few years ago, Fred Ferre gave a lecture at the Vancouver School of Theology. He told the story of his father, the distinguished theologian and author Nels Ferre. Fred said that his father had come from a family of ten in Sweden, and that when his father was only thirteen years old, he was sent away alone to find his future in America.

At the train station that day, all ten members of the family stood in a circle and held hands as young Nels's father led them in prayer. Then each person in the circle took a turn to pray. That's the last earthly contact Nels had with his family.

He boarded the train, a wisp of a thirteen-year-old. He sat at the window, watching his family standing there, crying, waving. His mother was saying something to him, but he couldn't hear her. He struggled with the window, trying to open it. The conductor blew his whistle, and the train began to move. Nels' mother ran alongside the train, right down the platform of the station. Finally Nels got the window open, and he caught his mother's voice as they drifted apart: "Nels! Nels! Remember Jesus! Remember Jesus!"

That, said Fred Ferre, was the key that opened the door for his father every time he found himself trapped in the dungeon of forgetfulness.

Do you remember Jesus? Do you remember the things God has done?

Postcards from the Edge

Some wandered in desert wastelands. . . . Some sat in darkness. . . . Some became fools through their rebellious ways. . . . Others went out on the sea in ships.
—Psalm 107:4, 10, 17, 23

Hollywood star Carrie Fisher's book, *Postcards from the Edge*, is a collection of scenes from her life that show just how close she came to losing everything: family, health, friends, sanity.

Psalm 107 can be read in a similar way: as four picture postcards from the edge of destruction.

Postcard 1: A Picture of Refuge (vv. 4-9)
Picture a vast desert. The sun is merciless, the sands shimmer with heat. A man staggers, his strength long gone. A woman stumbles. You want to reach out your arms to catch her as she falls. Your tongue starts wetting your lips.

But just as you turn away, your eye catches something you hadn't noticed: half hidden by the last sand dune is the green of trees and the blue of fresh water.

Then it strikes you: the lines in the sand and the shape of the hills form a giant hand. From your perspective it's clear. It's the hand of God—helping, holding, assisting the man and woman. They're going to make it!

Postcard 2: A Picture of Release (vv. 10-16)
This is Dachau. It's Auschwitz. It's Buchenwald. Prisoners lined up at the fences. Scarecrows of sticks and bones, tattered rags flapping against rib cages. Everything is gray: the sky, the grass, the buildings, the smoke from the furnaces, the human flesh, the sunken eyes.

On the far right, fat soldiers smash in a man's face because he stumbled as he worked in the fields. On the left, corpses rot in a huge pit.

You almost gag. But you can't tear your eyes from the faces of the children. And then it hits you. The gray clouds are parting, and in their shapes you can see the hand of God reaching down from heaven. Help is on the way!

Postcard 3: A Picture of Restoration (vv. 17-22)

Now you're in a cancer ward. Lightbulbs can't cut through the gloom of this place.

A man lies dying. His mouth hangs open, his breathing is labored. A woman moans. You hold your nose at the foul smell coming from her open sores. The place is quiet with death, yet the air is full of noise: groans and sighs, murmurs and cries, moans and whimpers.

You need to escape. But before you turn away, you notice something else: There's a slit in the curtains where the light shines through. And the folds of the curtains reveal the grip of the hands that are tearing them apart! You know that hope is on the way.

Postcard 4: A Picture of Rescue (vv. 23-32)

Suddenly you're on the high seas. Mountains of water push toward the dark skies. Lightning flashes, thunder rolls. Down in the trough between the waves, a ship founders. The mast is gone and cargo barrels roll around like marbles in the hand of an unseen giant. Those on deck stagger like drunks.

You feel the salty sea spray stinging your eyes. But when you rub them, you feel tears of horror and empathy. Enough, you say. As you move to drop the postcard, you realize that the line of the horizon, stretching between sea and sky, is the underbelly of a bird. A giant dove. And where the eye of the dove should be, the distant beacon of a lighthouse cuts the dark. You can almost see the lines of God's hand again, surrounding the ship, lifting it out of the grave, pushing it toward the harbor!

Perspective

What kind of psalm is this? Four times the psalmist tells the same story. Four catastrophes: but in each, a cry goes up to heaven. And the hand of God reaches into the picture, bringing help, and hope, and healing, and harbor.

In the last two verses the psalmist puts it all into place: "The upright *see* and rejoice." What do they see?

They see the hand of God in the picture of life. They don't always know what he's doing in each situation or experience, but they're positive about which direction he's leading. They aren't always sure of how he will act, but they're confident of his caring presence. They have perspective.

Verse 43 issues a challenge: Whoever is wise, let him heed these things and consider the great love of the LORD. Life is more than a morality play. It's a dialogue. It's a conversation between God and creation. It's a dance of divine and human partners.

Dawn

Awake, harp and lyre! I will awaken the dawn.
—Psalm 108:2

Some images dig their way into your mind and stick like glue. Listen to this description of dawn in Texas first published in *National Geographic* back in 1980:

> Anywhere in Texas, the best time is dawn. The sun flares above prairies and sere hills, caressing old Spanish missions, oil fields, remote ranches, the dew-kissed produce of early markets. It searches out the gaudy cities. Their neon signs, so bright with promise only a dusk ago, fade and expire as morning suffuses the sky. . . . Beside the Brazos River, the mesquites and cottonwoods take shape in the dim pewter light. A creamy fog clings to the bottom lands like a fallen cloud. . . . The world emerges from the little death of night.

Remember when you stood there one morning? Even if you've never been to Texas, remember when you've experienced that?

Light Welcomes Life

There's something powerful about the early morning, something new and vibrant and refreshing. When you stay awake all night, dawn seems to revive you. When you get up early in the morning, dawn welcomes you. Dawn "comes up like thunder" in one of Kipling's poems, and creeps "rosy-fingered" through the skies, according to Homer. Matthew Arnold remembers the "music" of the "bird-haunted" trees in an English garden at dawn. And who could forget Masefield's striking images in the poem "Sea Fever":

> I must down to the seas again, to the lonely sea and the sky,
> And all I ask is a tall ship and a star to steer her by,
> And the wheel's kick and the wind's song and the white sail's shaking,
> And a grey mist on the sea's face and a grey dawn breaking.

Remember? Even if you're not a morning person, there's something of the dawn that lingers in every great experience you feel. For dawn is the surge of life, and dawn is the power of rebirth, and dawn is the victory of the future over the past.

"Religion of the Dawn"

Leslie Weatherhead once called Christianity "the religion of the dawn." He pointed to the first dawning of light at creation as the irreversible testimony of God to this world. "It is a religion of unquenchable faith and hope and patience; unquenchable because it believes that the permanent thing is light and the passable thing is darkness; that however long the night, whether it be in world affairs or the poignant private world of the human heart, the night will pass." He pointed to the astounding power of Easter dawn. "After the great darkness, this amazing dawn! Within seven weeks they—the hunted, frightened fugitives—had become flaming missionaries and willing martyrs ready to lay down their lives rather than deny the truth of His risen glory and His transforming power. . . . From the East the dawn-light spread across the skies of the world. The religion of the dawn!"

David's song in Psalm 108 knows the power of the first dawn and anticipates the courage of the second. He sings at dawn of the strength of new life, for God is resplendent, exalted above the changing lights of the heavens (v. 5). And he heralds the dawn because it is the promise of greater things that God will yet do (vv. 7-13).

Remember?

In fact, it is not the dawn of sun's first glow that awakens him this morning, but he who awakens the dawn. Even in the blackness of midnight hours, when chills attack the bones, when eyesight strains at the mysterious movements of unseen attackers, when ears are bombarded with frightening sounds just at the threshold of distinction, David takes out his musical instruments and sings a song of grace and love and power. For other dawns remind him of divine strength, and other sunrises warm his heart in anticipation.

Remember?

Stand by Me

———

*With my mouth I will greatly extol the LORD. . . . For he
stands at the right hand of the needy one, to save his life from
those who condemn him.*
—Psalm 109:30–31

Different people read the biblical story of the creation of the human race in different ways. For instance, there's a male interpretation that says that since God made Adam first, he's obviously a superior being to Eve, and thus all males are superior in some respect to all females. Of course, countering that chauvinism is an equally chauvinistic female interpretation: God made Adam first. He stepped back and looked at the man, and said to himself, "I can do better than that!" And then he made Eve.

Far more wonderful, though, is the interpretation given by the ancient Jewish rabbis. They said that God made Adam out of the dust of the ground so that he would always love the earth and feel the wonder of it in his fingers. And then, because he was incomplete by himself, God made Eve to complement him as an equal. God didn't make Eve from his head, for then she would rule over him. And God didn't make Eve from his feet, because then he would be tempted always to walk all over her. Instead, God made Eve from one of Adam's ribs, at his side and close to his heart, so that together they would know the joy of friendship and partnership.

The Greatest Human Need
Certainly that last interpretation reflects what we know both from the rest of Scripture and from our own lives. We need friendship. We need companionship. We need another to stand there with us, to be close to us, to love us, and to support us.

That's the testimony of David in Psalm 109. Most of the song is an angry and sometimes vicious lament about the cruelty of some who proved to be far less than friends. They used their position in his family or in his circle of confidants to become tormentors and enemies. The pain of his cry is echoed by the people who've sat in my study, pouring out tirades against faithless marriage partners, shivering at memories of childhood abuse by parents, and weeping in agony because of traitorous soul mates.

There is no need greater in the human spirit than for kinship and intimacy with someone who knows us and who cares about us. The doctrine of the Trinity is not merely some theological or philosophical construct best left to the nit-picking debates of academicians; rather, it is the central badge of identity in the Christian religion. Because at the heart of the universe, at the core of all being, at the center of whatever reality we know, is a *community*. A community of three who know each other intimately. A community of three who love each other fully. A community of three who support and encourage each other without reserve.

If we are a reflection of that trinitarian God, created in his image, then it is no wonder that we also need supportive human companionship.

You've Got a Friend

Years ago, a young newspaper reporter got off a train in Detroit and came face to face with the great Henry Ford. Not wanting to miss a story or a contact, the man sauntered up and introduced himself. He spoke with undisguised admiration about Ford and sought some word of advice.

Ford startled him by asking a strange question: "Who is your best friend?"

The reporter stammered slightly, not knowing how exactly to answer. But Henry Ford knew what he was doing. He reached into his vest pocket, pulled out a scrap of paper, and wrote a single line. "Here!" he said, handing the note to the young fellow. To this day, that man, now in his nineties, keeps that paper in his wallet. It says: "Your best friend is he who brings out the best in you!"

That's what David prays for in Psalm 109. He's been betrayed by some who brought out the worst in him. Now he turns once again to the only Friend who has promised for time and eternity: "Never will I leave you. Never will I forsake you."

In the words of Ben E. King:

> When the night has come, and the sun is gone,
> And the moon is the only light I see,
> Oh, I won't be afraid, no, I won't be afraid,
> Just as long as you stand by me!

Melchizedek

You are a priest forever, in the order of Melchizedek.
—Psalm 110:4

The name "Melchizedek" has always intrigued me. I wonder what a "Melchizedek" would look like; rather imposing, I'm sure. The name rolls around for a while before it comes out. You begin with soft sounds and warm touches, and then you sort of sneeze the rest of it out. In my mind, Melchizedek would have to be rather tall; a short Melchizedek just wouldn't be Melchizedek. Maybe "Melchy" or "Chizy," but not the whole thing.

A Melchizedek would have to be fairly old, too. A handle like that could crush a baby. Can you imagine youngsters playing ball, and the coach calling for Melchizedek to get in the game? He'd be laughed off the field.

No, there's something old and tall and wise and authoritative about a person who fits the name Melchizedek.

Uncommon

You can't have too many people in your community by the name of Melchizedek, either. It loses its punch if you see it on every thirty-seventh mailbox. Melchizedeks are few and far between. They have to be, or they can't be Melchizedeks. Not that you don't want one around; a good Melchizedek in the family line sort of spruces it up. You can point to that name back in the pages of the family Bible, and it gives importance to your bloodline: "See! I come from a good family."

But it's not one of those names that you want to pass down from generation to generation, either. You can understand it when someone wants to call a baby Franklin, Jr., or Theodore Geisbert IV. But you have to handle a name like Melchizedek with care. One Melchizedek is enough; you wouldn't want to try to clone him or force someone else to walk in his shoes.

No Wimp

There's something royal in the name, of course. A Melchizedek deserves to rule. Maybe that's not putting it strongly enough: a Melchizedek *needs* to rule. Authority goes with the name. You can't be a Melchizedek and be a wimp at the same time.

In fact, you might find a Melchizedek in kingly legends, like the quest for the Holy Grail. A Melchizedek shouldn't just sit there on his throne and grow benignly old; he should have a mission, a purpose, a cause to champion, a crusade to march in. If a Melchizedek sits around too long you start calling him "the old man," or "the head honcho," or something demeaning like that. But when you see him on his steed, something in you stirs magnificently. His face is slightly weather-beaten, and his hair is brushed by the wind. You know he's a man of purpose. You know there's depth to him.

Where Legends Live

So what's this all about? Am I dancing around in ignorance, trying to make something out of a name that's only mentioned twice in the Old Testament (Gen. 14:18 and here) and in a single New Testament passage (Heb. 7:11)? Is this an exercise in theological silliness?

Not really. Melchizedek is a strange figure, scattered lightly across the Scriptures. Of himself, he doesn't really amount to much, I suppose. But his very insignificance, coupled with the single act of faith to which he's tied in the life of Abraham (Gen. 14:18-20) have given him the stature of prince among legends.

And that's really the point of this reference to him. With whom can you compare a divinely appointed king like David? Certainly he doesn't fit the mold of the other monarchs around him. In fact, when he resembles them most, he's least like his truest self. David is the stuff that becomes a legend. And before he becomes one himself, you can only talk about him and his sons in the hushed terms of larger-than-life figures. Like Melchizedek.

The Bible doesn't let you read too much theology into Melchizedek. But when it comes to thinking about David, your thoughts naturally turn to those few who stand slightly above the natural order of things. Melchizedek comes to mind.

That's probably why David's later, greater Son ran into the same family history generations further along. Someone probably bumped into him one day and started thinking, "That man's got a Melchizedek in the family tree, I'm sure."

Good Fear

The fear of the LORD *is the beginning of wisdom.*
—Psalm 111:10

Dennis the Menace climbs into bed between his mom and dad during a fierce storm. He says to them, "I wouldn't be scared of the thunder if I could only keep my mind off my thoughts." How true!

"Fear," said Michael Pritchard, "is that little darkroom where negatives are developed." All the largest negatives in our lives are developed in the darkroom of fear, where the thunder forces our minds to think all their worst thoughts: I can't. I won't. I don't know how. We've never done it before.

Raw Emotion

Someone once called fear "the rawest of all human emotions." It sneaks up from behind as apprehension. It looms over us as intimidation. It blankets us with dread. It tears at our hearts in anguish, our chests in panic, and our throats in terror.

A group of mountain climbers once were making their way up a steep, treacherous slope. They moved in unison, tethered together by a long cord. "Why the rope?" asked a spectator down below. Someone replied: "That's to keep the sensible ones from going home!"

Fear is the great debilitator. When it comes calling, all we want to do is run home and hide.

Neurotic Fear

In his little book on prayer, C. S. Lewis wrote that religion often breeds a kind of fear that is very neurotic. God is sometimes portrayed as a far and distant being, dreadful and awesome, harsh and vindictive, who will "jerk the rug out from under the offending creature."

Of course, says Lewis, even though we know that the Bible calls us to the fear of God, we also know inside ourselves that there's something wrong with religion that consists largely in anxious trembling. He writes: "Servile fear is, to be sure, the lowest form of religion."

So what do we make of the psalmist's declaration that "the fear of the LORD is the beginning of wisdom?" How is it possible for him to breathe praise of God and fear of him in the same utterances? When we look around ourselves, most would agree that greatly to be pitied among Christians are the quaking souls who spend a lifetime wondering whether they might sometime, somewhere, in some eternal destiny far beyond this dreadful existence, be loved by someone.

Unfortunately, recent conversations with three psychiatrists reveal that most of their "business" comes from people in the church. They owe their livelihoods to folks who have turned religious awe into neurotic fear. That's a tragedy.

Where Wisdom Begins

So what is the good fear of Psalm 111?

When I think of this verse, a vivid picture from Herman Melville's *Moby Dick* always comes to mind. Starbuck, one of the ship's officers, says loudly one day: "I will have no man in my boat who is not afraid of a whale." Melville goes on to explain: "By this, he seemed to mean . . . that the most reliable and useful courage was that which arises from the fair estimation of the encountered peril."

In other words, if you understand and respect the persons and circumstances that have a great ability to affect and shape and determine the course of events around you, then you are well on your way to living in genuine harmony with them. Blind blustering is neither courageous nor wise. It may not be neurotic, but it certainly becomes psychotic because it no longer responds honestly to its environment.

Real wisdom seeks the ground rules for responsible interaction with the major players on the field. And foolish is the person who thinks then to ignore God. One day he or she will find the thundering quite overwhelming. But by then any "good fear" will be lost in terror.

Is This for Real?

Blessed is the man who fears the LORD....
The wicked man will see and be vexed,
he will gnash his teeth and waste away.
—*Psalm 112:1, 10*

Fairy tales always paint things in vivid colors. There are no subtle tones, no shadows, no variations on gray. All is in stark contrast: "You may go to the royal ball, but be home by midnight!" "Don't open the box or the door or the window, or something evil will befall you!" "Say the magic words, kiss the princess or the frog, hug the beast, and you'll live happily ever after!"

And if ever there was a psalm that sounds like a fairy tale, it's this one. See this guy? asks the psalmist. He loves God, so his children are social and political leaders. He's rich and powerful (though, of course, also humble and pious). Everyone loves him. He has no worries. He lives the true fairy tale life—"happily ever after." All those who don't love God are jealous of him.

What World Are You Living In?
But we know it's not true. At least, that's not the way life meets us from day to day. Good things happen to bad people. Rotten things pile up on devout souls. Death stalks the young, while it evades the lonely elderly person who cries out for it. We don't live life in black and white.

This summer my high school class will "celebrate" in reunion the twenty years that have slipped through our fingers since those wonderful days when we knew all the answers. There will be good stories, and delight, and much to be thankful for. There will also be faces missing. And tragic tales. And class prophecies that sound hollow.

Psalm 112 comes from a different world than the one we know. It doesn't even really seem to belong, does it? Just stand it next to Psalm 73 and see how they argue against each other.

Where You Look
In 330 B.C., the Greek philosopher Aristotle gave a lecture that might apply here. He said that by observing a person walking, he could tell something essential about that person's character. Aristotle insisted that the di-

rection of one's gaze was tied to one's perspective on life. The person who looks downward most of the time is caught up with the past. His or her identity rests largely on tradition or past performance or the norms set down by previous generations.

The person who looks straight ahead was Aristotle's favorite. This one, he said, has a balanced view of things, able to take in the short vision as well as the panorama of the sky and horizon. This person, according to Aristotle, lives in the present fully, while being shaped by both past and future.

And then there is the dreamer, the visionary, the prophet. Aristotle didn't see much of a present life for those who only gaze toward the sky as they walk. But there is something deeply wonderful about them, and their presence is truly necessary for the rest of society. They may not be fully in touch with this world, but they have the uncanny ability to interpret all the grays of life under the spellbinding brilliance of future resolution. They tell fairy tales. They speak in parables. They use the language of Psalm 112.

You and I agree that life is more than fairy tales. And we may search a long time before we find a person for whom Psalm 112 seems fully to apply in this gray world of ours.

But poorer would be our lives if we didn't see these verses written across the sky.

MEDITATION 113

A Friend in High Places

---

*The LORD is exalted over the nations. . . . He raises the poor
from the dust and lifts up the needy from the ash heap.*
—Psalm 113:4, 7

Years ago, when our church missions board asked us to go to Nigeria, there was some question of whether we would be able to obtain the necessary visas. Nigeria was placing quotas on the number of missionaries that could enter. But there were some "friends of the church" in high places in Ottawa who made contact with the Nigerian officials, and in a very short while our papers were signed and sealed, and we were on our way. We were thankful for our unknown friends in high places.

Listen to the Cry
While we were in Nigeria, the economy went sour. In fact, it skidded sharply into recession. Certain food supplies became very scarce, including milk. Our youngest daughter was born during those days, and when we most needed milk powder, we could least find it. Suddenly the news came down on the radio: one of our mission personnel who had strong business ties in the Netherlands had managed to find a way to bring in a large supply of powdered milk. What a blessing to have a "friend in high places" at a time like that!

Many times during the Nigerian chapter of our lives we felt immediate and pressing needs that so seldom trouble us in North America. And it was during those days that we knew more powerfully the cry of millions in our world for a "friend in high places": someone to care, someone to know of troubles and miseries, someone to hear the whimpered cry in the night, someone to right the wrongs and open the prison doors and mend the wounds and feed the children.

Repertoire of Faith
Into that stumbling of despair comes the grand shout of Psalm 113: Look toward the heavens! The Lord is exalted over all the nations. You have a friend in high places. And the helplessness that now grips your soul will unravel till a song of praise erupts from your lips.

Sometimes God works it out in time. And sometimes it takes him till eternity. That's why misery often walks the path of life with us.

But praise is the announcement of faith. And even when we feel it least, it must become part of the repertoire of our souls, or we fade as those who have no hope. If, indeed, we have a "friend in high places," then life begins as Psalm 113 begins and ends on that note too: "Praise the LORD!" The dark time in between may call forth many other tunes, but they are not the first nor the last. Neither are they the best.

The Best of Us

Said Sir Edward Elgar when he finished *The Dream of Gerontius,* "When you remember me, remember me for this. This is my best. This is what my life is about."

So it is with us. "The LORD is exalted over the nations. . . . He lifts the needy from the ash heap. Praise the LORD." This is the best of us. And for this song, future generations will remember us.

Dominion

Judah became God's sanctuary, Israel his dominion.
—Psalm 114:2

Prior to 1939, each of the British Commonwealth countries was known as a "dominion." Record books throughout the nineteenth century contain no formal definition of that term, but apparently there was a general consensus as to what it meant. Canada's Sir John MacDonald called attention to it in his "Dominion Day" speech of 1867. With Nova Scotia, New Brunswick, and the Canadas (Ontario and Quebec) gathered into a larger political unit by the British North America Act, MacDonald proclaimed Canada a dominion among the possessions of God Almighty, under the protection of the British Commonwealth. He alluded to Psalm 114:2 as his guiding metaphor. God ruled, England explored and protected, and Canada stretched out as dominion.

Autonomous Communities
Of course, not everyone had such a theocratic understanding of the term. In 1926 a British Imperial Conference determined officially that dominions were "autonomous communities within the British Empire, equal in status . . . united by a common allegiance to the Crown." That definition includes less theology and more politicking.

Not surprisingly, in 1982, when the Constitution of Canada was patriated, "dominion" went out the window. Canada "grew up," so to speak, and became only one among several other independent distant Commonwealth relatives. But "something's lost, and something's gained," as the song puts it, in the shift. A newly flashing self-identity superseded the older and more romantic sense of "dominion"; no longer was Canada a realm of great importance called into being by an even higher power; no more was Canada a territory participating in the larger mosaic of things yet unfolding under the benevolence of grander global rule. Instead, Canada was simply an independent country—and Canadians' attitude became "don't bother us and we won't bother you." Our eyes turned to ourselves.

Ho-Hum Home-Rule

Unfortunately, nations self-contained, just like persons self-possessed, are left to wonder why so little good happens within them. Why do difficult hills grow into solid mountains of problems? Why do trickling waters of emotion overflow in violent torrents of passion?

Perhaps, as the psalmist puts it in Psalm 114, it's because we need to be owned in order to find a purpose. When Israel was created by God's covenant love, she began to find a place in the world. When the earth felt the rule of Yahweh through the movements and monuments of the Hebrews, mountains of difficulty danced away to the tune of temple worship. When the descendants of Jacob gained a divine identity, the storming waters parted for them and afforded them passage into their inheritance.

Obviously we don't expect any nation today, including the modern state of Israel, to write Psalm 114 into its constitution. But we're the poorer for giving up the richness of divine dominion in favor of home-rule.

Living Among the Living

---

*It is not the dead who praise the LORD, those who go down to
silence; it is we who extol the LORD, both now and forever.*
—*Psalm 115:17-18*

When archaeologists first began their investigations of ancient Roman
cemeteries, they noticed that one inscription occurred over and over
again. It was actually a series of seven letters: N F F N S N C.

What did those letters mean? What did they stand for? Why did the
Romans write them on so many graves? The researchers couldn't figure it
out at first.

But then they came to another stone that had the message of those letters inscribed in full. They were the first letters of a series of words: *Non
fui. Fui. Non sum. Non Curo.*

Seven short Latin words. Translated, they mean: I was not. I was. I am
not. I don't care.

Creed of the Dead

Can you imagine an ancient Roman funeral service? Here's a daughter
who lays her father to rest. Over his cold, lifeless body she places that
message: I was not. I was. I am not. I don't care. Could that be the message you would wish to speak from beyond the grave?

Or here's a husband who buries his wife. I was not. I was. I am not. I
don't care. Can that creed be the meaning of all her years with him? You
know that can't be the final word.

The cry of the psalmist in Psalm 115 comes from the edge of the tomb.
He needs to know that God is the God of the living, and that the epi-
taphs the nations wish to scatter through the cemeteries of this world are
not the true creed of our destinies. In life there must be purpose and
meaning. And in death there must be at least a remembrance of the dead
in succeeding generations by those who carry on the flame of godliness.

Easter Shadows

The psalmist doesn't seem to have a clear concept of life after death. That
would have to wait for the brilliance of Easter. But of this he was certain:
if God was worth any worship, he had to be the God of the living, the
God who brought life, fostered life, encouraged life, deepened life, blessed

life, made life, sustained life. Otherwise the dumb trinkets of the nations were satisfactory bedfellows, and the sleep of death was no different than the zombie walk of life.

Someone once put it this way. Suppose you have a magnificent house filled with the richest of treasure. And suppose that your young child runs through the hallways of that house in laughter and play. Then suppose that a fire breaks out in the basement—flames eat the curtains, smoke billows from room to room, heat melts the plaster. You have to make a choice: what will you save?

Will you grab for the paintings on the walls, leaving your child to die? Will you reach for the papers in the safe and not be overcome by the wails of your little son? Will you collect the jewelry from your bedroom, rushing past the offspring of your very body? If you should choose to keep the house and lose the child, we'd call you wicked or insane.

Our Best Treasure

So it is in this universe. Do the rocks stand while the children disappear? Do the mountains remain while the sons and daughters of God are cast aside? You know they don't. Easter says they don't. God won't let that happen. He didn't let it happen to his son, Jesus, and he won't let it happen to you either.

Alice Meynell once wrote a poem called "Christ in the Universe." It includes a line of great beauty: "Our wayside planet . . . bears as its chief treasure one forsaken grave."

Can you see it? The stone is still there in the garden, but the grave itself is abandoned. Not N F F N S N C. But Alpha and Omega, the Beginning and the End, the First and the Last, the Resurrection and the Life.

Remember the old saying: He who laughs last, laughs best. That is true indeed.

When Death Is Good

Precious in the sight of the LORD is the death of his saints.
—Psalm 116:13-14

Death wears many faces, most of them ugly. We see the tragic face of death in the slaughter of battlefields throughout history, in the wreckage of a sprawling scorched airliner, in the hideous killing of a murder victim. The painful face of death is visible on any cancer ward. And we feel the untimely face of death when children die before they've begun to touch the fullness of life. One grave marker puts it this way: If I am so quickly done for, What on earth was I begun for?

It's not without good reason that Death is called the enemy. "Death is a fearful thing," said Aristotle, "for it is the end." "Death takes no bribes," said Benjamin Franklin. Wordsworth put it this way: "A grave," he wrote, "is a tranquilizing object."

A Friendly Face
Still, there are times when Death wears the face of a friend. The lyrics of one song speak of the negative side of life: "It's the soul afraid of dying that never learns to live." But what of those blest souls who have never feared death because they have always lived life to the full? What of Simeon in the temple at Jesus' infancy? He faces death with joy because he's lived life to the full.

Sometimes Death can be a welcome friend when pain and illness make the days long and the nights endless. Moses wrote, in Psalm 90, that life could last for seventy or eighty years. But sometimes our times stretch well beyond that, and we come to the point of hoping that the next knock on the door is Death.

Wearing Out
Several years ago a pastor conducted a funeral for a woman who lived to be 107 years old. He told the gathering of a conversation they'd had shortly before her death. She'd loved that song "This Old House." As they sat talking, she pointed to the house of her body. "The roof's leaking," she said, pulling at the few thin wisps of silver hair that clung delicately to her wrinkled skull. "The underpinnin's shakin'," she said, lifting a wobbly leg carefully. "Telephone's out of order," she whispered, cracked

voice sliding out of a toothless mouth. "Even the windows are foggy," she said, looking out of hazy eyes.

When Death came knocking, she was ready to throw the door wide. As Paul put it in 2 Corinthians 5, our camping tents eventually wear out, and we long for the day when beautiful temples will house our spirits.

Goin' Home

Even more than that, though, Death comes as friend when it is a passageway into an even greater life. Jesus stood in the graveyard of his friend Lazarus and shouted, "I am the resurrection and the life. He who believes in me will live, even though he dies" (John 11:25). And that's why Death changes from an enemy into a friend.

Years ago, an elderly Black woman died in the South of the United States. At her funeral, James Weldon Johnson reflected on Psalm 116:15. He ended his message with a little poem, "Go Down, Dear," that he'd written for the occasion:

> And God said: Go down, Death, go down,
> Go down to Savannah, Georgia,
> Down in Yamacraw,
> And find Sister Caroline.
> She's borne the burden and heat of the day,
> She's labored long in my vineyard,
> And she's tired—
> She's weary.
> Go down, Death, and bring her to me.
> While we were watching round her bed,
> She turned her eyes and looked away,
> She saw what we couldn't see:
> She saw Old Death. She saw Old Death
> Coming like a falling star.
> But Death didn't frighten Sister Caroline;
> He looked to her like a welcome friend.
> And she whispered to us: I'm going home,
> And she smiled and closed her eyes.
> Weep not, weep not,
> She is not dead;
> She's resting in the bosom of Jesus.

That's when Death is good!

Praise

Praise the LORD.
—Psalm 117:2

Jascha Heifetz is one of the world's great violinists. When he gathers a violin into his arm and caresses it with a bow he can draw out melodies that speak and soar and sing and sadden. He's good. And he knows it.

Once when he hired a new secretary he said to the young man, "Now, you don't need to compliment me after every performance. If I play well, I know it myself. And if I don't, I shall only think less of you if you try to flatter me."

What's the Matter with You?
Eager to please, the young man held his tongue after each performance. No matter how beautiful the music, no matter how delightful the melodic display, no matter how moving the concert, he kept quiet as he tidied up after each show.

His silence was ended one night after Mr. Heifetz outdid himself with brilliance. This particular concert was more than spectacular; it was radiant. The glory of the music demanded praise.

Still, the dutiful young secretary, knowing his master's desires, kept quiet. Heifetz grew more and more upset, until he fairly shouted at the man: "What's the matter with you anyway? Don't you like music?"

It's the same way with us, isn't it? We need to express those things that move us deeply. And we must know that others feel the same way we do. Praise is the language of shared appreciation. It says as much about those who praise as it does about those who are praised. It tells of the values of our souls, and it speaks of the character of our hearts. To praise is to understand, to know, to appreciate, to find camaraderie, to deepen mutual delight.

Test of Faith
Remember Helen Keller? She was blind and deaf from her earliest years. When Helen was just a little girl and she'd first begun to speak with her hands, they brought the great preacher Phillips Brooks to her to teach her something about God. As he started to explain God to her with his talking fingers in her palm, little Helen got *so* excited.

She'd always known about God, she signed back, but until now she'd never known his name. How thankful she was to finally give expressions of praise to the God she'd always loved with her soul!

How well do you know God? The answer is found somewhere in your language of praise.

Building Material

The stone the builders rejected has become the capstone.
—Psalm 118:22

"The Philosophers' Stone." That's the title Christoph Wieland gave to his 1789 short story on the upside-down values of many in his society. The story tells how King Mark of Great Britain came to his throne at a very young age, and how he wasted the kingdom in the mad and rash pursuit of lavish extravagance. As his realm staggered under taxes, he realized his cash flow was limited. In desperation he dug up half the countryside looking for gold ore. But all he found was tin and copper.

Magic

Along came a strange man named Misfragmutosiris. With enchanting stories about magical secrets, he bewitched the king into a foolish conspiracy. Misfragmutosiris claimed he knew a spell for creating a "philosophers' stone." If the king would supply him with all the precious gems from his royal jewelry, Misfragmutosiris could use them to make a philosophers' stone that would then transform the tin and copper ore into gold.

Of course, Misfragmutosiris was a charlatan and his promises a charade. Wieland spins a delightful yarn about the manner in which King Mark regains his senses. The story ends with Mark and his queen Mabille reunited after some supernatural experiences. Two "divine beings" offer them a different treasure, the "philosophers' stone" from heaven.

Higher Power

What could that be? Interestingly, Christoph Wieland began his career as a student of theology. And in "The Philosophers' Stone," Wieland brings Mark and Mabille full circle to the love that first established their relationship, to the virtues of simplicity and freedom that marked their childhood, and to the devotion of divine benevolence that puts them in harmony with all creation. This is the true "philosophers' stone," they are told. They rejected it for a time in their sophisticated madness, but these angels of mercy have led them home.

Could it be that Christoph was thinking of Psalm 118:22? I suspect so. The psalmist tells of a frantic search for peace in a world of chaotic upset.

Was it one of David's sons who almost lost the throne when he strayed in bad political company? Was it a picture of wandering Israel finally finding herself again in one of the great festivals of deliverance? Was it those in Nehemiah's day who gathered divine strength amongst the muddle of stones torn down by their enemies and collected them together again into the temple of God?

Upon This Rock
Perhaps all of these. In each case, what once was tossed lightly aside by those looking for glittering gems to sustain fast living at last became a new treasure, a divine "philosophers' stone" that put lives back together.

No wonder Psalm 118 seemed an appropriate hymn for Jesus to sing with his disciples as they left the Last Supper (Matt. 26:30). Before the night was out, this Stone would be rejected as worthless by many.

But when the smoke of confusion melted away, and hungry souls looked beyond the wasted rubble to see the risen Christ, angels would tell the same tale that Wieland's divine messengers brought: "You've found the philosophers' stone in this wilderness" (see 1 Peter 2:4-10).

Wordsmith

Strengthen me according to your word.
—Psalm 119:28

Someone once asked Malcolm Muggeridge what epitaph he might like on his gravestone. Muggeridge paused for just a moment, and then, with a twinkle in his eye, replied: "He used words well!" That's how Muggeridge wanted to be remembered.

I like that idea. In an age of video and the visual, it speaks of human interaction, of communication, of the power of words to elevate the soul.

Words with Power

An old short story called "Wordsmith" tells of the coming of age of a young preacher. It describes him enjoying the sensation of words: "He rolled them off his tongue. He caressed them with his lips. He could feel the smoldering intensity of 'passion.' He trembled at the rumbling disquiet of 'mutter' and 'murmur.' His eyes grew misty at the thought of 'pride' and 'dignity' and 'honour.'"

Maybe that breed of speechmaker is vanishing. Still, as Rollo May pointed out in his most recent book, *The Cry for Myth*, what aches in the human heart is a longing for story, forged in the metal of language, that fashions for us identity and purpose.

To put it in Northrup Frye's phrase, "words with power" give us life. Frye took his theme from Jesus' teaching, as Luke refers to it in 4:32—"They were amazed at his teaching, because his message had authority." Surely there is something transcendent in the power of the word.

Echoes of Eternity

In the Hebrew language used by the poet in Psalm 119, the term *dabar* means both "word" and "deed." Words are never static records, ciphers on a page. They are alive with energy. A word must act or do something in order to be word. These verses are pages from a diary in which God's Word has become the creative energy by which he lives. He searches the alphabet from beginning to end (from Aleph to Taw) to find human terms to describe utterances unseen that have carried him along. The creative Word of God has been for him a boundary "law" of protection, a set of "statutes" that serve as pilot lights, "precepts" that create wisdom, "commands" that lead, and "promises" that draw toward the future. In short, the Word of God acts on him the way music operates on those magical little flowers you see in novelty stores: so long as there is sound, there is motion; so long as there is voice, there is identity; so long as there is Word, there is life.

One Final Word

Dr. Seuss (of children's books fame) once penned this verse:

> It has often been said
> there's so much to be read,
> you never can cram
> all those words in your head.

Any family that tries to use the Psalms for mealtime devotions knows how true that is when Psalm 119 comes up on the schedule. No child can rightly endure reading of "all those words."

Maybe that's why the last and greatest Word of God, the great Word-smith, became flesh and walked for a time with us. In him the "word" and the "deed" were one and the same thing. Truly, you could say of him: "He used words well."

Learning Your Limits

Too long I have lived among those who hate peace.
—Psalm 120:6

Every parent of young children can identify with this: A little boy was asked his name, and he replied, "John Don't."

Sometimes it seems that parents have only "no's" for their little ones. No, Sarah. You mustn't do that, Matthew. John, don't! It may sound harsh, but when we say "no" to our children it's often a matter of safety, a means of survival. We say it to keep them from falling out of a window or stepping out into a busy street or drinking poison.

Definition and Character

Adults need "no's" in their lives too. But for adults it's not always a matter of safety or survival. Usually it has more to do with self-definition. In order to truly say "yes" in life, we must also learn to say "no."

Think of it. If you can't say "no," then you lose the power to say "yes." If you are capable of doing anything, if there's nothing you wouldn't do, then you have no character. Character is something we define by drawing lines, by closing off possibilities, by saying, "I am this because I am not that. I cannot be that because I want to be this."

A Good "No"

That's really the point of the negatives in the Ten Commandments. God isn't trying to play the killjoy. He's dealing with us in grace. "Don't have any other gods before me," he says; "if you do, you'll miss the real thing your life is all about. Don't look for happiness in illicit sexual encounters; if you do, you'll miss the one greatest joy of your sexuality that you could find in troth. Don't speak an untruth, or you yourself will become a lie."

G. K. Chesterton put it marvelously. He said that art and morality have this in common: they know where to draw the line. That's definition. That's closing some things, and shutting other things out. Only when we draw lines can we develop some sense of character, some understanding of personality, some consciousness of identity.

Psalm 120 begins the pilgrimage of life there. "Woe to me," says the psalmist, for "I dwell in Meshech. Too long," he laments, I have lived "among the tents of Kedar." Meshech was thousands of kilometers from

Jerusalem, somewhere in southern Russia today. Kedar was a wandering tribe of Bedouin who moved around the desert sands of Arabia, always on the outskirts of community life, always hostile, always making scavenger raids on others.

The Grace of Limits

These were places and peoples that knew no limits. And one day the psalmist wakes up to the fact that his limits are gone too. He's said "yes" to everything and has suddenly become a slave of fad and fashion. He doesn't even know who he is anymore.

That's when the cry of desperation erupts from his lips: "Save me, O LORD" (v. 2). Grace works within limits: "No" to this and "yes" to that. No pilgrim will ever crawl to the road toward the kingdom of God until she or he learns the power of the word "no," a word that defines the beauty of God's great "yes."

The Hill Beyond the Hills

I lift up my eyes to the hills.
—*Psalm 121:1*

During the summer of 1978 I went on a study trip to Israel. We combed the lands of the Bible, reading both scriptural records and other historical studies. That summer the writings of Flavius Josephus (*Antiquities, The Wars of the Jews*) came alive for me.

Jerusalem Bound

But no part of Palestine is as fascinating as Jerusalem. Today you can marvel at the beauty of the city from a variety of perspectives. If you drive up the "miracle road" from Tel Aviv, rusted hulks of truck bodies memorialize the route and serve as sentinels guiding you into a modern, bustling metropolis. This is the way through the hilly wilderness pushed up in a matter of days by the freedom fighters in 1947 as they struggled to supply and fortify the Jewish citizens of Jerusalem during the first modern Arab-Israeli conflict.

A second way to come into Jerusalem is from the north, wandering down the ridge road that runs high on the "backbone" of Palestine's mountainous midsection. Jerusalem sort of grows around you from that vantage point, beginning some distance out as you pass through one small Arab village after another. This is not Jerusalem's flattering side. It's a bit like wandering slowly into a mega-city somewhere in the world by way of old industrial zones and miles of slums.

A third way into Jerusalem rises sharply from the Dead Sea and Jericho, peaking at the Mount of Olives. Suddenly the road tilts down, displaying all of the glory of Old Jerusalem before you in a breathtaking panorama. This was the route of Jesus on Palm Sunday. No scene of Jerusalem is more striking today: whitewashed limestone buildings shining in the sun, carrying along in shimmering splendor the blue tiles and golden crown of the Dome of the Rock atop the ancient temple platform.

Through the Hills

Then there is the fourth entrance to Jerusalem. It's the one my professor took some of us on one warm Israeli afternoon. We walked down into the southern wilderness, first, the wilderness of Judea, the wilderness of Jesus' temptations, the wilderness of barren wastes. Jerusalem, from that direction, is hidden among the hills. Every hill is a hill of fear. You are surrounded by "Is": *Isolation*—here you are really alone, shut off from all other people and communities. *Insignificance*—mounds of ancient rock tower as if in disdain of your tiny nothingness. *Insecurity*—the mountains house evil spirits, and the caves on the hillsides are home to bandits and robbers who slip out at night to slit your throat and steal your bags. *Inability*—the hills block your path at every turn; they taunt you to give up your foolish journey.

But every fifteen minutes, as we climbed back toward Jerusalem, my professor had us sit for a rest break. He pulled out his pocket Bible and read us, one by one, the Psalms of Ascents, the Pilgrim Songs, the Songs of the Road. First was Psalm 120, the cry from the bottom.

On to Mount Zion

Then came Psalm 121: "I lift up my eyes to the hills." He needed to say little to us of the gripping fear in those words. We felt it clamoring all around us. What an awesome testimony to make then, as the psalmist went on: "Where does my help come from?" Certainly not from these hills, these foreboding hills, these angry hills, these oppressive and frightening hills. No, "my help comes from the LORD, the Maker of heaven and earth."

And then explodes the doxology that sustains the pilgrim till the final hill comes into view, the hill of Mount Zion: "The Lord watches over you. . . . The Lord will not let your foot slip. . . . The Lord will keep you from harm."

Many roads lead to Jerusalem. But only this one reminds you of what the pilgrimage is really all about.

City Planning

Jerusalem is built like a city that is closely compacted together.
—Psalm 122:3

A couple of years ago *Saturday Night* magazine carried an interesting story about the layout of major cities in our world. Some spread and sprawl, some creep and crawl, and some rise ever higher to the skies.

Great Cities
"What makes a city great?" the author asks. The answer, it seems, has much to do with planning. Paris is great, he says, because it has a heart. The cathedral of Notre Dame stands gracefully proud on the Ile Saint-Louis, beckoning the rest of the city to gather round her like a brood hen.

Washington, D.C., is great too. Here the French engineer Pierre-Charles L'Enfant designed a city that would capture the vibrancy of the young United States of America. Not the church, but the halls of government would take center spot, with all of the rest of the city radiating outward from "the Mall." L'Enfant's vision was enormous for the time; it helped to create the myth that would become the nation.

An "Also-Ran"?
So, too, was David's vision for Jerusalem. The little city conquered by David early in his kingly career was barely more than a hillside village that happened to have great defenses. David saw its potential, somehow, and claimed it for his royal seat.

And then he did a surprising thing. Other kings would have immediately planted their palaces at the topmost heights of the city ("king on the mountain," you know), but David reserved that spot for another building. In fact, he spent most of his four decades in power planning for this other structure and collecting materials for its eventual erection. That building, of course, was the temple of God in Jerusalem.

It was left to Solomon to make the dream come to reality. And when he finally dedicated the temple after seven years of meticulous construction, it became the purpose for Jerusalem's existence. This was the palace of the true king of Israel—the God of heaven and earth.

So when the pilgrims of ancient Israel wended their way toward Jerusalem, they couldn't wait to see this great city, this city of importance, this city with heart. What greatness? And what importance? And what heart?

The City with the Heavenly Heart

In 1891, Scottish professor George Adam Smith traveled to Palestine to find out. Frankly, he was disappointed. Somehow Jerusalem didn't match up to all the promotional hype or tourist tripe. Until he read again his Bible. And then he wrote the following:

> [Judea] has no harbours, no river, no trunk-road, no convenient market for the nations on either side. In their commerce with each other these pass by Judea, finding their emporiums in the cities of Philistia, or, as of old, at Petra and Bozrah on the east side of the Jordan. Gaza has outdone Hebron as the port of the desert. Jerusalem is no match for Shechem in fertility or convenience of site. The whole plateau stands aloof, waterless, on the road to nowhere. There are none of the natural conditions of a great city.

> And yet it was here that She arose who, more than Athens and more than Rome, taught the nations civic justice, and gave her name to the ideal city men are ever striving to build on earth, to the City of God that shall one day descend from heaven—the New Jerusalem. For her builder was not Nature nor the wisdom of men, but on that secluded and barren site the Word of God, by her prophets, laid her eternal foundations in righteousness, and reared her walls in her people's faith in God.

> —*George Adam Smith,* The Historical Geography of the Holy Land, *London: Hodder and Stoughton, 1939*

With heart like that, how could Jerusalem's city planning fail?

The "Eyes" Have It

As the eyes of slaves look to the hand of their master, as the
eyes of a maid look to the hand of her mistress, so our eyes look
to the LORD our God, till he shows us his mercy.
—Psalm 123:2

Once when Henrik Ibsen, the Norwegian playwright, was traveling in Rome, he noticed a crowd of people gathered around a large red poster. They were talking rather excitedly among themselves about the message it announced, so he reached into his coat pocket for his eyeglasses. Only then did he realize that he'd left them back at his hotel.

So he turned to the fellow next to him. "Sir," he said, "could you please tell me what that sign says? I've forgotten my glasses."

"Sorry, Signore!" said the other, with a knowing look in his eyes. "I don't know how to read either."

Open the Windows
Eyes are marvelous windows. Jesus called them the lamp of the body. Emerson said that a person's eyes "indicate the antiquity of the soul." George Herbert spoke of the power of the eyes when he remarked that they "have one language everywhere."

That's the insight of the poet in Psalm 123 as well. How should we posture ourselves in prayer? Well, he says, remember the last time your slave bowed before you? Remember the trust, the searching, the readiness to help reflected in the eyes of your maid? Remember the dependence and submission you took for granted? If you do, then you're well on your way to finding the attitude of your soul when you approach God.

Choose the Target
Eyes need to be trained, of course. Moshe Dayan, the famous Israeli soldier and statesman, wore a trademark black eye patch over the eye that he'd damaged in combat. Once when he was speeding along like Jehu, Israeli police stopped him. He talked himself out of a fine by saying, "I have only one eye. What do you want me to watch—the speedometer or the road?"

His humor is true in this sense: we cannot focus everywhere. And where we decide to settle our eyes is as much determined by our hearts as it is by our heads.

So it is with prayer. The "eyes" have it. And they get it from the heart.

Find the Focus

One thing more. Glasses are a necessary evil for me. I can't get along without them. Our youngest daughter once told me I was lucky in that way because at night I take them off when I go to bed. She was sure I could never have bad dreams because without my glasses, I couldn't see the monsters chasing me. Isn't that interesting wisdom?

It's certainly true that we can't see what we don't bring clearly into focus. No servant will serve his or her master without keeping an eye on his location and circumstances and desires. We see what we want to see. And that we focus on.

But the opposite is also true. The last verses of Psalm 123 talk about troubles and enemies that have long produced anxiety and dread. Now, however, the psalmist expects them to go away. Why? Because they vanish in an instant, as if by magic? No. Rather because he changes his focus. He deliberately removes the glasses that forced him to gaze on them for too long. And then he finds his new focus on God in prayer.

The "eyes" have it. They find it. And they show it. How's your eyesight?

If . . .

If the LORD had not been on our side . . .
—Psalm 124:1

"If wishes were horses, then beggars would ride."

I still remember those lines from my childhood school days. There are so many of those "if" poems around. Remember these lines of Robert Browning?

> If thou must love me, let it be for naught
> Except love's sake only.

Or the way Shakespeare ended his play *As You Like It:*

> If it be true that 'good wine needs no bush,'
> 'tis true that a good play needs no epilogue.

Or Robert Burns's devotion to his true love:

> The desert were a paradise,
> If thou wert there, if thou wert there.

If: Regrets

"If" is a powerful word. Sometimes we use it to express regret. A young woman involved in an accident, with the blood of her child spilled around her in the car, cries: "If only I had been paying more attention!" A middle-aged businessman sobs at my desk, on his way to jail for a heinous crime: "If only I had thought about what I was doing!" One of our daughters mourns from her bedroom after a particularly difficult day that ended with some punishment: "I wish I didn't have to be naughty. If only I could be a better girl!"

What's gone is gone, though, and all the "if-ing" in the world won't make the past come back for another try.

If: Wishes

Sometimes we use the word "if" as a wish and a hope and a prayer. That's what Robert Burns did in the verse above. He could cope with a lot in life, he thought, if only his true love would be around to grace the day.

Or think of Rudyard Kipling's famous poem to his son:

If you can keep your head when all about you
Are losing theirs and blaming it on you,
If you can trust yourself when all men doubt you,
But make allowance for their doubting too;
If you can wait and not be tired by waiting,
Or being lied about, don't deal in lies,
Or being hated, don't give way to hating,
And yet don't look too good, nor talk too wise:
If you can dream—and not make dreams your master;
If you can think—and not make thoughts your aim;
If you can meet with Triumph and Disaster
And treat those two impostors just the same

If you can talk with crowds and keep your virtue,
Or walk with Kings—nor lose the common touch,
If neither foes nor loving friends can hurt you,
If all men count with you, but none too much;
If you can fill the unforgiving minute
With sixty seconds' worth of distance run,
Yours is the Earth and everything that's in it,
And—which is more—you'll be a Man, my son!

Beautiful, isn't it? You can guess the title: "If."

If: Testimonies

There's a third kind of "if" we speak as well. It's something of the "if-wish" but stronger. It's a kind of "if-testimony." We know where we are today because of what we've come through. We know what we are today because of where we've been. We know who we are today because of those who've loved us.

That's the "if" of Psalm 124. It begins with "if" and records a journey. And when it's ended, there's only one final thought: "Our help is in the name of the LORD, the Maker of heaven and earth."

No "ifs" about that.

Surrounded

As the mountains surround Jerusalem, so the LORD
surrounds his people both now and forevermore.
—Psalm 125:2

Five hundred years before Christ, the Greek philosopher Sophocles summed up the fears of our world in this pithy statement: "To the man who is afraid, everything rustles."

You can see examples of this picture all around. The story is told of a woman who came into a police station. She didn't approach the officer on duty. Instead, she took a seat in a corner of the lobby, pulled a book out of her handbag, and began to read. After a while the duty officer went over to her and asked if he could help her with something. "No, thanks!" she replied. "I only came down here because I'm reading this murder mystery, and it scares me so much that I wanted to finish it here, under police protection."

Surrounded by Enemies
Psalm 125 is the song of those who know fear firsthand. It's for those who feel the lump in the breast and hear the doctor's hesitant speculation. It's for those whose lives are suddenly grinding to a halt because of the economic recession and the loss of a job. It's for those who are struggling through the first year of university, and who can only see the dark clouds of exams billowing on the horizon. It's for children who hear things that go bump in the night, and for teens who walk on the edge of the "in" crowd, and for lovers who feel they can never meet the expectations of the other person, and for parents who sense their children slipping away from them, and for widows and widowers who don't know how they can carry on.

As the mountains of trouble surround the person in the depths of despair, so it is for those who fear. "To the person who is afraid, everything rustles."

Surrounded by Grace
Do you remember what chased the fear away when you were a child? When the dog barked at your heels, your father scooped you up into his arms and made you brave. When the bogeyman threatened from under your bed, the blankets surrounded you with their warmth. When hurts

and pains made going back to school difficult, your mother hugged you tightly in the embrace of her love.

So, says the psalmist, it is with us. Surrounded by evil and loss and hopelessness and enemies, only one thing can bring relief. Remember the story of Elisha and his servant in 2 Kings 6? The armies of Aram circled Elisha's house one day, threatening the both of them with death. Elisha's servant quaked in fear. But not so Elisha. "Why not?" asked his servant.

Elisha prayed that God might open his servant's eyes. And then he saw that the armies of Aram were surrounded by an even mightier army—the hosts of the Lord God Almighty, shining in their heavenly power and splendor.

We're surrounded by evil. But the evil that surrounds us is surrounded by an even greater power: the loving arms of a Father.

Laughter

Our mouths were filled with laughter . . .
—*Psalm 126:2*

Once, when a French diplomat had been appointed as ambassador to a distant nation, he asked for a last audience with then French president Charles deGaulle. "Monsieur le President," he exclaimed passionately, "I am filled with joy at my appointment!"

Mr. deGaulle's response was as decisive as a rapier thrust: "Sir! You are a career diplomat. Joy is an inappropriate emotion in your profession."

Inappropriate?

There have been times in religious history when a remark like that set the tone for the church as well. In her autobiography, Ellen Glasgow writes about her father, a lifetime elder in the Presbyterian church. She describes him as "full of rectitude" and "rigid with duty." From her vantage point as a young girl, "in his long life he never committed a pleasure." Can you picture him?

Someone once defined a certain branch of Christianity as being alive with "the haunting fear that someone, somewhere may be happy." And Alexander Cruden, famed Bible scholar of the eighteenth century, put on his best "Sunday face" when he declared that "to laugh is to be merry in a sinful manner."

Surprise

No one planned to laugh in the community where the psalmist of Psalm 126 lived. Picture a scene like that after a battle: a few destitute people are trying to carry on. The men have been led away as slaves, houses lie in ruins, animals have been slaughtered across the fields, and crops are wasting in decay. No one feels good. Though the children might sing "Happy Birthday," there's no twinkle in any eye. Those left behind struggle on, their energy gone.

But then one day, as the children drag a stick along a dusty road, as the elderly sit in front of broken-down houses, strangers appear on the horizon. All the villagers freeze in their tracks. It's like somebody hit the pause button on the VCR. Who is it now? Have the enemy armies returned to strike again?

The youngest child moves first. "Abba! Abba!" she cries. "Daddy! Daddy!"

And then the whole community is on the move. Cousins see faces they thought they'd forgotten. Wives shudder with overwhelming joy as they tuck unruly strands of hair into place and smooth worn and dirty dresses. A man too old to walk makes new creases on his face when he laughs a toothless grin.

The exiles have returned!

Do It Again, God!

Once you've learned to laugh, you can't give it up. Eugene O'Neill, in his delightful drama *Lazarus Laughed*, imagines what it must have been like for Lazarus of Bethany after Jesus called him from the tomb that day described in John's gospel, chapter 11. He pictures a man whose skin never fully recovered from the decay of death, who walks around white and scaly, who has to stay out of the hot sun. But he also portrays a man who has this incredible tendency to giggle as he strolls along, to burst out with laughter in the most embarrassing situations, to start a community joke that's as contagious as the plague.

How could someone who had been "surprised by joy," as Wordsworth named it and C. S. Lewis claimed it, ever think that life or religion is meant to be dull? Those who have once been touched by the resurrecting powers of God can never live a sourpuss faith again.

That's why Psalm 126 ends with a prayer. "You made us laugh once, God. Do it again!" Do it in the parched places of our lives. Do it through the tears of pain. Do it over the cries of death.

Those who think frowns are the mask of holiness will never understand, of course. But someday soon God will tickle them!

Home Building

Unless the LORD builds the house . . .
—Psalm 127:1

Homes come in all shapes and sizes. There's a house in Asheville, North Carolina, that boasts 250 rooms and lays claim to being the largest private home in the world. Or, if you live on the 110th story of the Sears Tower in Chicago, you can truly boast about living in the clouds.

Strange

Of course, if you're into the weird and wacky, there's the home of Mrs. Winchester in southern California. After her husband and her only child died early this century, Mrs. Winchester believed spirits were telling her that she should buy a particular seventeen-room house, then under construction, and that she would continue to live so long as she kept building it. She did manage to survive another thirty-eight years, dwelling in solitude as the construction continued on around her. But even the builders couldn't keep death from going in to visit her one night. Her house is now one of the strangest curiosities in the world.

Strong

But perhaps the most unusual story of house-building happened in Detroit. Henry Ford erected a marvelous home called "Fairlane" on the upper slopes of the River Rouge. It's a masterpiece of craftsmanship and artistic design. Ford had learned early in life that he could never really count on anyone else, so he spent an extra $200,000, already back in 1917, to put in his own electric power plant for the whole estate.

In all his years at Fairlane, the power plant served faithfully, lighting and heating his impressive home. Except for one time: in early April of 1947, torrential rains lashed the Detroit area. The River Rouge rose from its banks. And on the night of April 7, the floods entered the Fairlane boiler room, smothering the fires and causing the steam pressure to drop. That night the lights went out at Fairlane. And that's the night that Henry Ford died in his bed at the age of eighty-seven.

Striking

That story is something like a parable. Here was a man who put North America on wheels, who invented one gadget after another to make life less tedious and more enjoyable, who helped to usher in our modern technological society. Here was a staunchly independent man, one who took care of himself and didn't owe anybody anything. Here was a man who even managed to separate his wiring grid from that of the public utilities. And the very night he dies, forces beyond his control snatch away his source of power!

It reminds me of Jesus' parable about a rich man who built bigger barns. Wealth, said Jesus, was not the issue. Self-sufficiency was. We can each build our own houses, rich or poor, luxurious or humble, extravagant or miserly; but only love can turn a house into a home.

And love is the business of the greatest Builder of all time.

The Good Life

Blessings and prosperity will be yours.
—Psalm 128:2

When Ryan Barbarisi was in fifth grade at Grace Community Christian School in Tempe, Arizona, his teacher asked each member of his class to finish this sentence—"I would be rich if . . . "—and then to draw a picture of what he or she was thinking about. Here's what Ryan wrote: "I would be rich if I had enough money to buy a mansion and a red Ferrari. I would like to have these things because if I had a mansion, I would have a good life. If I had a Ferrari, I would burn up the streets."

Blueprint?
I've heard that song and dance before, and so have you. In fact, we've both heard it from people much older than Ryan. I've heard words of that sort coming out of my own mouth. Maybe you have too. We're all looking for the "good life." That's the human quest.

Well, then, what is the "good life"? Some might point to Psalm 128 as God's answer to that, and so it is. But if you try to read this psalm as a blueprint for the "good life," there are some gaping holes. For one thing, singles might find the family talk quite embarrassing or rather annoying. Those who were widowed early in life might feel harshly judged. And those who've given up this picture of the "good life" for mission service under difficult conditions in far-away places might begin to feel a bit dismayed at the image of a successful middle-class farmer or businessman that the psalm calls to mind.

Details
On the other hand, if you read through Psalm 128 a few times, a number of things might be distilled. For one thing, the picture of the good life here has a lot to do with relationships. Relationships make life meaningful, and tragic is the lot of those who walk alone. The psalmist points to meaningful *family* relationships, but the sense is that *all* quality human relationships are at the heart of life. Our doctrine of the Trinity is all about that, in fact. I remember when I first came to realize that the doctrine of the Trinity is more than some intellectual game of mad theological conjuring; in fact, it means that there is a community of persons who stand at

the center of all that exists in this universe. Can you see it? At the heart of reality is not some impersonal power, but a fellowship of three who wish to share their fellowship with others. That's what the "good life" is all about.

Second, a sense of dependency sifts from Psalm 128. "Blessed are all who fear the LORD" (v. 1), not merely those who have the red Ferrari or the mansion on the hill. Blessed are those who know they can't make it on their own and realize it early enough in life. Blessed are those who find power in weakness, who find strength in inability, who are led to depend on others and on God through the limitations of their own skills.

Happy Days

Third, there's a great urgency of hope in the closing lines of the Psalm. The future beckons, and it's a good future because it's full of the promises of God. It is linked to the fortunes of "Zion." In other words, there's a sense that our hope is tied, not to our own ability to make it, but to God's own character and identity. If there's a "good life," then it is "God's Life" or it's nothing at all.

Maybe someday I'll get a red Ferrari. I doubt it, but who knows? If it should ever happen, it will only be an extension of the "good life" I know now, and not the source of it.

True Grit

They have greatly oppressed me from my youth, but they have not gained the victory over me.
—Psalm 129:2

Sometimes the circumstances of our lives take more than a little guts to endure. John Bartel, out in British Columbia's Fraser Valley, knows that. It was silage time some years ago, and John was at the blower, pumping the chopped alfalfa into the silo. The conveyor belt stopped suddenly, jammed by a chunk of the fresh cuttings. Without a thought, young John jumped on the machine and forced the wad into the blower with his foot. Before he knew what was happening, there was a tug on his leg, and his foot went up the pipes with the silage.

John prayed and pulled and fell backward onto the ground. He struggled to loosen his belt and then used it around his leg to stop some of the bleeding. He dragged himself along the ground to the milking parlor and found the telephone and called for help.

Courage

Later, when he was alone in the hospital, he wished that he had died. He even thought of suicide. What good was living now, if you could even call it that? But then one day he met a man with no legs. That man had more courage than he. John searched his Bible till he found the motto for his life: "I can do all things through Christ who strengthens me!"

Today John is back on the farm. He's married and has three children. He milks seventy cows. He skies and swims, and does hundreds of things that people with two legs wouldn't even dream of doing.

He knows the sentiment of the psalmist in Psalm 129—"they have not gained the victory over me."

Brooding

That's part of Psalm 129. Guts and courage, fostered by deep faith and a sense that God will deliver and strengthen. But Psalm 129 has another side that's a lot darker. Most of the turbulence that it speaks of has to do with human cruelty: enemies, injustice, painful relationships, oppression. That kind of hurt can go a lot deeper than the tragic circumstances that otherwise fall on us.

And those dark times can produce the moody brooding of the last half of Psalm 129. It's angry and almost spiteful. And it's not the kind of song we like to equate with New Testament Christianity: May those who hate me be shamed and hurt and pained and die and not be blessed by God.

Out of Date?

Can we sing Psalm 129 today? Certainly the first half is the victory shout of those who have found the courage to endure hardships through their faith in God's unshakable care. That's true grit.

But maybe we need to sing the second half of the psalm as well, when injustices prevail too long, when diseases won't die, when children are abused, and when societies dehumanize and enslave and oppress those who are down and out.

If that restlessness for deliverance ever leaves us, we'll forget what gives courage to life, and where true grit comes from: "But the LORD is righteous; he has cut me free from the cords of the wicked" (v. 4).

Waiting

I wait for the LORD, my soul waits, and in his
word I put my hope.
—Psalm 130:5

The songwriter of Psalm 130 begins in a spot we don't like: "Out of the depths I cry. . . . " Have you ever been there with him—a place where there are no buttons to press, no credit cards to hand over, no magical fingers to snap?

It's the story of Job all over again. God was rather proud of Job, you know; he even bragged about Job to the devil himself: "Have you seen my servant Job? Now there's a man whose heart you'll never own."

Satan wasn't so sure. He'd cracked a lot of tough nuts in his day, and he took on Job as a special challenge. "Sure Job loves you," he said to God, "but that's because you've bought his soul. You give him everything he wants. Why shouldn't he serve you? Even I would do that."

"Alright," says God. "Take it all away from him, and see what happens. Just don't harm him personally."

So Satan does his thing. Job loses everything: his children, his flocks, his buildings, his servants. He's as poor as a church mouse. But *still* he loves God. *Still* he serves the Lord!

The Silence of God
The wagering in heaven heats up. Satan gets another shot at Job. He touches Job's body so that he's wracked with pain. And he touches Job's mind so that he can no longer clearly hear God's whisper of love.

Job is all alone. His wife calls him stupid, his friends call him a liar and a sinner, and the world calls him nothing.

Here's Job. But where is God?

Where is God? That's the hardest challenge in life. Some time ago I sat with a mother in University Hospital. We prayed for the life of her daughter. She had no peace that God was there. And then, after we prayed for God's healing, her daughter died anyway. Where was God?

The Armenians are one of the oldest civilizations in the world. They turned to Christ early in the history of the Church. Then the Turks slaughtered them and drove the remnants like orphans off the map. Where was God?

The question of Job is the question of every generation: "Where are you, God?" Sometimes the only answer is silence. The promises of Scripture become dead fantasies. The Holy Spirit leaves and the heart grows chilly. The newspapers report events that make no sense. Where is God?

Then Satan looks down from heaven with glee. He knows he's got Job now. He knows we'll never get out of this one. He knows the cards in his hand are the winning draw. Can faith remain when God is silent? Can trust carry on when there seems to be no one at the other end of the line?

"No!" shouts Satan.

But Satan doesn't have the last word.

Patience

"Yes!" whispers Job. "Even though I can't see him, even though I don't understand what's happened to him, even though every human wisdom tells me he's not there, I know that my Redeemer lives. And with these eyes I shall see him."

That's the deepest level of patience in the human spirit. That's the waiting of Psalm 130. In the New Testament, the apostle James would call it "perseverance." We love God, not because of what we get out of it, but because it's the only way life makes sense. We trust in God, not because we always feel the wonder of his presence, but because, even in his absence, there is nowhere else to turn.

That's the waiting of Psalm 130. You can't explain it. Those of us who have been there can never really share the experience with others. We may talk about it later, when God seems closer again, but it's the awful agony of faith when we stand undressed and alone.

Psalm 130 doesn't explain the silence of God. But take it from one who's been there: no night is endless. And those who know the meaning of life wait for the morning.

Listen Slowly

I have stilled and quieted my soul. . . .
—*Psalm 131:2*

"All the evils of life," said Pascal, "have fallen upon us because men will not sit alone quietly in a room." Do you think he had a point?

Chuck Swindoll tells of the time that he had been "caught in the undertow of too many commitments in too few days." He says he reacted the way most of us do: by snapping at his wife and children, choking down his food at mealtimes, forcing down irritations when people interrupted his over-scheduled schedule.

Speed Demon

But the worst of it was that everything around him suddenly had to catch up to his speed. If his daughter wanted to talk with him, he danced impatiently till she blurted out quickly what she had to say. One evening, as he was rushing out the door, his youngest daughter, Colleen, caught him by surprise. Something important had happened to her at school, and she sort of yelled out to him as he breezed by: "Daddy-I-wanna-tell-you-somethin'- and-I'll-tell-you-really-fast- . . . "

Suddenly, Chuck realized her frustration and stopped for a moment. "Honey," he said, "you can tell me. . . . And you don't have to tell me really fast. . . . Just say it slowly."

Her response cut deeply. "Then," she said, "*listen* slowly!"

Into the Quiet

Listen slowly!

That's not a bad command to remember now and again! Rupert Brooke once wrote a powerful poem about catching the meaning of life in the silence, and losing it again in the banging of noisiness. He said:

> Safe in the magic of my woods
> I lay, and watched the dying light.
> Faint in the pale high solitudes,
> And washed with rain and veiled by night.
> Silver and blue and green were showing.
> And dark woods grew darker still;

And birds were hushed; and peace was growing;
And quietness crept up the hill. . . .

In that moment, Brooke says, he felt all his puzzlement unfold, as God seemed about to speak to him the key to the mysteries of life. He knew, as he lay there, that in the next moments the meaning of his existence and the depth of his love for one special person would whisper out to him.

Crash!

"And suddenly," he goes on, "there was an uproar in my woods." Who should it be but his love, "crashing and laughing and blindly going," stomping with her "ignorant feet," dragging the small creatures of the forest to destruction with her "swishing dress," and "profaning the solitudes" with her voice.

"The spell was broken," says Brooke, "the key denied me." His love prances around, "mouthing cheerful clear flat platitudes," and quacking trite noise till the anger welled inside him. "By God!" he thought to himself, "I wish—I wish that you were dead!"

Strong language, that. And strong sentiments. But maybe we, in our noisy world, need to be moved once in a while to covet the silence of Psalm 131. Does grace always find us in the crowded business of life? Is there no urge within to capture the meaning of our souls again in silence?

Sabbath

Leslie Weatherhead once preached a sermon called "The Significance of Silence." "There are two ways of getting through life," he said, "and I think we must decide which we shall follow. . . . The first way is to stop thinking. The second way is to stop and think."

Many of us, he said, try the first way. We fill up every hour with rushing, with noise, with radios and television, with action and reaction. There is no silence, and therefore there is no real thought.

But, he said, there are some who long for Sabbath. And Sabbath, that old Hebrew word, means to stop doing, to find silence, to tune one's heart, to commune with God. Those who long for Sabbath, he said, find more than just rest. They find themselves. They find the immensity of creation. And they find God.

Maybe this is the day we ought to read Psalm 131 twelve times, once each hour, and then, in between, learn again what it means to "listen slowly."

Remember David

O LORD, remember David and all the hardships he endured.
—Psalm 132:1

A Texas oilman was showing his Canadian cousin around. In true Texas style, he exaggerated everything about his homeland. "We've got the biggest oil fields in the world right here in Texas," he swaggered. "And we've got the biggest ranches with the biggest cattle anywhere. And our cities are the grandest, and our . . . " The list went on and on. Everything in Texas was bigger than anywhere else.

Even though he knew it couldn't be true, the Canadian cousin was beginning to think there was some truth to the oilman's boasts by the time they stopped for lunch. Texas *was* incredible! They walked into the biggest restaurant he'd ever seen. When the coffee came, it was served in cups the size of soup bowls. His hamburger looked more like a T-bone steak stuck in the middle of a loaf of bread. He couldn't swallow down more than half of all the food on his oversized platter.

Badly in need of using the washroom, he asked for directions and was told to go down a hallway, then turn right. But he was more than a little overwhelmed, and at the end of the hallway he turned left instead of right. He opened the door and fell right into the swimming pool. In the muddle of his mind, overwhelmed by Texas, all he could shout was: "Don't flush!"

Bigger Is Better
Texans aren't the only ones to boast. In fact, we're all prone to it now and again. We know that sometimes "small is beautiful," but we also know that bigger can be better. Remember, for instance, when you were taking piano lessons, and there were days when you didn't want to practice? You kept asking, "Is it a half-hour yet?" You wanted to know how little you had to do before you could leave the keys. But if you want to become a great pianist, can you imagine saying, "How little music do I have to know?"

Or put it this way: when you look for a friend, what do you think of a person who says to you, "Well, how little will you ask of me if I'm going to be your friend?"

Or picture a couple standing at the front of a church. She's wearing white; he's got his penguin suit on. She turns to him and says, "I'll do as little as I can, Gustave, to be your wife. Just let me know what the minimum requirements are."

You know it's wrong. Some things only live when they become bigger and bigger in our lives. Bigger is better when it comes to music. Bigger is better when it comes to friendship. And bigger is better when it comes to love.

Religion Too?

But what of religion? I remember a fellow who sat in my study years ago. He had his eye on a young woman in our church, and he wanted to impress her. He knew she was a Christian, so he wanted to become one too. "What do I have to do?" he asked me. "What's the minimum requirement before you'll let me become a member?"

He wanted to know how small his religion could be. He wanted to know how little he could get by with and still be called a Christian. The less it cost him, the more he would appreciate it.

Remember David

We may laugh about that, or shake our heads; but perhaps that young man was more honest than we sometimes are. We may not say it, but there are times when we live that way. A religion of the minimums.

And then we read Psalm 132. "Remember David. . . . " Why? Because David didn't live a small religion. Because David opened his heart, he poured out his soul, he gave it all he had, he emptied himself in service. When it came to his relationship with God, David only had one testimony: Bigger is better.

God rewarded David's devotion, but you know that that's not why he gave his heart to his Lord. The temple, the Davidic kingdom, the strength of Israel—to call those blessings a payoff would cheapen everything about David. Tribute is nice, but devotion is bigger. That's why God should remember David. That's why we should too.

Unity

*How good and pleasant it is when
brothers live together in unity!*
—*Psalm 133:1*

This is a true story. It happened only a short while ago, but it has happened again and again in similar ways over the course of time. A family had not been attending worship services at a particular church for a number of years. The elders of the church had tried, with varying degrees of success, to maintain contact with the family and provide pastoral encouragement.

Finally a new elder, younger and more forthright than some, said to the couple, "Look, it doesn't sound to me like you really want any contact with us. Are we just kidding ourselves? Do you want to be part of this church or not?"

Then they admitted it. There was a sense of some need for spiritual attachments, yes. They certainly weren't non-Christians. And, no, they hadn't given up their faith. But it was true that they didn't want contact from this church again.

Root Cause
Why? What was behind it all? The elder probed a little deeper.

To tell you the truth, they said, it has to do with our parents. Every Sunday after we got married, we'd go to one home and then the other for coffee or a meal. We'd sit around one coffee table and we'd hear all the criticisms of the church: the sermon was no good, the minister wasn't doing his job, theological controversies were dividing the church. Then we'd go to the other parental home and the conversation around the meal table would be the same: who was doing what to whom, how the church was no good, how the consistory and the classis and the synod were making all those wrong decisions.

We finally got sick of it. We haven't left God; he hasn't left us. But we really don't want to ruin our spirituality anymore by going to that church.

Heresy vs. Hypocrisy
Sound familiar? Sometimes, perhaps even many times, to be sure, people are looking for excuses, and comments like these come off as rather hypo-

critical. But not always. In fact, a recent speaker at a church development workshop said that there is a significant dividing line through our North American society: those who were born in the 1940s and earlier tend to be more concerned about *heresy* than they are about *hypocrisy*, while those born after 1950 tend to sit easily with persons whose theological stripe is slightly different, but they can't stomach hypocritical double-talk or two-faced living.

It has to do, he said, with the intermingling of cultures and societies and the exploding population of our post-World War II era. If he's right, there may be a reason for the lack of denominational loyalty that seems to mushroom every year. People won't stick with something that talks theology but lives criticism and controversy.

Getting Back to Basics

Is the new trend a lower form of spirituality than the staunch devotion to church structures in past eras? Some might think so. But it's hard to square critical and divisive spirits with true godliness when you look at the Bible. David pictures unity as the prime quality of saintliness in Psalm 133. He points to the anointing of the priests as a teaching image: the oil of God symbolizing his Spirit of leadership is poured only on the head. But it then runs down over the entire person, beard, robe, and all, touching every quarter with its same empowering essence. Where there is one Spirit of anointing, there is one unity of identity and purpose.

There's where the blessing of the Lord is, says David. Jesus, of course, says the same thing (John 14-17). Maybe it's time we catch up with some old-fashioned spirituality like that once again. Who knows? The souls we bring back to the church may be those of our own children!

Culmination

May the LORD, the Maker of heaven and earth,
bless you from Zion.
—Psalm 134:3

Do you remember the song that Helen Reddy made popular years ago, "Delta Dawn"? It tells the story of a forty-one-year-old woman who lives in Brownsville, Texas. She spends her days wandering around the downtown streets, carrying a suitcase and waiting for "a mysterious dark-haired man" who loved her once and promised to return to make her his bride. I can see her in my mind's eye wearing a rumpled wedding dress, a crazy glint in her stare, muttering to herself, peering into the faces of the men she meets, looking for her lost lover. But he never comes.

Sad Song
The crowds on the streets of Brownsville stop and shake their heads. They laugh a little, and they raise that sad, sad chorus:

> Delta Dawn, what's that flower you have on?
> Could it be a faded rose from days gone by?
> And did I hear you say he was a-meetin' you here today
> To take you to his mansion in the sky?

It's a sad song, ominous in its overtones. The part that scares me, though, is this: sometimes that song seems to be a picture of what the church looks like in this society—a half-crazed bride pledged to a no-show husband, wandering around muttering to herself while the world shakes its head in disbelief.

Did the peoples surrounding Israel three thousand years ago think that way about her? Can you see the pilgrims gathering at the temple on one of those high holidays like the Passover or the Day of Atonement? Here they come, singing the psalms of Ascents. Now they stand in the holy courts, and the choirs of Asaph chant these lines of Psalm 134 over them in blessing. Is it another version of "Delta Dawn," played out in tragic comedy?

Parallel Worlds

Some might think so. That's the strangeness of God's eternity and our time running parallel to one another. The road seems to go on forever for us, and it can be lived as if there is no "mysterious dark-haired man" who beckons us from worlds beyond.

But those who have stepped away from the road and peered over the brink of eternity know that there is much that joins the spiritual realms with our physical world. The road ahead may seem like an endless, godless pilgrimage, but it runs next to the greatest wonder possible for those with eyes to see.

In one of his novels, Charles Williams tells the story of Nancy. Most of her life she's stumbled down the road, safely asleep to things spiritual. Then one Christmas morning, out of a sense of duty, she attends a worship service at a tiny country church.

Time to Wake Up

The voice from the front announces the first hymn. Around her the pages flutter as the congregation stands with the choir to sing. The words begin, and Nancy mouths them with the rest:

> Christians, awake! Salute the happy morn
> Whereon the Savior of the world was born.

Suddenly Nancy wakes up. Her voice catches. She can't go on because the words stare up at her and bring her to tears. "Rise to adore," they say, "the mystery of love. . . . " Suddenly she wants to see Jesus. Suddenly she wants to look into eternity. Suddenly she wants to know and to feel and to do the best she can in life. She finds herself, in that instant, turning from the road ahead in order to lose herself on the brink of eternity.

Delta Dawn was a little bit crazy, tipped over the edge by jilted love and psychological need. But there is more than meets the eye in the devotion of religious pilgrimage. All traffic does not move down the road of life; some of the best traffic stops and stares and worships in the open mystery of divine love that runs parallel to our physical journey.

Those who know it sing Psalm 134.

My God Is Bigger Than Your God!

I know that the LORD is great, that our Lord
is greater than all gods.
—Psalm 135:5

Boasting can be an invigorating sport. Two young lads found a stray puppy one day. Both wanted to take it home. They finally decided to hold a contest of skill in order to decide the winner of this prize. They would each tell a story. The teller of the most fantastic, the most unbelievable, the most exaggerated story would earn the furry friend.

The stories were good. The boys' pastor happened to walk by. He was amazed at the lies and fairy tales they were spinning. "Boys, boys!" he said. "You shouldn't tell false stories like that. Why, when I was your age, I never told a lie!"

The youngsters looked at each other regretfully. Then the oldest said to the minister: "Well, that's got to be the biggest fib of all. Here's your puppy, sir."

Haughtiness
Some people boast out of pride. In his story "How the Camel Got Its Hump," Rudyard Kipling took a potshot at prideful boasters. In Kipling's story, when God first created the earth and all the animals, he gave each of them a different job to do. Quickly the animals went about their business. Except for one. The camel refused to do anything. Whenever any of the other animals asked the camel to help them, he just said "Humph!" and walked away.

The camel, you see, thought that he was so much better than all the other animals. When God saw what was happening, he began collecting all of the camel's "Humphs" until they created a big pile in heaven, and then he dumped them back down on the camel's back. And that, according to Kipling, is how the camel got its hump.

Even though we know that the true story of the camel's hump doesn't read quite that way, it's an accurate description of prideful people. They stand out in a crowd. You can almost see them "humphing" up above everyone else.

Earlier this century, people used to say of the pompous Italian dictator Mussolini things like, "He could strut sitting down" and "He was a solemn procession of one." In your mind's eye you can see him "humphing" along.

The Trouble with Our Measuring Sticks

A little boy wanted to know how tall he was. So he made a ruler by which to measure himself and found that he was *nine* feet tall! Those around him realized that the standard he set was his own.

Usually that's the problem with pride: it measures us and ours by rulers we create to our own dimensions.

But there can also be good pride, honest pride, pride that has its measuring stick firmly grounded in reality. Isak Dinesen spoke of it in her book *Out of Africa*. She said, "Pride is faith in the idea that God had when he made us. A proud man is conscious of the idea and aspires to it."

Looking Higher

The boasting of the poet in Psalm 135 is like that. "My God is bigger than your god!" he shouts to whatever little powers might vie for his allegiance. He's not measuring by standards he created out of his own school kit; he just happens to be in touch with reality.

The true way to be humble, said Philips Brookes, "is not to stoop until you are smaller than yourself, but to stand at your real height against some higher nature that will show you what the real smallness of your greatness is."

No one need stand against a greatness greater than the God of Psalm 135. In that context, the shout of pride is very, very good.

Repetition

His love endures forever.
—Refrain in every verse of Psalm 136

Not long ago I was reminded again of Solomon's famous saying: "There is nothing new under the sun. . . . What has been will be again, what has been done will be done again . . ." (Eccles. 1:9). It happened when our daughters came home from school with a "new" joke to tell. The joke goes like this: "Pete and Repeat were out in a boat. Pete fell into the water. Who was left in the boat?"

Of course, when you give the answer "Repeat" they go back and tell you the story from the beginning once again: "Pete and Repeat were out . . ." And it goes on and on until somebody breaks down with silly laughter.

That same story, so new, so fresh to our daughters today, was one I myself told in another age and in another country long ago. In fact, as we might have put it then, it's so old the dinosaurs are digging for it!

Tedious
The fun of that old story isn't only in the silly punch line that goes on forever; part of the fun is in the dry humor of the repetition itself. "What is so tedious as a twice-told tale?" asked Homer in the *Odyssey*. Shakespeare repeated his words 2,500 years later in *King John*, drawing out the sighs of a fellow who no longer laughed:

> Life is as tedious as a twice-told tale,
> Vexing the dull ear of a drowsy man.

Juvenal said the same thing in his Latin satires in the first century: "That cabbage hashed up again and again proves the death of wretched teachers." More than a few students would agree with him.

Memories
Repetition may be tedious and tasteless at times, but in some situations it can become downright hurtful. In Shakespeare's *King John*, Constance speaks to King Philip of France about the death of her son Arthur in words that describe her love/hate relationship with grief:

Grief fills the room up of my absent child,
Lies in his bed, walks up and down with me,
Puts on his pretty looks, repeats his words,
Remembers me of all his gracious parts,
Stuffs out his vacant garments with his form:
Then I have reason to be fond of grief.
Grief's repetitions of memory soothe and scathe at the same time.

So it is with gossip, a lesser form of death. Says Solomon: "He who covers over an offense promotes love, but whoever repeats the matter separates close friends" (Prov. 17:9). Repetition can be the scandal of friends who break confidence and bare secrets.

The Mother of Learning

But there is also another side to repetition. As my daughters have found, some jokes bear repeating, ancient as they might be. Nathaniel Hawthorne picked up Shakespeare's line about "twice-told tales" and then accumulated a marvelous collection of stories that will never grow old or tedious through the retelling. According to Oliver Wendell Holmes, anything worth saying is also worth repeating: "What if one does say the same things—of course in a little different form each time—over and over? If he has anything to say worth saying, that is just what he ought to do." Repetition of the best of us is the test of our truest character.

In spite of Juvenal's idea about repetition being "the death of wretched teachers," others have known the wisdom that says "repetition is the mother of learning." In one of his books, H. G. Wells said: "After people have repeated a phrase a great number of times, they begin to realize it has meaning and may even be true."

No doubt that idea about repetition was in the mind of the composer of Psalm 136. The psalm calls to mind a picture of temple worship in Jerusalem: the cantor shouting each phrase in celebration of God's glory and power, and the worship choir chanting back again and again: "His love endures forever."

By the time the song is finished, the crowds will find themselves drifting away with that refrain lingering in their hearts.

Aliens

How can we sing the songs of the LORD
while in a foreign land?
—Psalm 137:4

Three people were watching a news documentary on television. The announcer declared that she was about to lead her audience through the dark underworld of humankind's "oldest profession," as she put it, the pathos of prostitution.

"That's not quite correct," said the doctor among the three. "After all, before there was even sexuality among humans, God took a rib out of Adam and formed it into Eve. He performed a nice piece of surgery, so I think medicine is the world's oldest profession."

"True," responded the engineer. "But don't forget that the act of creation was itself the greatest engineering feat ever accomplished. My profession is older than yours."

"Well," came the word from the politician, "before God made the world, the Bible says that there was nothing but chaos, darkness, and void. Wouldn't you agree that that's the business of politics? My profession dates back further than anyone's."

The Politics of Alienation

However you might feel about that last remark, it proved true for the writer of Psalm 137. Exiles in a strange land, the leftover Jews found themselves wondering about the politics of chance and the curse of foreign domination. The closing notes of vindictiveness sound more cruel than devout to those of us who have never lived the constant death of alien loneliness in a mean and spiteful culture.

The question for us is whether we can sing Psalm 137 in the context of the freedom and tolerance of North American society. Perhaps it is reserved for the voices of displaced peoples only?

Not so, according to St. Augustine. Fifteen hundred years ago, in an age dominated by the church, Augustine used Psalm 137 to speak of the natural cry of the godly soul while living, as he put it, between Jerusalem and Babylon. Our tendency, he said, is ever to conform to the norms and culture of Babylon which surrounds us. "Sing us a song . . . " we're told, but always for the sake of sport and dance in societies that find their definition in the self-sufficient world of Babylon.

Said Augustine, "if ye wish not to be willows of Babylon fed by its streams, and bringing no fruit . . . sigh for the everlasting Jerusalem: whither your hope goeth before, let your life follow. . . . "

Lest We Forget

Several generations ago, Augustine's reminder and the psalmist's song came together in another powerful way. The year was 1897. Queen Victoria had ruled the British Empire for sixty years, and England decided to throw a party in her honor. The Union Jack flew above every continent in every corner of the world, and schoolchildren learned with pride: "The sun never sets on the British Empire."

Rudyard Kipling was the storyteller and poet of the day. He was commissioned by Parliament to "write a little something" for the celebrations. But when the poem "Recessional" appeared, the nation was shocked by its dark and somber tone. It didn't fit with the mood of merriment.

> Far-called our navies melt away—
> On dune and headland sinks the fire—
> Lo, all our pomp of yesterday
> Is one with Nineveh and Tyre!
> Judge of the Nations, spare us yet,
> Lest we forget—lest we forget.

Some sing Psalm 137 in the pain of political exile. May their sojourn in captivity be brief. All of us, however, who know with our anticipated memories the New Jerusalem of Revelation's visions, sing Psalm 137 in the aching of spiritual exile. It's what the Heidelberg Catechism, in its first major section, terms *Das Elend*—alienation, displacement, and exile.

The moment we grow comfortable with that "misery," we'll have forgotten Jerusalem.

Face to Face

Though the LORD *is on high, he looks upon the lowly. . . .*
—Psalm 138:6

In an interesting tale called *The Man with the Good Face,* Frank Luther Mott describes Mr. James Neal, law clerk, who has a single absorbing interest in life: the search for a man with "the good face."

Riding on the New York subway each day, James Neal spent the time studying faces. After several years, he became an expert at the state of the heart told in the lines of the face. So many showed sadness and suffering, emptiness and evil, lust and lechery, woe and weakness. But one thing he seemed never to find: a face in which shone simplicity, transparent truth, and the spiritual strength of meekness coupled with gentle power. In fact, after a while, it became an obsession for him to find such a face. He called it "the good face."

Accidental Sighting

Then one day it happened: as he sat in the 14th Street Station, he glanced at an express train across the way. There, framed by a window, was the face of a man shining with all he'd ever hoped faith and love to be. He left his seat and raced toward the man's rail coach. But the doors closed, and the train fled without him.

Still, thought, James Neal, he was the better for having seen that face. Indeed, it gave him hope that he would see it once again. Then a strange thing began to happen: those who knew Mr. Neal began to see him change. Once a loner, hovering at the fringes of society, he slowly began to reach out to others in friendliness and grace. Not only that, but his heart warmed to the suffering needs of those whose faces he had studied so long.

Those who knew James Neal wondered at the change that had come over him. If he told anyone anything, it was only that he had seen "the good face."

The Face of a Stranger

Mr. Neal's death came in a sudden and shocking way. He was crossing a street at lunch hour when a car struck him. He was rushed to a hospital, and doctors performed emergency measures to save his life. Now, however, a doctor entered his room and addressed the nurse at his bedside: "How about the skull fracture?"

"He is dead," said the nurse.

"When?" asked the doctor.

"Just now."

The nurse brushed past the doctor, leaving to make further arrangements, but the doctor stopped her. "That tall man," he said, "who was with him: where has he gone?"

The nurse looked at the doctor in surprise, knowing that no one had come to see Mr. Neal. "Oh, yes," said the doctor. "I saw a man bending over the bed—a very tall man with a remarkable face. I wondered who he could be."

For a while they mused together at this mysterious sighting, and then the doctor looked down at the peaceful face on the body that once had been the living man James Neal. "He was very fortunate," said the doctor in a low tone, "to die with a face like that looking into his."

Smile on Me

Interesting, isn't it? To see a face, "the good face," among all the faces in the crowd, and then to have that face change your life. Something of that seems to have happened to David, as he reflects in Psalm 138. It's mysterious; it's miraculous; but it's also the way of God with us in this world. No one who needs rational explanation for every event of living will experience this.

But God is companion to those who call to him from the crowded streets of life; perhaps more so since the Word of God took on a human face. Wrote John Drinkwater about those New York streets of James Neal:

> Shakespeare is dust, and will not come
> To question from his Avon tomb,
> And Socrates and Shelley keep
> An Attic and Italian sleep.
> They see not. But, O Christians, who
> Throng Holborn and Fifth Avenue,
> May you not meet, in spite of death
> A traveler from Nazareth?

Have you seen a "good face" in the crowds lately?

Personal Testimony

All the days ordained for me were written in your book before
one of them ever came to be.
—Psalm 139:16

Fifth-century B.C. Roman historian Heroditus told this interesting story: The Egyptians always prided themselves on being the oldest civilization on the earth. However, when Psammetichus became their king in about 660 B.C., he decided that this assumption wasn't enough. He set out to prove "scientifically" which race on earth was the most ancient.

Experiment
He took two newborn children of ordinary parentage, and gave them to a shepherd who grazed his sheep in a lonely area. He charged the shepherd and his family to keep the children in an isolated dwelling, to care for their physical needs, and to guard them from harm. But, he said, never allow a single word of any speech or language to be uttered within the range of their hearing.

Whatever language came naturally to them would obviously be the original language of humankind and thus would serve as a record of the antiquity of the founding people on earth.

So it went for two years. Then one morning, as the shepherd entered the dwelling of the youngsters, they grabbed his legs and stretched out their arms in delight and cried out the word *bekos*.

Knowing the gravity of the situation, the shepherd neither responded orally nor reported this incident until it had recurred several times.

King Psammetichus immediately went to hear the children and their "native" speech. He called in his linguists, demanding from them the source of the word *bekos*. When they found a group among the Phrygians who used that term for bread, Psammetichus and the noble Egyptians had to concede that their race was derived from older stock.

(And if Heroditus is correct, political games entered the picture at that point, and Psammetichus instituted a cover-up of "Watergate" proportions!)

Who Am I?

I've thought often about that experiment over the years, especially as a father watching three daughters grow and develop. Who are these young beauties, anyway? Yes, their mother and I are in them . . . certainly in their rawest moments the worst of us oozes out! But who are they inside? Where did they come from? How can they be living creatures, so unique, so complex, so wonderful? What would they be like if we were not their parents? If they were bred in isolation from our genetic material, would they still be the persons we've grown to know in part and to love in unmeasured measure?

Who are they? For that matter, who am I? How did I come to be the person I am?

Many years ago, Dr. Peter Eldersveld was the preacher for a radio ministry. Back in 1965, he preached a sermon based on Acts 16. Most of us are self-made people, he said. At least that's how we like to think of ourselves: self-made, self-directed, self-sustaining.

Even our Christian testimonies hint in that direction. He told about some of his friends who delight in telling how, after years of destructive living, they came to know God and got turned round, and then made new commitments of service.

Boring?

Then, said Dr. Eldersveld, they politely look to me and ask about my "personal testimony." I always feel like a second-rate Christian, he said, because I have no amazing before-and-after stories to spread. In fact, his whole testimony could be summarized in a single rather "boring" statement. He said, "I have never known a day in all my life when I could not believe that I was a child of God."

But as he reflected further, he came to realize that this simple statement was really an earth-shaking confession. Is it possible that from the time a child draws its first breath, it could belong to God, be part of the family and community of God, be found in the loving care of God? Is it possible that the first language a youngster could speak would be the language of faith, and the dialect of divine love? What a testimony that is!

Maybe, he thought, Psalm 139 would be a rather spectacular life story to tell. Do you think so too?

Song of the Abused

Rescue me, O LORD, from evil men;
protect me from men of violence.
—Psalm 140:1

In an issue of *Perspectives,* Thomas Boogaart tells the wrenching story of his friend Jim and a horrible cry in the night. Jim was a young pastor, fresh in his first congregation. On a steamy, sultry summer night, as the atmosphere hung heavy and sleepless exhaustion dogged everyone who lived in non-air-conditioned environs, Jim and his wife tossed restlessly.

Of course, it happened to be a Saturday night as well. The tension of Sunday morning preaching always teases at the edges of a preacher's consciousness on Saturday nights. And Jim wasn't all that sure he had a handle on this particular sermon. Numbers 14—the Israelites whimper in their tents, fearful of what might happen to them if they enter Canaan as God—through Moses—has instructed. They're afraid they'll be whipped. Their substance will be ripped away from them. Their wives will be raped and their children abused.

Listen!
After another restless romp with the text in his study, Jim came to bed. It was 1:00 A.M. Sandy was there, also wide awake. "Shhhh. . . . " She put her finger to her lips. "Listen!"

The night was definitely not silent. From the little white frame house next door came noises. Not unusual, actually, since it seemed as if every night for the past two weeks had been party time for the newly-arrived family.

But tonight was different. The pounding rumble of an angry man's voice. Then the high whine of terror: "No, Daddy! No, Daddy! No, Daddy! Please, no!" Then the shrill eruption of agonized screams and deep pain. And then the soft whimpering of a young girl's private horror.

Before the black scene evaporated, Jim found himself whimpering too.

Help!
I have lived an enormously blessed life. I read a lot of history, and it never ceases to amaze me how carefully preserved and calm and safe my existence has been, compared to so many throughout the ages. Maybe that's

why I have such difficulty appreciating prayers like the one raised in Psalm 140. It seems to me too caustic, too vengeful, too mean-spirited.

But one thing my pastoral ministry has revealed to me is the darker side of even what sometimes appears to be a bright and delightful life in twentieth-century North America. More regularly than I care to retrace are the moments I spend with the abused and abusers. Women, children, even men sit in my study and tell me of the merciless pounding, the sickening incestual "love"-making, the belly-kicking, the "special secrets," the verbal shredding. . . .

And then come the moments when I sit with the abusers, listening to the stories they need to tell to recover sanity, to relocate a sense of dignity, to plead for forgiveness.

Strange Comfort

And when later I sit alone, images and scenes in my mind that I don't want there, I find prayers like David's in Psalm 140 strangely comforting.

Harry Emerson Fosdick once told his congregation that no one should ever think that a pastor has a nice, clean job, out of touch with reality, set apart in scrub-polish cleanliness. We see more of the dregs of society, he said, than we should ever have to admit. And if, on occasion, a prayer like that of David's escapes our lips, it's only because, like Jim, we've heard the soft whimpering in the night and wondered about the cruelty of abusers and about the reality of our own faith in God.

Wrestling

Let not my heart be drawn to what is evil. . . .
—Psalm 141:4

Elizabeth Achtemeier, great teacher of preaching at Union Theological Seminary in Richmond, Virginia, says that one of the greatest errors of young preachers is their desire to tell people that it's very easy to know the will of God. It's so easy, she says, to preach in black and white, to declare either this or that, with no shades of gray in between.

But life's not like that, she says. We know that too. We wrestle every day of our existence. What job should we be looking for? Who should be our life partner? Where will we send our children to school? How do we care for the sinner while condemning the sin? Do we walk out of the grocery store with paper bags that destroy trees, with plastic bags that use up oil, or with cloth bags that pollute the water when we wash them? How do we watch the starving children of Somalia on television and then turn back to our rich and excessive meals, throwing the scraps away as garbage?

War Within

The answers are rarely easy. Our lives reflect the struggles of choices made and often choices regretted. Think of Corrie ten Boom, who tells her story in *The Hiding Place*. During World War II, her family hid some Jews to keep them from the gas chambers. She and her father needed to find a safe place for one Jewish mother and her very young child.

One day a local clergyman stepped into their watch shop. They decided to ask him if he would take these two frightened ones into his home. He refused, however. Corrie couldn't believe it at the time, so she impulsively ran to the mother and grabbed the little baby from her arms. She brought the child to the pastor and tried to thrust him into the pastor's hands.

Again he refused. "No!" he said. "Definitely not! We could lose our lives for that Jewish child."

Who could blame him? How could he help others, if he himself were dragged away to the concentration camps? That was his decision as he wrestled with himself in the gray area of his circumstances.

Father ten Boom gathered the little one in his arm and said to the pastor, "You say we could lose our lives for this child. I would consider that the greatest honor that could come to my family." Another self. Another choice. You and I wrestle with such choices every day of our lives.

Who Am I?

Think of the things we say:

"I don't really feel like myself today."

"I'm so ashamed of myself!"

"For a moment there I forgot myself."

"I just *hate* myself!"

What are we saying? What's really happening to us? A father had abused his daughter, time and time again, for years on end. Eventually he got out of jail on parole. The first time he got together with his daughter, he said, "I'm so sorry for what I've done to you. I don't know what to say. I wish I wasn't myself."

We think we're making our way in life. We think we know the self that's best for us. We think we can find a way to swim outside of the ocean, a way to fly without looking up to the heavens or to grow without digging deep. But we can't, can we? We can't and we can't and we can't, till Love wrestles us in the night and gives us a new name.

For in the end, as David knew in Psalm 141, God must wrestle with us as he did with Jacob many generations before. God must wrestle with us, or the choices of our hearts will lead us astray.

Fading

When my spirit grows faint within me,
it is you who know my way.
—*Psalm 142:3*

Tinkerbell is the delightful sprite in *Peter Pan* who drifts between the world of senses and the world of magic. She sprinkles "fairy dust" to make children fly; she sparkles around Peter Pan as a comrade adventurer.

Once, I remember, on a "Wonderful World of Disney" broadcast, Tinkerbell ingested some poison. There was nothing to be seen of her, tiny thing that she was, other than the brightness of her little light. But with the poison, her light began to fade. Before our very eyes she grew dimmer, pulsing with a weakening glow.

Miracles

But miracles do happen in fairy tales and on television. Peter Pan turned to the audience. "You've got to believe!" he pleaded. "You've got to believe in Tinkerbell. Everyone out there, clap your hands together now, and show Tinkerbell that you believe in her."

Across North America, children of all ages who were watching must have clapped. I know we did.

As we watched, we could see Tinkerbell's light grow strong and bright. She flitted back to life, and then the story could go on. She almost had faded away, but we believed in her, and she lived.

Believe in Me

All of us need someone to believe in us. In Psalm 142, David says, "I was fading, fading, almost gone, pursued by those who didn't believe in me, who treated me like an object to be tricked and tossed: "No one is concerned for me . . . no one cares for my life" (v. 4).

Then David says to God, But you believe in me. You know who I am. You rally to my side and clap your hands for me in strength and faith. "When my spirit grows faint within me, it is you who know my way."

The Touch of the Master's Hand

Myra Brooks Welch wrote a rather earthy poem years ago that expresses the difference it makes to be valued:

'Twas battered and scarred, and the auctioneer
Thought it scarcely worth his while
To waste much time on the old violin,
But he held it up with a smile.
"What am I bidden, good folks?" he cried.
"Who'll start the bidding for me?
A dollar, a dollar—now two, only two?—
Two dollars. And who'll make it three?
Three dollars once, three dollars twice,
Going for three!"—but no!
From the room far back a gray-haired man
Came forward and picked up the bow:
Then, wiping the dust from the old violin,
And tightening up all the stings,
He played a melody pure and sweet—
As sweet as an angel sings!
The music ceased, and the auctioneer,
With a voice that was quiet and low,
Said: "What am I bid for the old violin?"
And he held it up with the bow.
"A thousand dollars! And who'll make it two?
Two thousand! And who'll make it three?
Three thousand once, and three thousand twice,
And going and gone!" said he.
The people cheered, but some of them cried,
"We do not quite understand—
What changed its worth?" The man replied:
"The touch of the Master's hand!"
And many a man with life out of tune,
And battered and torn with sin,
Is auctioned cheap to a thoughtless crowd
Much like the old violin.
A "mess of pottage," a glass of wine,
A game—he travels on.
He's going once, and going twice,
He's going—and almost gone!
But the Master comes, and the foolish crowd
Never can quite understand
The worth of a soul and the change that's wrought
By the touch of the Master's hand.

SOS

Answer me quickly, O Lord; my spirit faints with longing.
—Psalm 143:7

Somewhere today a woman sits quietly at the window of her hospital room. She absentmindedly plays with the cord that fastens her dressing gown. It was a routine check-up. . . . She's always taken care of herself. . . . She feels fine. . . .

But the doctor said the lump looked suspicious. Now he says there's nothing more he can do.

"But I'm still young," she tells him. "What about my kids?" she cries. "My husband needs me," she pleads.

A nurse comes in with the meal tray. With no appetite, the young woman stares at the food. Then she flings the plate against the wall and cries: "It isn't fair!"

Somewhere today a young man in a wheelchair rolls himself along a cracked sidewalk. He gazes at the glistening bodies of bronzed fellows in shorts as they toss a football in an impromptu game. He watches lovers lying side-by-side on a blanket, talking and laughing, teasing and touching each other. He remembers the strength of his legs and the girlfriend who never calls anymore.

It was a freak accident, and now he's a "freak," tied to this chair like a limp doll. The sidewalk narrows. A wheel gets caught in a rut. He tips and slams into the dirt. The tears sting as he cries out: "It isn't fair!"

Unfair

Somewhere today the aching of a million hearts will be covered over with polite smiles and ignored by forgetful friends. Somewhere today a child will die in a riot, simply because it was born in the wrong community. Somewhere today a fifty-seven-year-old man will lose his dignity because a change in corporate policy in some distant boardroom put him out on the street with no job. Somewhere today a teenage girl with a beautiful face will scream at herself in the mirror because a drug prescribed for her mother during pregnancy left her with no arms. Somewhere today a young husband will miraculously survive a terrible car accident, only to waste away with AIDS, contracted from the blood that saved his life. It isn't fair!

What do you do with the unfairness of life? Don't you look for two things? First, you look for someone who will listen to your moans, hear your tormented ranting, feel your raging pain. Second, you plead. You plead and you plead and you plead: "God, make it right. I can't stand it anymore. Do something about it!"

Distress Signal
SOS! SOS! SOS! That's the prayer when life's unfair.

Will there be an answer? Is there any substance to religion? Does God exist, and can he hear, and will he do anything about it?

David thought so, as he sobbed Psalm 143. I might be tempted (as I have been at times in my life) to think his prayer was pious nonsense, except for one thing. One day, long after David prayed, God stepped into this unfair world and wound up on a cross. Why? Simply because he wanted to let all who pray David's prayer know that he cares. That he hears. That he wants to help. That he was willing to go through some pretty unfair things with us, if that's what it took to balance the scales of life and death.

Psalm 143 spills out of our hearts easily. But that doesn't mean it disappears into oblivion. For, as David knew, there's always someone monitoring the airwaves. And no distress call goes unanswered.

Warrior

Praise be to the LORD my Rock, who trains my hands for war, my fingers for battle.
—Psalm 144:1

Pyrrhus was a Greek military commander in the third century B.C. Under his leadership, a combined expeditionary force landed in Italy and began a sweeping conquest aimed at Rome. After one preliminary struggle, which gained victory for the Greeks at the expense of many soldiers' lives and the entire supply caravan, a subordinate congratulated Pyrrhus on his success. His reply was less enthusiastic: "Another such victory and we are ruined."

Now you know where the phrase "Pyrrhic victory" comes from. It means a battle won at too high a price.

Battlefield Images

I think of that phrase when I read Psalm 144. There's something about it that I don't like. It has to do, I think, with the combat imagery. God is a warrior for David, someone who "trains my hands for war, my fingers for battle," someone who "subdues people under me," someone who "scatters enemies" by "shoot[ing] your arrows," someone "who gives victory to kings."

I'm not sure if I'm a convinced conscientious objector for all forms of war and violent expression, though I have tendencies in that direction. I remember standing in the back room of our radio station at college, late at night, reading with others the lottery numbers of the U.S. Selective Services military draft that came across our United Press International teletype. My number was seven. And that year they ended the compulsory draft for the Vietnam War. I was thankful I didn't have to make a decision about conscientious objection at that point. I just stayed in school and earned a degree.

"Just War"?

My Christian faith, shaped by the Scriptures and the community of God's people, has increasingly pushed me in the direction of pacifism. That's not an easy position to take—my father distinguished himself in World War II military service, and many of the older people in my congregation know firsthand the great evil of Hitler's Nazi machine and the place armed resistance had in defeating it.

But I was sickened again by the Persian Gulf war in 1991, as I am on a continued basis with the fighting in Somalia, Czechoslovakia, Yugoslavia, Northern Ireland, South Africa, Bosnia. . . . A friend of mine recently threw these statistics at me—for every 100 people who are killed in modern warfare, 5 are babies, 31 are children, 2 are pregnant women, 21 others are women, 18 are male laborers and businessmen, 7 are senior citizens, and 1 is a mentally incompetent person housed in a psychiatric hospital. That comes to a total of 85. Out of 100 war casualties.

The other 15 are soldiers, of course. But these days, no arms merchants die in war. Nor do generals. Nor do any who are speculators on international markets. Nor do any politicians.

That's why I have a bad taste about war. Who calls it, and who pays?

Powerful Deliverance

Because of those feelings about war, images of God as Warrior are hard to stomach. I don't want a wimp for a God, but neither do I believe that the one who teaches me love and grace is a bloodthirsty military general.

I understand David's desire for protection from enemies. I appreciate his joy at release from slavery and slaughter. And maybe that's where I should leave it. Because Psalm 144, regardless of its militaristic overtones, emphasizes the great divine gifts of salvation and relief.

Perhaps my distaste of battle sometimes arises from the safety of my rather protected circumstances. It might be that if I were in David's shoes, threatened by "foreigners whose mouths are full of lies, whose right hands are deceitful," God, in my personal picture, might wear more stripes on his sleeves.

Celebration

My mouth will speak in praise of the LORD. Let every
creature praise his holy name for ever and ever.
—*Psalm 145:21*

Nineteenth-century Welsh manufacturer Robert Owen became increasingly discouraged with conditions in England's coal mines. He personally toured the coal districts and was appalled at the degradation of human life. One evening he stopped a twelve-year-old boy, coal-black, trudging off to a squalid rooming house after another day in the night below.

"Do you know God?" Owen asked him, concerned for his spiritual development.

"No," said the boy. "He must work in some other mine."

May I Introduce You?

Too many people bow to the truth of that sentiment. "No, I can't say I've ever heard of him. He must work in some other department, on some other floor, in some other building. Maybe he lives in another apartment building." Life is consumed in the small experiences of the mines or the mills or the factories and the tunnels one must endure to travel to and from them.

And even where the name or the idea of God is bandied about, often there's little appreciation for what it might mean to know and love and celebrate him. When our congregation began a new Saturday night expression of music and drama designed to introduce people to the message of the gospel for the first time, one young man thanked us profusely. He came only because he wanted to hear one particular young lady sing. But he wouldn't leave until he told us that he received so much more. He said that he had heard about God now and again through his teen and early adult years, but he'd never before met people who actually helped him understand the reality of things larger than the experiences he encountered from day to day.

Crisscross to Love

Some time ago cartoonist Bill Keane captured a beautiful expression of that serendipitous delight of love and passion in his "Family Circle." Little Jeffy asks, "Who will I marry, Mommy?" Mommies know everything, of course. She looks down at him with all the emotions of motherhood—pride and hope and wonder and love: "Nobody knows, Jeffy, but someday your paths will cross."

Little Jeffy skips out of the front door, wondering about that other person and that other path.

Then, under the caption "Meanwhile, hundreds of miles away—" Keane shows a little girl coming out of her home. Inside, a Mrs. Wilson, with a thoughtful smile on her face, says to her husband, "Melinda just asked me who her husband would be someday. . . . " Keane concludes the strip with this note: "Congrats to Jeff and Melinda who were married yesterday!"

Wedding Song

What a priceless picture! Isn't that the veiled excitement of David's song in Psalm 145? In essence it dances like a wedding song that humbly boasts of how two paths crossed in life—David's and God's—and how, when it happened, love was the only choice and joy the natural outcome.

Do you know God? Has your path crossed his yet? Just wait! When it happens, you won't be able to stop humming David's song.

Follow the Leader

Do not put your trust in princes, in mortal men, who cannot
save. . . . Blessed is he whose help is the God of Jacob, whose
hope is in the LORD his God. . . .
—Psalm 146: 3, 5

The year was 1934. Times were difficult around the world, especially in the repressed economic and political climate of post-World War I Germany. But recovery was in sight. A group of theologians at Wurtemburg saw a rising star of hope and penned together a declaration of faith that would be signed by six hundred pastors of churches and fourteen theology professors at seminaries.

Their promising statement included these words: "We are full of thanks to God that He, as Lord of history, has given us Adolf Hitler, our leader and savior from our difficult lot. We acknowledge that we, with body and soul, are bound and dedicated to the German state and to its Fuhrer."

Astounding, isn't it? In retrospect we can only shudder at the demonic twists of history that could produce such unqualified devotion to a man who would later rip God's world apart, and destroy, insofar as he was able, both the church and children of God.

History's Hinge

That same year, 1934, Hitler summoned a group of church leaders to his office. Martin Niemoller was among them. He had been a great hero in the German Navy during World War I, commanding a submarine that caused great destruction to the Allied fleet. Now he was a pastor, much loved in his new vocation.

The meeting with Hitler began cordially enough. Suddenly, however, Hermann Goering burst into the room with a charge of treason against Niemoller. Hitler raged in angry tirade. Finally he regained his composure and told Niemoller, "You confine yourself to the church. I'll take care of the German people!"

But Niemoller knew Psalm 146, and he marched to its challenging beat. He stood quietly and replied, "Herr Reichskanzler, you said just now: 'I will take care of the German people.' But we too, as Christians and churchmen, have a responsibility towards the German people. That responsibility was entrusted to us by God, and neither you nor anyone in this world has the power to take it from us."

Heaven's Heartbeat

Hitler knew a showdown when he saw it. Niemoller went to trial, and was convicted of misusing his pulpit for political purposes. Hitler refused to pardon him, declaring, "It is Niemoller or I."

Not all political confrontations are that dramatic. Neither Mr. Chre'tien nor Mr. Clinton would ask North Americans to make a choice between themselves and God. But the gray area of compromise, whether social, economic, emotional, physical, or political, always takes place with the slow staccato of drum beats in the background. And conflicting rhythms tear at our souls till we find a way to isolate the heartbeat of the God we will follow.

Medicine Man

He heals the brokenhearted and binds up their wounds.
—Psalm 147:3

Over the entrance of the famed Columbia Presbyterian Medical Center in New York City is this inscription: "For of the Most High cometh healing." Nice words, aren't they? But one wonders how they temper the minds of those who walk beneath them.

Prescriptions for the Heart

Benjamin Franklin once quipped: "God heals, and the doctor takes the fee." John Quincy Adams heard that and told his doctor: "I inhabit a weak, frail, decayed tenement; battered by the winds and broken in upon by the storms, and, from all I can learn, the landlord does not intend to repair!" No fees were collected that day.

Healing is a strange thing. The most obvious wounds and sores are not necessarily the most deadly. And even where doctors attack the traumas of the flesh, they often say that no true healing can take place till the mind and spirit and soul desire restoration. Thomas Moore's well-known hymn reflects that thought:

> Come, you disconsolate, where'er you languish;
> come to the mercy seat, fervently kneel.
> Here bring your wounded hearts, here tell your anguish;
> earth has no sorrows that heaven cannot heal.

When Fingers Don't Reach

But our desire for healing doesn't always match the ability of heaven to perform, even through modern medical means. "Gypsy Smith," a widely touted evangelist earlier this century, preached a powerful sermon based on an incident from his own childhood.

His people worked the fields of hops near Tunbridge, England. One day, a force of fifty people finished one section and boarded a horse-drawn wagon for transport to the next site. The wagon overflowed with people singing and laughing. But when they crossed a flooding stream on an old wooden bridge, a woman's sudden scream spooked the horses.

When the wagon crashed against the side of the bridge, everyone was thrown into the raging waters.

A young boy caught hold of a horse and then reached for his drowning mother's hand. Their arms flailed desperately, but the currents pulled her away to death.

At the mass funeral for thirty-nine victims, crowds gathered in humbling numbers. Over the drone of words of mourning and hope, the boy who had lost his mother crawled into the gaping grave, hugged her casket, and cried: "Mother, Mother! I tried to save you! I did all a man could do to save you, but you would not let me."

Beyond Doctoring

Gypsy Smith called his sermon "The Saviour of All" and told how another Son reaches for others who are drowning with other arms of mercy. And he does not let them down.

Louis Pasteur knew that the expansion of human knowledge can lead us to excessive self-sufficiency. But he knew, too, that when we probe the inner workings of disease and disaster and death, no science in the world can replace the Great Physician. He said: "A little science estranges men from God; much science leads them back to him."

Do you want to be healed?

Two-Part Invention

Praise the LORD from the heavens. . . .
Praise the LORD from the earth. . . .
—*Psalm 148:1, 7*

Do you know what a "two-part invention" is? Composers might call Psalm 148 a "two-part invention" because it's formed as a short musical piece with two related themes that come together in a single final refrain.

Love Story

Author Madeleine L'Engle used that term as the title of a book she wrote about her marriage. She and her husband, she says, were like two parts of a song, woven together sometimes in dissonance, sometimes in harmony, but always bound together by the same lines of music and love. Their lives together were a "two-part invention" of melody and counterpoint, always in creative tension.

Creation itself is a "two-part invention," sings the psalmist. The glory of God is shouted in the heavens. Then it's resounded by the creatures of earth. The music they make together is a refrain that wafts throughout the contours of time and eternity, space and infinity.

Day and Night

George MacDonald wrote a story about "The Day Boy and the Night Girl." It was really a "two-part invention" of love and praise. The girl had been raised in a dark cave by a witch and never was allowed to see the light of day. The boy, on the other hand, was raised by the same witch to live and breathe and romp during the daylight. Never was he allowed to sleep during the day. Never was he put in dark spaces. He went to bed before the sun went down, and his room was brightly lit by candles and torches.

So, says MacDonald, these two roamed their separate worlds. The Night Girl managed to find her way out of the cave, but only during nocturnal darkness. And the Day Boy spread his flights of fancy further abroad, always making sure to be home before sunset.

Of course, destiny draws this pair together. On one day's hunt, the Day Boy strays too far and too late to avoid the onset of twilight. Falling asleep in bewilderment at the growing gloom, he's later awakened by the Night Girl, who is searching for friends.

"You are a creature of the darkness and love the night," he told her reproachfully.

"I may be a creature of the darkness," she replied. "But I do not love the night. I love the day—with all my heart. . . . "

Wedding Bells

But she's never had a guide to the light, nor he a teacher of the night. So they become fast friends, playing out the same youthful delight on either side of dawn and dusk. And when they come to marry, this is the Day Boy's prayer: "She has got to teach me to be a brave man in the dark, and I have got to look after her until she can bear the heat of the sun and he helps her to see, instead of blinding her."

Perhaps the marriage of heaven and earth is something like that. I have a feeling that on the day of that ceremony, portrayed in festive terms in the book of Revelation, Psalm 148 will be a fitting selection for the choir to sing.

Double-Edged Sword

May the praise of God be in their mouths and a
double-edged sword in their hands. . . .
—*Psalm 149:6*

The poet Robert Browning used to boast that he had perfect eyesight. That may not seem like much of a boast until you understand that he was nearsighted in one eye and farsighted in the other. When he wanted to peer at things close to him, he covered the farsighted eye, and when he gazed at things distant, he covered the other. His unique malady was a conversation piece.

Out of Focus
Sometimes we suffer from a kind of spiritual "double vision" when we want to praise God at a distance. We want the warm fuzzies of having God as our pet or bodyguard, but we don't want him to get so close to our lives that he might affect how we live.

One of Robert Louis Stevenson's poems includes these mournful lines:

Sing me a song of a lad that is gone,
Say, could that lad be I?

His question includes a touch of wistful repentance that speaks at once of both praise and judgment. Obviously there was something to be admired about that lad, something good and right and noble and kind. But just as obviously something's gone wrong in the person he's become.

Check It Out
The chant of Psalm 149 is about recovering good vision. It praises God and things righteous. But that praise becomes a double-edged sword when it casts its reflected gleam on the dark and spotted places of life, the things that breed violence, corruption, and hatred. One cannot praise God lovingly without also calling evil sin and vileness unacceptable.

A father put his arm around his daughter as she was about to leave on her first date. He said to her: "Just remember who you are." That's enough, isn't it?

Maybe that's why Psalm 149 looks out of two eyes at once and sees both the glory and the gory. "Just remember who you are!" One who praises God sincerely cannot stomach godlessness at the same time.

The Haunting of Grace

You see, it's not so much that we're hunted into the kingdom of heaven, but that we're haunted into it. We're haunted by the selves we know we were, the selves we know we could be, the selves we see ourselves becoming in the eye of God. In the haunting of our lives, through praise and prayer, God brings us to our senses, restores our right vision, and helps us to see ourselves and our world truly.

Do you remember when you were soft, not hard? Do you remember when you were warm, not cold? Do you remember what you felt when you first brought songs of praise to God?

Then you know the haunting of full vision that weeps and rejoices at once in Psalm 149.

Dance in the Desert

Praise the LORD.
—Psalm 150:1, 6

Even though we like laughter and enjoy praise and celebration, it doesn't always come easily.

One fellow tells of his work as a hospital volunteer. He couldn't believe the pain and suffering he saw there. Burn victims. Deformities. Terminal cancer. He watched the little ones cry. Some were so lonely: their parents couldn't take the trauma, so they never came to see their own children. How horrible!

A Taste for Tears

Somebody has to bring a little cheer to this place, he thought. So the volunteer got a clown's nose, one of those bright red foam balls. Someone gave him a pair of oversized shoes. Then he painted his face and pulled on a wig. When he went to work dressed like that the next day, some of the children were scared, some were captivated, and some even showed hints of a smile for the first time in ages.

But others couldn't stop crying. They were consumed by agony. What could he do for them?

The next day the clown brought along some popcorn. When he came to the side of a crying child, he took a kernel of popcorn, placed it against the child's cheek, and soaked up the cascading tears with its fluff. Then he popped that kernel into his mouth and ate it.

It was a stroke of genius, a gift given to him by God. The only time some of those children stopped crying was the moment they knew that somebody else cared enough to swallow their tears.

Searching for Sanctuary

The psalmist brings us to a place like that. He takes us, at the end of our journey, to the "sanctuary" of God for a time of praise. "Sanctuary" is refuge, fortress, safe house, security, arms of love, a place where someone cares enough to swallow our tears and protect us from the worst that could harm us.

Madeleine L'Engle paints a picture of such a sanctuary in one of her children's books. She tells of a young couple on a desert journey through wilderness in a rough caravan. They're on their way to Egypt. Someone is after them; someone wants to kill their little boy.

The journey is a rugged one. The desert is alive with ferocious beasts. All eyes cast about uneasily as darkness settles. There'll be little sleep in the camp tonight.

They build a great fire to drive back the shadows and keep away the world that belongs to monsters with glowing eyes. Suddenly they start in terror; a great lion appears at the bonfire. The mother reaches for her child, desperately trying to draw him to safety.

Lost in Wonder, Love, and Praise

But the child stands and laughs. He opens his arms wide to the lion. The lion lifts his front paws and hops around on his hind legs. He's dancing!

And then, from the desert, come running several little mice and two donkeys and a snake and a couple of clumsy ostriches. Three great eagles swoop in from the purple skies. From the other side of the camp a unicorn emerges, and a pelican, and even two dragons.

They all bow before the child and then dance together, round and round him. He stands at the center of their great circle, laughing in delight.

It's a dance in the desert, as L'Engle calls it. In essence, it's the sum and substance of our worship here on earth, pilgrims passing through the wilderness of ghastly beasties and mournful hurts.

Worship and praise don't come naturally to us. But when the Child lights up the darkness with his laughter, even the wild creatures in us want to dance!

Page 304 blank.

Made in the USA
Monee, IL
04 January 2024

51086671R00168